HF240618

THE GENIUS OF LIES

François Noudelmann

THE GENIUS OF LIES

Translation by the author, with the assistance
of Kathryn Parker and Francesco Mercuri

Max Milo

© Max Milo Editions, Paris, 2024
www.maxmilo.com
ISBN: 978-2-31501-200-8

From the same author

- Authored:

Les Enfants de Cadillac, Gallimard (Blanche), 2021

Un Tout Autre Sartre, Gallimard (Blanche), 2020

Penser avec les oreilles, Max Milo, 2019

Édouard Glissant. L'identité généreuse, Flammarion (series Grandes biographies), 2018

Le Génie du mensonge, Max Milo, 2015, Pocket paperback, 2017

Les Airs de famille. Une philosophie des affinités, Gallimard (Blanche), 2012

Tombeaux. D'après La Mer de la fertilité *de Mishima*, Cécile Defaut (series Le Livre La Vie), 2012

Le Toucher des philosophes. Sartre, Nietzsche et Barthes au piano, Gallimard (Blanche), 2008 (grand prix des Muses 2009), Folio Essais paperback, 2014. *The Philosopher's Touch* (Columbia University Press, 2012)

Hors de moi, Léo Scheer (series Variations), 2006

Samuel Beckett (with Bruno Clément), ADPF publications, 2006

Jean-Paul Sartre, ADPF publications, 2005

Pour en finir avec la généalogie, Léo Scheer (series Non & Non), 2004

Avant-gardes et modernité, Hachette (series Contours littéraires), 2000

Image et absence, essai sur le regard, L'Harmattan (series Ouvertures philosophiques), 1998

Beckett ou la scène du pire, Honoré Champion (series Unichamp), 1998, new edition 2010

Sartre : l'incarnation imaginaire, L'Harmattan (series Ouvertures philosophiques), 1996

Huis Clos et Les Mouches de Jean-Paul Sartre, Gallimard (series Foliothèque), 1993, new edition 2006

- Edited:

Voix, Figure, Pensée (with Florence de Chalonge), Presses Universitaires du Septentrion, 2022

Archipels Glissant (with Françoise Simasotchi-Bronès and Yann Toma), Presses Universitaires de Vincennes, 2020

Soundings and Soundscapes (with Sarah Kay), Journal *Paragraph* (Edinburgh University Press), 2018

Édouard Glissant, la pensée du détour (with Françoise Simasotchi-Bronès), Journal *Littérature* (Colin/Dunod), 2014

Filiation and Its Discontents (with Robert Harvey and E. Ann Kaplan), SUNY-SB papers, 2009

Dictionnaire Sartre (with Gilles Philippe), Honoré Champion, 2004

Les 20 ans du Collège international de philosophie (with Antonia Soulez), Presses Universitaires de France, 2004

Politique et filiation (with Robert Harvey and E.Ann Kaplan), Kimé, 2004

Politiques de la communauté (with Gérard Bras), Presses Universitaires de France, 2003

Le Matériau, voir et entendre (with Antonia Soulez), Presses Universitaires de France, 2002

L'étranger dans la mondialité, Presses Universitaires de France, 2002

Roland Barthes après Roland Barthes (with Françoise Gaillard), Presses Universitaires de France, 2002

Scène et image (with Dominique Moncond'huy), La Licorne, 2000

Ponge : matière, matériau, matérialisme (with Nathalie Barberger and Henri Scepi), La Licorne, 2000

Suite/Série/Séquence (with Dominique Moncond'huy), La Licorne, 1998

Le Corps à découvert, S.T.H., 1992

La Nature, de l'identité à la liberté, S.T.H., 1991

Conversations:

Penser l'avenir (with André Gorz), La Découverte, 2019

L'Entretien du monde (with Édouard Glissant), Presses Universitaires de Vincennes, 2018

To Gio.

*Man's mind is so made that he is more impressed by lies
than by the truth.*
Erasmus, *The Praise of Folly*

*We should not be upset that others hide the truth from us
since we hide it so often from ourselves.*
La Rochefoucauld, *Maxims*

Introduction:
For an Amoral Approach to Lying

The moral condemnation of lying prevents us from appreciating its complexity. Observing the springs and richness of lying attitudes becomes fascinating and instructive if we suspend our judgment toward someone who lies. Like Darwin scrutinizing the joy and pain on his children's face to record them in a study on animal emotions, we discover the extent of the signs and languages specific to lying. Ordinary life offers multiple scenes, intimate and collective. Adultery has long been a field of experience in which to see the unfaithful invent scenarios, twist words, and maneuver with varying degrees of skill. In a political spectacle, a corrupt official also comes to swear by all the saints that he is innocent. Of course, we can hardly contain our feelings—jealousy or contempt—because we are shocked by the outrage against the truth. Still, a little clarity about humans' nature and discourse allows us to glimpse the incredible richness of lies and their infinite forms. Without always reaching the rigor of the scientist or the calm of the cynic, we can at least question the creativity of lies.

The ability to tell the opposite of the truth both fascinates and worries people. Once a liar has been exposed, he is discredited for a long time. All his speeches become suspect, even when he is telling the truth, like the cry of the child who cries "Wolf!" and is no longer believed because he lied the first time. The human propensity to lie casts suspicion on all speakers. How might one spot a false statement behind a clear voice or a frank look, what science would allow one to find out the most seasoned liar? Small mythologies offer the hope of countering false speech thanks to police investigation and psychological techniques. Thus, the "lie detector," which has become a cliché in American films, transcribes the emotions of the subject being questioned onto a graph. As its name suggests, the polygraph writes a lot based on speech and body language. It restores the hidden secret. The device connected to the test subject's body measures the reactions to multiple questions and records the answers that provoked an emotion, sweating, or an accelerated heartbeat. Recently, detection techniques have been refined through analysis of microexpressions or functional imaging that identifies brain areas activated during a lie. The television series *Lie to Me* has been a great success with its pseudo-savants who observe the slightest fold of a face, the movement of a finger, the size of a pupil, or the timbre of a voice. In order to find the truth for the police, they pierce souls and point out the most devious false claims. Whether these tests are reliable or not, they take up a long-proven idea: the body reveals the truth when the soul hides it. The greatest psychologists, such as Racine or Proust, have shown characters who betray their intentions and feelings by a tone, a tremor, or a blush. Odette's lies to Swann can be guessed by her painful look and plaintive voice, which add too much expression to her sadness.

The body exposes the conflict between truth and lie, incarnating the wrong committed against the truth. Physical troubles, discreet and intense, illustrate how the lie does not remain hidden in a malicious soul, but causes an external disorder. It produces a particular bodily manifestation, unfaithful to the message it is supposed to express. The lie develops a little controllable substance between pus, cyst, sweat, and hysteria. This dynamic engages as many bodily materialities as well as inventive figures, choreographies, scenarios, and speeches that escape conscious control. The study of such productivity leads to a relativization of the dualism inherent in the sciences of lie detection. There is no interior zone proper to the thought, where the lie is forged, juxtaposed with a carnal envelope whose fragility reveals the background. The body is neither the trembling vehicle of a false word nor the transparent surface of a conflict between trickery and truth. Instead, it participates in the constitution of an unstable complex made up of words and gestures, alibis, and comedies. The lie may assume an integral and metamorphic behavior because it associates passions and reasons and mobilizes intellectual and inextricable impulses. Speaking, writing, judging, feeling, and loving...

all these activities can provoke deceitful fabrication, active or passive, spiritual or carnal.

The detection of a lie is subject to various resistances, the most well-known of which is the control of a seasoned liar. The parameters of a lie detection test are tailored to each individual, measuring their emotional responses to their lies and establishing a unique scale based on their different reactions. However, some personalities manage to control themselves, sometimes aided by tranquilizers, and escape detection. Like a perfect actor, the liar puts himself in the shoes of a truthful character.

But the biggest objection to such techniques is the supposedly intentional nature of a lie. The ordinary definition suggests that an individual lies intentionally: he knows the truth and decides to hide it or even to say the opposite. They are lying *knowingly*. However, there are many situations where lies are unidentified. Specious presentation of facts and the twisting of language allow for several "versions" of the truth. When asked questions such as "Did you cheat on your wife?" Or "Did you receive money illegally?" multiple responses and postures demonstrate that the line between truth and falsehood is drawn through linguistic and legal quibbling. The statements made by President Bill Clinton, convicted of lying under oath, were the subject of extensive commentary on whether oral sex with his intern was a criminal sexual act.

Lacking the ability to fathom hearts and minds, the denunciation of a lie comes up against the obscurity of intentions. Does the liar always lie deliberately, and to what extent is he aware of his lie? Sharp moral principles are unsuitable for a nuanced analysis of the liar's motives or involvement in his statements. And sometimes the liar, without becoming psychotic, can convince himself of his lies. A child who denies having broken the teapot or a murderer who denies having stabbed a victim in the heart will undoubtedly be thwarted by evidence. However, the truth is only sometimes based on authenticatable facts. The liar's perception of their lie may vary, to the point that truth comes in sizes and colors: small or half lies, or what are in English called *white lies*, appear inconsequential and do not provoke a sense of betrayal or wrongdoing. Ordinary life forces us to lie a little or even requires it to avoid offending others. Demanding the truth in all circumstances, like Alceste in *The Misanthrope*, leads to solitude, even madness. Those whom he denounces, the liars of civil convenience, are moreover not convinced that they lie. As each person's acknowledgment of their lie may be suspended by their own definitions or feelings, the intention to betray the truth cannot be held up as an absolute criterion. Some people manipulate the truth, while others feel strong scruples about lying. Here lying is similar to acting: individuals are not equal when faced with the possibility of breaking the moral law.

So, how can we identify a lie that is not lived as one? Here, we come to the most widespread and interesting lies: the ones that we all practice regarding ourselves. Lies become an immense question that goes beyond moral and legal judgments. Confronting the power of lies requires an analysis of their effectiveness, compared to that produced by the truth, in its utterance, fabrication, and autonomy. More than a simple lie detector is required to accomplish this task. We need a science as much as an art of observation is needed, a science that could be conducted in the form of a "psychology," like the one practiced by the moralists of the 17th century or by Nietzsche and Freud. The thousand and one ways in which a subject deceives himself, believes in his lies, and gets caught in the traps of his self-love lead to extending the investigation on lying well beyond the intentional act. Liars do not always know they are lying, especially since they deceive themselves as well as others. The notion of *intention* seems too crude to appreciate the multiple nuances and means by which a subject disguises, arranges, and manipulates the truth.

An amoral investigation of the lie analyzes, without judgment, the inventive logic of a subject who builds a coherent and powerful world intended to draw others in its lures. In ordinary situations, liars show great talent in supporting their lies because they have to feed them with many other stories. While the straight talker, once he has confided the truth, no longer needs to bother with arguments, the liar, on the other hand, composes multiple and infinite fictions. He invents and entangles many stories, adding to them unceasingly as contrary proofs appear. Often, this accumulation of details or this effort to counteract the truth leads to the revelation of the lie. By telling too many stories, the liar "overdoes it" and exposes himself. However, such constructions also come from unintentional liars, those who lie without their own knowledge. They present an astonishing aesthetic and psychic richness in the twists and hypertrophies of their language. Faced with such verbose and devious figures, suspicion arises from the subject's insistence on displaying a truth or a quality.

Insisting, repeating, and hammering are suspicious linguistic gestures that reveal an anxiety opposed to the assurance exhibited by the enunciator. Freud observed that we repeat what we cannot say once and for all. According to him, the repetition of behavior refers to a past trauma that the subject cannot articulate. From a linguistic point of view, it rather indicates a dissonance experienced in the present, even a contemporary conflict between the statement and its meaning. Why does such a subject feel the recurrent need to say that he is fine, that he is not afraid, or that everything is going well? Doesn't hear him continually trumpet his good health suggest that we seriously doubt it? We can also detect this insistence in a tone of voice, a sentence rhythm, and a paradoxically assured flow. Finely tuned ears will be able to detect the subtext of sometimes minute phenomena that bear the trace of a lie.

The use of persuasive rhetoric in politics and advertising confirms this psychological intuition. Opinions abound in voluntarily contradictory formulas where the affirmation of the false is given the appearance of the true. We can understand the tactical aspect of the reversal as long as we detect the procedure. "I don't need to remind you of my fight for the workers of the metalworking industry," says the one who displays it as a pretense for better betraying them. Or, again, a politician provoking a split within his party will name his new group "rally." Such verbal manipulations are part of the techniques of persuasion, and advertisers are well aware of their mechanisms. This is the case with products whose defect, rather than being hidden, is converted into an asset, such as a car that is too expensive and whose promotion insists on its modest price in relation to the exceptional qualities it offers. These procedures remain sketchy as the intention to disguise the truth is based on a simple inversion and maintains the bipolarity of truth and falsehood. On the other hand, specific constructions of the mind testify to a much more complex work, which confers astonishing creative power to the lie.

Theoretical speeches, apparently detached from any intention to lie, combine the evoked features: a psychic complex and a verbal strategy. On the one hand, they manifest a will to affirm, to discover, to declare; on the other hand, they utilize verbal forms that mask the motives of their affirmations. A suspicious listener of these great speeches will thus detect their obsessive character, the recurrence of an idea, a sentence, or a word that knocks and returns unceasingly. "Theorists" or "affirmers" use images, phrases, and expressions that play the role of fetishes. It is not enough to spot a style because these forms are connected to the lie that motivates the theorist's activity. The subject's architecture and the arguments' sophistication offer a linguistic veil that hides the motives of these so-called "works of the mind." Thus, Idealism is adorned with abstraction to hide the kitchen where the idealities are made. However, the demonstrative words and the theoretical treatises are also *bodies that* expose and produce sublime lies.

Systematic recourse to the most abstract language leads to a particular interest in philosophers who use generalizations and claim the universality of their thoughts. These ideas are meant to be understood by all, at least in the major tradition of philosophy; they must be detached from their author and from their conditions of enunciation. The particular investment of the philosopher, the motivations that pushed him to develop such or such concepts, theses, or demonstrations, fade away in face of the elevation of a work coming from the spirit, intended to address other spirits. To be interested in the life of those who discover or create ideas seems, therefore, anecdotal, even inappropriate. However, historical studies on ancient philosophers and their practices have, in the last few decades, rehabilitated this interest in the concrete existence of thinkers. They suggest that philosophy is not limited to the elaboration of doctrines but is built by life choices. It is still necessary to specify the meaning of this "philosophical life."

This interest in the life of thinkers usually presupposes a coherence between their thought and their existence. They are supposed to embody an idea of existence by their attitude—insubordination, wisdom, and self-control. However, there is no guarantee that they lived out a perfect harmony of their ideas and their behavior. The "exemplary" and legendary value given to "philosophical" acts (the provocations of Diogenes, the suicide of Seneca...) prevents us from approaching the psychological motivations of their author concretely. Acting against this illusion of an ideal coherence, Nietzsche adopted a purposefully polemical style towards the great figures of philosophy: Did Socrates display his independence towards the world? Was he not afraid of death? He hated life and was incapable of any existential joy, wrote the author of *Twilight of the Idols*. According to him, the source of philosophies that value the afterlife and hide their true motives is resentment. This nasty apostrophe has the merit of drawing our attention to the reputation of pure and virtuous thought, leading us to suspect it of obeying a hidden strategy.

The distortion between ideas proclaimed and the life lived reaches its maximum curve when a thinker enacts the opposite of what he professes. There is a great benefit to understanding this paradoxical link between an intellectual construction and an opposite practice. Of course, the most common reaction to such a discrepancy is to denounce those who proclaim themselves virtuous while behaving immorally. However, this hypocrisy concerns intentional acts, and we prefer to focus on the unconscious lie, on the theoretical elaboration produced by contrast with the lived existence. It is no longer a simple contradiction, a negligible accident, but a devious verbal invention that expresses *a truth in the form of a lie*. The discourse does not develop "in spite of" a contrary behavior; it is constructed "because of it"! We must reverse the formula "this thinker displays this principle, *even though* he behaves otherwise" and say instead, "This thinker displays this principle because he lives the opposite of what he theorizes." Thus, Rousseau wrote an excellent treatise on education in which he presents himself as a caring father, not in spite of but thanks to the abandonment of his five children.

What we call contradiction is more a psychic process by which a thinker enacts a division of his self that leads him to utter a truth antinomic to what he lives. This *lie-truthfully ("mentir-vrai")*, according to the word of Aragon, assembles a body of concepts in which he invents a theoretical existence. Foucault, at the moment when he professes the courage of the truth, hides the AIDS that will take him away a few months later. He delivers a last speech that is the opposite of the practice of secrecy that he meticulously organizes. It is not enough to take note of this, and denouncing it leads to understanding nothing. Analyzing it, on the other hand, allows us to access the fertile torsion by which a denial produces a conceptual performance. By addressing itself to our rationality, philosophy hides from us the psychic springs at work in its theses. We take the theoretical constructions at face value and believe in transparency between the person of the thinker and the author who enunciates truths. However, it is not obvious that these two instances are the same. Who are we when we think? Ourselves or someone else? Such a question concerns both those who master reasoning and everyone else. Once we install this doubt and recognize the opacity, it becomes possible for us to question the adherence of the thinker to his thought and discover its multiple facets.

The identification of a philosopher with his ideas is fiction. Listening to their demonstrations from a new ear encourages us to question the reasons for their intellectual choices and their investment in a concept. The scholastic hagiography agglomerates an author's name and a thesis—Descartes and the cogito, Pascal and the wager, Kant and the moral law, Hegel and the dialectic, Sartre and commitment...—and prevents us from seeing the distortions and the complex motives that lead an author to choose an idea and persist in supporting it, sometimes contrary to what he may have experienced and felt, and which he could have supported with equal legitimacy. Why did Sartre suddenly defend the notion of commitment with fierce conviction? What happened in 1945 to make him identify with the figure of the interventionist philosopher when he had done little to mobilize during the Occupation? Rational and moral explanation is not enough, nor are his own justifications. Why did Deleuze, who hated travel, become the champion of nomadism? And why did he want to disappear behind his concepts, supporting the idea of an impersonal life of thinkers? Many philosophers have devoted themselves to the construction of a flagship word that has radiated over all fields of thought to the point of acquiring an autonomous existence of its own, detached from any referent. Thus, the hypertrophy of the word "other" in Levinas's work has become the paragon of otherness and solicits the imagination of readers amid a displayed rationality. These great notions, these "keywords" as Adorno analyzes them, are like fetishes. They hold a communicative magic and proceed from powerful denials.

As soon as we admit the part played by fiction in forming and using concepts, we reach the psychic forge of the philosophers. Their apparent contradictions uncover in the same author multiple lives that oppose, articulate, deceive, and recompose themselves. At the same time that Beauvoir was writing *The Second Sex* and laying the foundations of feminism, she was living out a consuming passion with an American writer. On the one hand, she theorized about women's independence; on the other, she wrote hundreds of pages about her servile enjoyment. Even if it is impossible to say where the "real" Beauvoir is, analyzing this double life is of the most significant interest to understand the psychic investment of thought and the contradictory turns that authorize her to affirm great theses. These multiple personalities of a philosopher are seldom acknowledged, although they can raise a strategy of thought, as Kierkegaard experiences, thanks to the numerous pseudonyms that allow him to support and live contrary theories. He writes religious speeches when leading a libertine life, and he writes a seducer's diary when living as an ascetic. This *lying-truthfully* stands at the heart of philosophical reason.

The word "lie", freed from its moral charge and inscribed in this psychic way, must be nuanced and refined because it designates a great variety of figures. It is necessary to unravel its agglomerated contents and distinguish its processes and symptoms. If we no longer limit it anymore to the intentional negation of the truth, the lie takes complex verbal forms whose multiple works, systems, and intellectual postures will show extraordinary

Introduction: For an Amoral Approach to Lying

diversity. Some common traits unite them, however, such as *the desire to affirm*—even if the affirmative mode can be officially contested—which extends into a desire to argue, demonstrate, and link ideas. The overvaluation of "concepts," general ideas that cover more or less sensitive and disparate realities, offers another sign of the fabulation and its linguistic fetishism. A third trait, more thematic, is the necessity for the liar to formulate a theory of truth. Here again, several different names of truth proliferate: sincerity, authenticity, and veracity... however, the liar always encounters this antithesis of truth and falsity that he must reconstruct in order to lie even better.

Though I may repeat this so many times that it becomes suspicious, my remarks are far from denigration and never from the point of view of the one who escapes lies or, worse, of the one who knows the truth. The word "liar" is never, here, an accusation. All the same, I am interested in the gap between what can be held as verifiable and the fabricating practice of certain theoretical discourses. The truth of the lived experience of this or that thinker remains forever inaccessible, like that of any psychic life. However, there are incongruities between truth and falsehood according to the values of discourse that are admitted by the liars themselves, which allow them to point out the "contradictions" between what they affirm and what they practice. In this discord between them and themselves, psychic power is uncovered, giving a new reading to their writings and abstract discourses.

The choice of authors for this analysis of lies is based on one criterion: my present or past admiration for their works, with which I have spent a long time. That admiration should restrain any form of resentment and any temptation to denounce ugly liars. Writing to slander authors has always seemed to me a dubious exercise, proper to the hatred of prominent authorities. A minimum of generosity is necessary to understand these works and reread them while crediting them with a meaning irreducible to a single interpretation, even if it means passing them afterward through the sieve of an unfaithful reading.

Certainly, one of the least important reasons for this investigation is my knowledge of many professional philosophers I meet in academic and media circles. And I have always been surprised, probably naively, to notice a vast gap between principles, values claimed with brilliance, and the lives led in opposition to these virtues. This discrepancy is all the more striking because the speech is so loud. But, in the end, why should there be fewer fabulists among philosophers than among the population as a whole? They have nothing to envy of the political staff or any manufacturer of counterfeiters. Instead, they offer "cases," allowing us to understand beyond the aforementioned philosophy the inventive power and the paradoxical construction of lies about oneself. This incongruity, so widespread among the thinkers, is often transformed into a fascinating theoretical delirium, a source of joy, and a generator of thoughts for their readers. The defect becomes excess; the twist becomes creation.

The Pathos of Truth

"Loving the truth" expresses a moral and spiritual ideal that is easy to accept. Who, on the other hand, could claim a love for lies? The search for truth and the fidelity to the *truth* are immediately taken for granted. However, it is advisable to specify exactly what these formulas refer to since they designate different motives and require specific virtues. The metaphysical truth of God or the suprasensible world is not the moral truth that engages an attitude of the conscience. Nor is it the factual and judicial truth. Far from tracing a history of truth in the philosophical tradition, we question the affects accompanying references to truth. Why do we "love" that which is professed as true? What satisfactions does the commitment of oneself to the truth bring? What are the reasons for publicly declaring one's love for the truth? A series of antitheses orchestrates the felicitous choice of truth, transparency, sincerity, and natural purity, in contrast to the opacity of falsehood, error, lies, and hypocritical acting. All these notions stress at the same time the moral sides and the imaginary aspects of the truth, which are associated with so many positive qualities.

It is not surprising then that the proclamation of the truth is so enthusiastic, except that a liar would declare it just as willingly. If the liar were suddenly caught in a fit of frankness, he would encounter the famous logical paradox pointed out by Eubulides. The formula "I am lying" is impossible to sustain since it implies its opposite: I am lying by saying that I am lying; therefore, I am telling the truth. If this statement has been much glossed after the Greek philosopher, on the other hand, the opposite sentence, "I tell the truth," remains underestimated. This statement can also be pronounced by a liar as well as by a sincere individual without logical paradox. From the point of view that interests us here, we must question its enunciative support since it manifests the joy of asserting by concentrating its energy on a significant property of the assertion: truthfulness. "I know what I'm saying, and I insist: it's true," the asserter proclaims with a force of self-conviction to convince his interlocutor. The demand for trust is implicit in the statement "I am telling the truth": the asserter must be taken at their word. It appeals to our shared love of truth, to the credit we give it. "Believe me, I am telling the truth!" But why does he feel the need to appeal to the truth of his saying, impose it, and claim a certificate of authenticity instead of simply stating what he means? Such a claim leads to our suspicion, and we are prone, maliciously, to doubt a discourse as soon as such a demand has been made.

All Liars, Except Rousseau

The lover of truth takes us as witnesses of his love. He makes us captives of the credit given to his words because he needs us to guarantee his sincerity. Insidiously, we become his debtors. In Rousseau, this alliance of hyperbolic proclamation and hostage-taking found one of its most brilliant incarnations. The writer-philosopher never ceases to display his love of the truth. He carries it as the common essence of philosophy and of his personality. His favorite motto, taken from Juvenal, is *Vitam impendere vero*—"to devote one's life to the truth"—and he made it his seal, engraving the phrase to sign his name.

However, with Rousseau, practical truth prevails over general truth. If he wants to "tell" this truth, it is officially to repair the wrongs done to him and also to confess some faults in secret. He wrote *The Confessions* for this purpose. He continuously displays his honesty, and his frankness in front of the readers, telling them the multiple situations where he has exposed himself without falseness. The man who hated theatrical artifice does not end his long enterprise of confessions, his hundreds of "sincere" pages, by a spectacular staging of his public declaration. He shows himself to the reader affirming before witnesses:

"I have written the truth: if any person has heard of things contrary to those I have just stated, were they a thousand times proved, he has heard calumny and falsehood; and if he refuses thoroughly to examine and compare them with me whilst I am alive, he is not a friend either to justice or truth. For my part, I openly, and without the least fear, declare, that whoever, even without having read my works, shall have examined with his own eyes, my disposition, character, manners, inclinations, pleasures, and habits, and pronounce me a dishonest man, is himself one who deserves a gibbet."[1]

The audience remained silent, according to the assertor. The truth made itself evident through the spoken apology, as its messenger embodied the victorious truth in itself. The one opposing it deserves death, as the lie itself must be overcome and punished because nothing is more hateful. A fine psychologist, La Rochefoucauld, observed that "the aversion to lying is often an imperceptible ambition to make our testimonies considerable and to attract to our words a religious respect."[2] In fact, through faith-statement, Rousseau imposes devotion on his speech. He has given himself the last word; he offers his "declaration" as a spectacle, and he forbids any possibility of contesting it. Is it necessary to say it a thousand times? Everything has been declared; that is to say, he has told the truth!

However, doubt arises in the mind of a slightly informed psychologist: so much pathos and so much huffing and puffing, so much exposition and repetition indicate that not everything has been said once and for all. In fact, after *The Confessions*, Rousseau again felt the need to explain himself, to justify himself with *Rousseau juge de*

---

1. Rousseau, Jean-Jacques. *The Confessions of Jean-Jacques Rousseau: Complete*. Translated by W. Conyngham Mallory. Auckland: The Floating Press, 2012, pp. 769-770.
2. François de La Rochefoucauld, *Maxims and Moral Reflections*, London, 1791, p. 133.

Jean-Jacques. Does a virtuous person so badly need to exhibit his virtue? Self-presentation necessarily involves masks and tricks. Rousseau is moreover aware of the difference between "the genuine man" and "the man who tells the truth." The first acts without even feeling the desire to present himself to others. Why, then, does he insist that he is for the truth, that he is its defender? Because I am unjustly attacked! answers Rousseau.

What exactly is he accused of? When reading, it is difficult to identify his faults, as the author proliferates the examples of slander—plagiarism, treason, theft, lechery, blasphemy... However, one of them, obsessive and disguised, constitutes the core of a general trial that is carried out until the end of his days: the abandonment of his children. Our great virtuous man claims his truth and cries out against injustice in many cases, but at the end of the day, this lack of responsibility towards his offspring remains his inexpiable crime. In *The Confessions,* he reconstructs his moral path and tries to cover this stain with varying degrees of skill. Meeting Thérèse, whom he gets pregnant, is presented as a decisive step in his access to virtue. "I have always considered the day on which I was united to Theresa as that which fixed my moral existence,"[3] he claims.

How can placing five children in a public institution be justified? A first defense consists in relativizing the event. Pregnancy is made to be only a matter of body size and

____

3. Rousseau, Jean-Jacques. *The Confessions of Jean-Jacques Rousseau: Complete, op. cit.,* p. 480.

does not implicate those who have caused the increase in volume. Rousseau relates the news in this way, obscuring the term "paternity": "Whilst I was increasing my corpulency at Chenonceau, that of my poor Theresa was augmented at Paris in another manner, and at my return I found the work I had put upon the frame in greater forwardness than I had expected."[4] The issue seems to be averted by an almost playful casualness that reduces procreation to trivial physiology. Moreover, in *Emile*, the educator compares childbirth to peeing with pain, which Rousseau knows well from having problems with his urethra.

The second explanation is more surprising because it contradicts the self-image presented in *The Confessions*. While Rousseau began his autobiography by asserting his absolute singularity, incomparable to other men, he takes refuge behind habits and customs. The man who said he was "intoxicated with virtue" now adopts the corrupted mores of his time. Populating the "Enfants-Trouvés" hospital because one is poor or debauched is an ordinary conduct, even approved. "Since it the custom of the country, they who live here may adopt it,"[5] observes the father who must, despite everything, overcome the mother's resistance. Does he really believe in his own arguments? Does he clear himself of the fault by admitting it? The truth is given here in the form of a confession. But isn't Rousseau lying to himself?

---

4. *Ibid.* p. 395.
5. *Ibid,* p. 397.

The denial of fault and its paradoxical admission produce an infernal spin between truth and lies. The wrongdoer reverses the prejudice and becomes the victim: this abandonment of his children will follow Rousseau all his life, and his detractors will use it to denigrate him, unfairly in his eyes. Did he feel remorse? Rousseau had left a numbered card in the swaddling clothes of his firstborn, keeping open the possibility of future recognition of the child, but he abandoned the following ones without any trace of their origin. Each time, the abandoner gives new justifications, not only the precariousness of his social condition but also the bad education Thérèse Levasseur and her family would have provided. Moreover, he wanted to believe that the public institution raised orphans better, even though the mortality rate of *Les Enfants Trouvés* was reputedly very high. However, this excess of reasons makes one suspect some concern, some bad faith intended to hide the responsibility of the crime.

The bid to absolve the philosopher continued among his biographers. The affair of his abandoned children has indeed known astonishing glosses, and Rousseau's defenders continue today to plead his innocence: his urinary disease, his impotence, Thérèse's infidelity, and the hypothesis of children by adultery have provided theses justifying the abandonment. It is common to see admirers transform their author into an irreproachable idol. So many specious arguments aim at reversing the wrong: the injustice was no longer committed against the orphans but against Rousseau himself. However, such an accumulation of truths and untruths suggests a lie or at least an inexpiable fault. It is necessary to affirm the "truth" and proclaim this word loudly and clearly to better conceal the crime better. The tone is exaggerated, the utterance too firm, to the point that it sometimes cracks, as the contemporary Dorat notes, observing that Rousseau's voice never trembled, except at the moment when he evoked the abandonment of his children.

The love of the truth, invested and overexposed, reveals itself as a lie. Rousseau lived out this paradox passionately, identifying himself with the outraged virtue. He increasingly constructed an image of himself as a martyr for truth, suffering the humiliation of "liars," the others, those villains who conceal their motives. At the end of his life, he claims he is hated for what he is, a good man, more than for any faults. This masochistic delirium leads him to love the general calumny against him since it transforms him into an allegory of the martyred Good: "I find nothing so great, nothing so beautiful than to suffer for the truth. I envy the glory of the martyrs."[6]

What we can call the *pathos* of truth takes diverse and sometimes dramatic psychic forms. With Rousseau, the scene organized by the *affirmative lie* is a paranoia that summons all the liars in the world around a single, unjustly accused subject. The obsession with a plot against him is a discourse familiar to readers of Rousseau. And this fiction is built early, before the abandonment of his children. Its

---

6. Jean-Jacques Rousseau, « Lettre à M. de Saint-Germain, 26 février 1770 », in *Correspondance complète*, t. XXXVII, ed. R. A. Leigh, Oxford University, The Voltaire Foundation, 1980, p. 261. My translation.

origin can be found in the death of his mother when she gives birth to Jean-Jacques and in the attitude of his father, who holds his son involuntarily responsible for this death. But a psychoanalytical approach to Rousseau as a subject exceeds our intentions here, and we will remain at the analysis of a discourse that feeds on both a *denial* and an *affirmation of truth.*

Rousseau's paranoia constantly revolves around *Emile*'s publication in 1762, which seems to him to be the cause of all his misfortunes. In fact, the book was condemned by the Sorbonne, seized by the police, and burned in front of the Palais de Justice. A decree of arrest forced Rousseau to take refuge in Switzerland, and there, once again, the work was attacked, and its author had to flee again. The "Profession of Faith of the Savoyard Vicar," which constitutes the fourth chapter of *Emile*, provoked the clerical wrath in Europe. However, this objective cause—the condemnation of an essay on ideological grounds—is minimized by Rousseau, who interprets his persecution in the light of another, more personal motive. In *The Confessions*, he recalls the difficult process that accompanied Emile's writing, which is quite different from that of *The Social Contract*. Jean-Jacques conceived the treatise on education as his final work, after which he would retire. Unfortunately, he is constantly delayed in his undertaking due to repeated hassles in printing the book and the worsening of his psychological state as he writes the treatise. A scene reveals his masochistic fixation: when he is advised to publish anonymously this text that will cause him serious trouble. Rousseau refuses: *Emile* will make him triumph for posterity, and it will return his honor. Instead of adopting caution, he asserts his authority and presents this treatise as a full-length portrait.

Imagining that a crowd of liars are slandering him, Rousseau hides his own lies from himself. However, the truth continues to work in the heart of denial, in excessive paranoid writing. After evoking the abandonment of his children, Rousseau dates the beginning of his misfortunes to the publication of *Emile*, and obsesses over a worldwide plot against him. He soon imagines himself burned at the stake among his books, all for an increasingly specious reason: his conception of education. Guilt constructs this paranoid motive: the subject feels unjustly attacked for a thousand reasons because, deep down, he believes himself guilty of an absolute, existential fault.

The conspiracy thesis thus serves to conceal the fundamental flaw; it substitutes faults that are not faults for another, unsurpassable one: Rousseau is accused of being a supereducator, so he is not reproached for being an undereducator. The tourniquet turns to delirium when Rousseau believes he can read the signs of his persecution everywhere, even among his protectors. Mme de Luxembourg, Hume, Mirabeau… all plot against the author of *Emile*. "The ceiling under which I write has eyes; the walls of my chamber have ears. Surrounded by spies and by vigilant and malevolent inspectors, disturbed, and my attention diverted, I hastily commit to paper a few broken sentences [...] I know that, notwithstanding the barriers which are multiplied around me, my enemies are afraid truth should escape by some little opening."[7] This truth that others are supposed to covet is, in fact, Rousseau's lie, which hides behind the ramparts of assertions that he has built around himself.

The affirmative lie—"Rousseau is a great educator"—constructs a machinery that can activate without the subject knowing it. The whole world is transformed into multiple accusing glances, which sharpen the feeling of injustice and push the imaginary victim to cry out "his" truth until self-sacrifice. The pathos of truth is due to the over-investment of a verbal idol with which the subject identifies, ready to die for his victory. And the more pressing the need to repress the lie becomes, the more dramatic the glorification of the truth becomes. The subject, caught in the trance of a hyperbolic affirmation, splits up by becoming the idolized character of a fetishized word. Rousseau shows the spectacular logic of this: the world has constituted itself into a tribunal to judge and condemn him, he pleads his case by dividing his word in *Rousseau juge de Jean-Jacques*. Three dialogues show him answering a "Frenchman" and justifying his behavior. This self-advocacy takes up the conviction of a plot, dated precisely on June 18, 1762—the publication of *Emile*—and turned into a "universal conspiracy" against his person. His self-portrait is so invested in the representation of himself as a martyr for truth that it produces a cleavage between the hypostasized victim Rousseau and Jean-Jacques debating

---

7. Rousseau, Jean-Jacques. *The Confessions of Jean-Jacques Rousseau*: Complete, *op. cit., p. 318.*

with their accusers. "Rousseau the truth" has become an icon. All that remains is a multitude of scattered, delirious *selves* defending and recriminating themselves. The cries are no longer aimed at convincing any juror because the subject, thus fragmented, has lost the ability to address anyone. He lives in a theater where he incarnates at once the actors and the spectators of his martyrdom.

When affirmed so passionately, truth can be proclaimed without any interlocutor. This proclamation goes so far as to forbid any possibility of response and deliberation, feeding on its own delirium. The outcome of the trial that Rousseau conducts against himself leads to abandoning all charges. In the third dialogue that the author imagines with the Frenchman, the latter exonerates him, in a move equivalent to a self-absolution. Rousseau, the author of the *Dialogues*, produced an actor, Rousseau, who quoted texts of Rousseau the philosopher, without providing real arguments against the accusation. His goal is no longer to convince anyone but to exhibit his martyrdom as an innocent saint of truth. He ends up taking his text to God by planning to place his *Dialogues* on the high altar of Notre Dame. On the envelope, he writes: "Protector of the oppressed, God of justice and truth, receive this deposit that is placed on Your altar and entrusted to Your Providence an unfortunate stranger, alone, defenseless on earth, outraged, mocked, defamed, betrayed by a whole generation."[8] But on February 24, 1776, he discovers that

---

8. Rousseau, Jean-Jacques, *Rousseau, Judge of Jean-Jacques: Dialogues*. Translated by Judith R. Bush, Christopher Kelly, and Roger D. Masters.

a gate protects the altar, and paranoia takes over again: Rousseau is convinced that it has been installed on purpose to prevent him from reaching God and claiming justice.

The pathos of truth, in Rousseau, is revealed in its paroxysm as a Christ-like passion. In spite of its exceptional energy, it testifies both to the symptomatic nature of the great declarations in the name of truth and to the creative power of a lie that lingers in the consciousness of a subject. The one who constantly refers to the Truth has something to hide, and he unwittingly develops a hypertrophied and transferential representation of his lie. Faith in the truth goes hand in hand with paranoia in Rousseau, who paints himself as a supplicant of all the liars in the world. The model of such an injustice, committed against the one who embodies the truth, or at least the desire for truth, is the *Apology of Socrates.* But in the absence of one Plato to report the trial, Rousseau appeals to his readers' empathy rather than to a critical reflection. He turns away from philosophical analysis in favor of his self-presentation as a martyr. In his excess, did he not manifest, through his paranoid delirium, the propensity of any subject to over-invest in a concept, to identify with it, and to transform himself into its valiant knight? Heroes of truth, freedom, justice... how many have not given in, in their small intimate theater, to this scenario that enchants ordinary life? Such an over-investment seems crazy when it takes on a delirious and spectacular appearance, but it

Hanover: Published for Dartmouth College by University Press of New England, 1990, p. 247.

gives us an insight into the psychic motives of those who adhere faithfully to a concept, claim to embody it, and believe themselves to be its flag-bearers.

Theories and Practices of Lying:
Montaigne, Rousseau, Kant, Constant, Nietzsche

If we admit that lies are exposed in their full power when presented under the auspices of truth, observing how liars feel the need for a theory of truth becomes fruitful. They can formulate it positively, praising true discourses, or negatively, deciphering falsity. According to this second version, the liar hides himself by talking about the lie or even by denouncing all liars. Pointing out the defects of others is often the revelation of one's own defects. From this point of view, professional informers should always be suspected. But, in a more refined way, liars can resort to a great discourse on the meaning of truth and falsity or the digressions of lies. Rousseau, again, offers us a fine example, proposing a thesis on lying in *Reveries of the Solitary Walker*. In the fourth walk, the philosopher foresees a problem that could undermine the sincerity displayed in his *Confessions*: a subject may indeed *feel that he* is telling the truth but could be *lying to himself* without knowing it. Unintentional lying, even more so when it is to oneself, is difficult to detect and ruins the claim of authenticity. Rousseau admits that "know thyself" is difficult to follow and that one can be fooled by its frankness.

To speak of "the" lie as if it could have a single definition is inappropriate for the varied uses of lies. There is no such thing as a "lie," and beyond a moral discussion of its intentional nature, its forms and motives require a much finer analysis than a conceptual synthesis. Why do we lie, how do we lie, what are the types of lies, do we enjoy lying, do we control it? So many questions call for a pragmatic and psychological approach. In the 16th century, Montaigne already observed the extraordinary diversity of lying and proposed distinguishing between the lie and the lying.[9] In his time, the language easily used substantivized verbs, making it possible to underline the lie as an activity: the *lying*—which will find topicality with the expression of Aragon, lying-truthfully.

Montaigne suggests, on the authority of grammar, that a lie is simply saying something false without intention to harm, whereas lying concerns invention or deception exercised with knowledge of the facts. He takes up a distinction that has been made since antiquity, from Plato to Cicero and then to Augustine, whose discourses on lies have constantly differentiated between the liar and the one who "tells a lie." The liar is condemnable in principle because he knows he is lying, and does so to deceive others by misleading them. On the other hand, the one who tells a lie sometimes does not know it, and his motives may be praiseworthy even if they remain illicit. A few rare situations justify a departure from the truth, and even

---

9. Montaigne, *Essais,* ed. Pierre Villey, P.U.F., 2 vols, 1978, *loc. cit,* Book I, chap. IX, t. I, p. 35. Black, Cyril E. *Essays* of Montaigne, Volume I. Cambridge: HUP, 1924, Book I, Chapter IX, p. 43.

then, not everyone is entitled to this departure, because only the wise man, who knows how to distinguish truth from falsehood, has the right to use a lie for noble ends. In his two works on the lie, Augustine precisely describes its variety, suggesting that there are "lies" rather than "the" lie. Uncompromisingly, however, he condemns lying as an abomination and admits no exceptions to the duty of truthfulness: "There are many kinds of lies, all of which, indeed, we should detest uniformly. There is no lie which is not contrary to truth."[10]

Far from such intransigence, Montaigne opens a new way to understand the forms of lying without condemning them outright. "If falsehood, like truth, had but one face, we should be better off, for we should take for certain the contrary of what the liar said. But the opposite of truth has a hundred thousand shapes and a limitless field."[11] The author of the *Essays*, not very dogmatic, observes that truth and lies are not symmetrical and obey different logic than that of the true and the false. Lying is a matter of the multiple and the diverse; it cannot be defined because it knows no limits. Though Montaigne does not give it moral credit, considering it a vice, he distinguishes between lies with a background of truth and invented lies. The former call for the art of disguise; they manipulate

---

10. Augustine, *Treatises on Various Subjects : The Christian Life, Lying, against Lying, Continence, Patience, the Excellence of Widowhood, the Work of Monks, the Usefulness of Fasting, the Eight Questions of Dulcitus*. Translated by Roy J. (Roy Joseph) Deferrari, and Mary Sarah. Muldowney. 1st pbk. reprint. Washington, D.C: Catholic University of America Press, 2002, p. 129.
11. Montaigne, *Essays, op. cit.,* p. 45.

reality and must constantly transform it as it comes back to challenge these fallacious versions. The latter requires a certain *genius* since they create a reality out of nothing and infuse it with the force of truth that convinces listeners of the lie. Montaigne's originality and insight come from his theoretical position: he does not judge, he does not condemn, he analyzes, and he lets himself be surprised. He glimpses the playful part of lying, its fragility, and its madness. Liars are dizzy with their own lies, they deceive themselves to the point of no longer controlling their fictions. Lying then becomes intransitive: one lies to lie and finally loses one's head. The spiral of lies leads from the pleasure of invention to the delirium of the personality.

Rousseau, the champion of truth, occasionally admits the exhilaration of this game with lies. The most astonishing thing happens at the turn of his reflection on a bad memory. Rousseau is beating his chest by confessing that he has, throughout his life, regretted a particular lie, but he suddenly remembers other little lies committed almost innocently. And suddenly, the reader understands that it is not so much the content of the lie as its activity: lying is a pleasure in itself, without motive. Inventing facts, asserting their truth with "absolute faith," is a childish taste for imagination, a desire to bend reality to the most unbridled fantasies. Rousseau, who never ceased to proclaim his hatred of lies as the worst ignominy, confessed that he could have lied out of joy!

Lying for pleasure, without intention to harm, gives us a glimpse of the complexity of lying, and its underhanded infiltration into many behaviors. Morality would easily settle its fate if the lie aimed only at counterfeiting the truth out of self-interest. It escapes moral reason if it can be exercised without a goal and free itself from any utility. According to a popular saying, truth comes out of the mouths of babes, but so does lies, at least in another disposition, joyful and malicious. It is linked to the imaginary and the suspense of the meaning. Everything becomes possible for those who know how to lie for the pleasure of lying in an intransitive way. It doesn't matter if a statement is true or false as long as it allows one to invent by telling it.

Often, a child's lies are the object of relentless repression because it is necessary to educate the child in the truth as soon as possible. However, behind the pedagogical and moral motive that leads to reprimanding the little liar, a panicked fear is hidden: the contract of trust no longer functions and no longer guarantees with certainty that the verbal exchange obeys the order of the meaning. Nothing is guaranteed any longer as soon as doubt is introduced and language is stripped of its referents. And worse still, the referents become interchangeable: if the imaginary had only substituted one reality for another, lies would have the status of acceptable untruths, and, in fact, people or societies assume lies with a certain stability. However, the volubility of lies prevents any certainty since everything can be reversed into its opposite, since everything is false, even the truth. One reality can be arbitrarily presented under the aspect of another through a playful assertion. What to believe, who to believe, when the reversal becomes king? The lying child makes you dizzy, he deserves to be punished!

And what if the choice to tell the truth was based solely on conformism? The duty that obliges us to the truth has undoubtedly moral grounds, but gregariousness is also part in it. The most suspicious psychologist among philosophers, Nietzsche, observed this motive undermining the glorious claim to truth. In ordinary life, those who speak the truth act out of laziness. Once they have told it, they feel free of any further speech. Lies, on the other hand, require imagination, disguise, and memory. In order to firmly ground a lie, it is necessary to invent many others. It thus requires talent and courage to lie, Nietzsche remarks in *Human Too Human*: "Why do men, as a rule, speak the truth in the ordinary affairs of life? Certainly not for the reason that a god has forbidden lying. But because first: it is more convenient, as falsehood entails invention, make-believe and recollection (wherefore Swift says that whoever invents a lie seldom realises the heavy burden he takes up: he must, namely, for every lie that he tells, insert twenty more). Therefore, because in plain ordinary relations of life it is expedient to say without circumlocution: I want this, I have done this, and the like; therefore, because the way of freedom and certainty is surer than that of ruse.—But if it happens that a child is brought up in sinister domestic circumstances, it will then indulge in falsehood as matter of course, and involuntarily say anything its own interests may prompt: an inclination for truth, an aversion to falsehood, is quite foreign and uncongenial to it, and hence it lies in all innocence."[12]

---

12. Nietzsche, Friedrich Wilhelm. *Human, All Too Human : A Book for Free Spirits*. Translated by Alexander Harvey. Auckland, New Zealand: The Floating Press, 2013, aphorism 54, p. 60.

While the straightforward path of truth offers comfort and security, the path of lies is steep and welcomes only the adventurous. This reversal of moral evidence may seem like a provocation, as the praise of lies is so subversive in its rhetoric. However, Nietzsche goes further than an immoral suggestion; he aims at a state before moral meaning.

Lies are childish, and this polymorphous play with meaning suggests an available world that has not yet been crushed under the weight of duty and guilt. This moment when children play parts and can exchange their roles of policemen or thieves evokes a joyful and theatrical existence. Surely, the philosopher who has freed himself from the specter of metaphysical truth and no longer believes in backward worlds can assume this masquerade of the world without lament. However, it is still important to distinguish between lies because not all of them are equal, as we shall see later. And precisely, for Nietzsche, the biggest lie is to make people believe in a supernatural reality preferable to the present life. In his aphorism, the figure of the child makes it possible to emphasize a *cheerful lie*. And as other texts on the child testify, this moment is situated both before the age of reason—these are the children we have been—and after it, since the ultimate metamorphosis Nietzsche hopes for reaches this innocent freedom of the masked player. The first child lies to hide his misdeeds; to avoid punishment, he instinctively follows his immediate interest and locks himself in his fanciful allegations. On the other hand, the child to come lies without interest because he has gone beyond good and evil because he has stripped the truth of its metaphysical and moral charge. The two children join together to lie in total innocence, devoid of depth.

Such a practice of lying is supposed to have left behind its moral significance, and certainly, it cannot be set up as a universal maxim. If it does not offer a guide to follow, it nevertheless opens our ears to singular tunes—not only those of slander—linked to multiple lying discourses. Once again, it is not so much a question of "types" of lies, identified according to their content or their purpose, as of activities, of ways of "lying at leisure." Rousseau, the great scorner of lies, thus glimpsed, in his infinite introspections, what Nietzsche would underline with malice a century later: the pleasure of lying. In his fourth walk of the *Reveries*, Rousseau opens the box of lies and perceives their complexity. There is no longer "the" lie, odious and condemnable, but "different" lies. Some of them even seem minor, to the point that they can be divided.

The denunciation of lies gives way to a *casuistry of lying*. Thus, there are "half lies," told with no intention to harm and without serious consequences. Meticulous, the solitary walker dissects ambiguous situations as to the intention to lie; not telling the truth when one is not obliged to tell it is not a lie, according to him. And even when one tells the opposite of the truth, one does not lie if the truth is not required. From then on, Rousseau dares to think, it becomes conceivable to "make a lie innocent,"[13]

---

13. Rousseau, Jean-Jacques. *Reveries of the Solitary Walker*. Translated by Russell Goulbourne. Oxford: Oxford University Press, 2020, p. 38.

The Pathos of Truth

with caution certainly, but rejecting the intransigent moralists. A complex discussion follows on the duty of truth: when the truth is not useful, when it does not imply justice, and when it concerns only unimportant facts, not touching the universal, then it is possible to keep it quiet or to disguise it without lying! By definition, this "innocent" lie is just one that does not harm, and innocence does not involve a philosophy of play and childishness like the one that Nietzsche will promote. However, the innocence of the one who fights against his accusers, who believes himself unconsciously guilty, is a moral and existential value. Rousseau thus tries to accept that he could have lied without lying, that he lied while remaining innocent.

If lies become acceptable as long as one's intentions are not malicious, the morality of truth is then subjected to the most ambiguous situations. Is the subject who lies authorized to deceive if he has good reasons? Who can be sure of the validity of his reasons? If the universal maxim disappears in favor of a particular judgment, a personal evaluation of what is good or bad, the frontier between truth and lies remains blurred. Rousseau makes many moral concessions that move him away from the austere and glorious attitude that presided over his pathos of truth. Not only does he accept the possibility of deceiving with good intentions, but he also considers that a will to deceive is not so serious if the one lied to does not suffer from it. Saying good things, making someone believe in a reality that does not exist... this does not constitute a fault in itself; only the result counts. Rousseau becomes a consequentialist at this moment: he evaluates the morality of an action on the basis of its effects. The argument passes like a flash and is not followed up, but it surprises the reader accustomed to good faith statements about truth.

The philosophical and moral argumentation concerning the search for truth and the duty to tell it takes on a new inclination if we refer to its psychic motivations and its discursive turns. Rousseau again offers a good example because he invests excessively in his declarative speech and struggles furiously with his contradictions. The energy he expends is commensurate with an immense denial that never ceases to inflate and agitate the forms he invents. The moral contortions that arise in the *Reveries* are all the more clearly visible if we compare them to an almost contemporary reflection on lying, that of Kant in the *Foundations of the Metaphysics of Morals*, and the discussion it has provoked. The austere and radical conception of the duty of truthfulness that is asserted there shows Rousseau's deviations and twists more clearly.

In the name of an intangible principle, Kant affirms the impossibility of justifying lying, whatever the circumstances, intentions, or consequences. The autonomy of the will supposes a categorical imperative: I must forbid myself to lie, not out of fear of incurring opprobrium since "I ought not to lie even if it did not bring on me the least disgrace."[14] And if I were in extreme danger and could only get out of it by lying, the lie would always remain a

---

14. Kant, Immanuel, *Groundwork of the Metaphysics of Morals.* Revised edition / translation by Jens Timmermann. Cambridge, UK ; Cambridge University Press, 2012, p. 52.

moral fault. Benjamin Constant objected to this absolute position, which disdained any particular experience or situation. He observed that a duty to tell the truth in all circumstances abusively assumed a right to the truth for everyone: according to this excessive right, a subject should tell the truth to respect the right of others to access it. However, *not all truth is good to tell*, especially when it can harm the person receiving it or others it concerns. For example, someone suffering from an incurable disease does not always want to know. Should this truth be forced upon them? Should we also inform the insurance company that guarantees a long-term financial loan? Numerous cases thus testify to the complexity of situations and lead to doubts about reducing them to a single general principle. And above all, the duty to tell the truth obeys motives that are rarely as clear as a moral imperative.

At the political level, the revelation of truths, even when it is exercised in the name of virtue, depends on the situations in which it is exercised. It is part of information management strategies from which even the best-intentioned informers—especially those who are now called "whistle-blowers"—cannot escape. What is the purpose of such and such a truth, and who does it harm? These questions cannot be devalued as secondary consequences with regard to the duty to tell the truth. The right to know the truth is undoubtedly legitimate, but this truth is never spoken out of context. It exists both absolutely and in a situation. Exposing a state secret, such as revealing espionage activities, may seem at first glance an ethical and democratic duty to make political information available to all. However, the ideal of transparency, as we will soon discuss, cannot ignore the context and consequences of uncontrolled dissemination of information, especially when it involves the lives of individuals. This critique of the duty of truth, formulated by Benjamin Constant, thus legitimizes secondary principles under the primary principle of truth at all costs. Common sense leads Constant to observe that the absolute use of this principle would lead society to its ruin.

If everyone told the truth to everyone else, war would immediately spread. It is, therefore, necessary to evaluate the beautiful, rational principle in the conditions in which it is exercised. Kant was incensed by this objection and the examples that ridiculed him, such as this practical fiction: Let us imagine assassins looking to kill a man a friend has hidden; the friend would have to say where the man is hiding if asked. Even assassins should not be lied to, even if the consequence is murder! Kant then wrote, in 1797, a small text entitled *On a pretended right to lie out of humanity*, in which he reminded us that if a subject lies, he harms himself first and, through him, humanity in general. Every liar thus undermines the foundations of law and language. Since truth remains the basis of any contract, being faithful to it is a sacred commandment. This proscription of lies also guarantees the elementary faith in dialogue and, more generally, in the link between words and reality. If everyone doubted the word of others, mistrust would inevitably settle among men. The slightest lie puts humanity in danger! To tell the truth is thus an absolute imperative, and no circumstance could justify shirking such a duty. Derrida, who considered this little text of Kant as "one of the most radical and powerful attempts in the history of the West, after Saint Augustine, to think, determine, reflect the lie, but also to proscribe or prohibit any lie,"[15] points out the example which serves to reaffirm the imperative: the lie of feigned pleasure during sexual relations. He observes that this motif recurs several times in the book as subtext, joining the vast file of female lying and misogynistic discourses. He ironizes this unconditional prohibition of a simulated orgasm even if, or because, she is deceiving others for her supposed benefit. Through this irreverent reading, Derrida suggests that another motive than practical reason informs Kant's text. In fact, the moral discourse masks the psychic motives of great philosophical arguments.

The incoherence between words and thoughts, between a theory and acts—an incoherence designated by the word lie—obeys much more complex mechanisms than those of conscious and intentional cunning. Faced with any general discourse on lies and truth, we should always question the claim of an author to embody the truth. This doubt leads us to suspect obscure relations with certain lies, like the one Derrida points out in Kant, and to question the illusion of an asserter when he assures with certainty that he can delimit the border between truth and lie. Doesn't it take, precisely, a singular experience of the lie to describe

---

15. Jacques Derrida, *History of the Lie: Prolegomena,* in Bennington, Geoffrey, Paul Davies, Jacques Derrida, Peter Fenves, Werner Hamacher, Jean Rabate, and Elisabeth Weber. *Futures : Of Jacques Derrida.* Edited by Richard Rand. Stanford, CA: Stanford University Press, 2022, p. 74.

its figures with such precision? The position of enunciation as herald of truth does not guarantee this enunciator is not a victim of his own lies. Not recognizing that we can lie to ourselves at the moment when we are so sure of the truths we tell testifies to a blindness of motives that lead us to assert a thesis as truth.

The theories of lying expounded by many philosophers do not come only from observation but also from practice. Underneath rational argumentation, there are forces at work that go beyond the reach of morality and law. These motivations do not call into question the law but suggest that the law itself serves as a screen to hide the causes that lead to *telling* the truth or a lie. When Rousseau proclaims his love for the true man who accepts all the consequences of the truth, even to his disadvantage, he seems close to the uncompromising morality formulated by Kant a few years after him. But his statement is not entirely based on a rational argument, and it is in the depths of his individual conscience that he experiences both the necessity of truth and the pitfalls of bad faith. His assessment of truthfulness is animated and disturbed by the unspoken words, even the lies, that underlie his reflections.

Is it characteristic of Rousseau to maintain a discourse on generality when he is thinking of particular and personal cases? Certainly not, especially since this is often the function of generality: to mask intimate experiences and to find resolutions for them thanks to an abstract legitimizing language. The case of Rousseau fascinates us for its spectacular character and its beautiful inventiveness, and also for its concern. Rousseau is not a quiet subject, and his theories on truth or lies testify to great psychic pressure. They expose and intertwine questions on which philosophers have always clashed. The dissonances of the fourth walk of the *Reveries* are audible in the pragmatic arguments of Benjamin Constant, but upstream, they dialogue with thinkers of lies. Rousseau draws on Grotius and Pufendorf, Helvetius, and Fontenelle, who allow him to legitimize his moral instinct as much as his reasoning.[16]

The compromise is stated as follows: *general* and abstract *truth* is the most precious good, and one owes it unconditionally; on the other hand, *particular truth* is indecisive, even perverse, and the duty to tell it is neither universal nor unconditional. Thus, it becomes acceptable to lie about small things without engaging the ethics of truth. This distinction resolves the conflict, but we can understand it differently from a psychic point of view: the more the particular truth is lived with guilt, the more hyperbolic the allegation of the abstract truth is. It is impossible to hide the intimate wars of the conscience in the beautiful discourse of reason. We listen then to great declarations on veracity and truth as signals of the difficulty of assuming them for the enunciating subject.

The opacity of our motivations leads us to question the duty of truth not only towards others but also towards ourselves. How can we avoid lying to ourselves? Do we recognize the motives that push us to deny or hide the

---

16. See Jean Starobinski, *Accuser et séduire*, Gallimard, 2012, pp. 185-194.

truth? The investigation carried out in this book revolves around these problems, not so much to answer or remedy them as to show both the deception and the inventiveness of subjects who lie to themselves. According to these philosophers, the lie committed against oneself is the worst of all, and one must fight mercilessly to avoid it. It horrifies them as if the devil had entered their consciousness. It divides them without their knowledge and undermines the authority of their words, whose veracity becomes doubtful. The degree of lucidity or deception with regard to oneself is never clear nor assured. Thus, Rousseau ends up listing different types of lies, whereas until then, he vilified lies as the opposite of the truth and as a supreme offense. He glimpses their obscure causes while exposing confessions meant to guarantee his transparency. Among the quoted lies, some of them reveal astonishing psychic knots linked to the functions of speech. They underline the passionate investment of the lies that we cannot reduce only to the intention to deceive.

What if we lie to be unmasked? The pleasure of lying is not only exercised at the expense of those we deceive. It also comes from certain situations that encourage it, from words themselves or from mixed feelings where shame and cruelty are combined. Rousseau knows these ambiguous and devious reasons, although he professes a beautiful moral rigor. Let us return one last time to the fourth walk: as he confessed to heroic and altruistic lies intended to protect little comrades, he evokes other lies at once pure and perverse—the confession of the valorous lies assured him a moral retribution, a portrait of himself as a generous man. These other lies obey a kind of mechanics of lying that gets out of hand and follows an uncontrolled course associated with compulsion and pleasure. He affirms that he has never lied out of personal interest but sometimes out of necessity to speak, to spout fables in order to converse. Silence would often be preferable, but in certain situations, it is necessary to *speak to say nothing*, and so we invent. This peril of the conversation also evokes the specter of Kant, who gives rules to order the discussions without heads and tails during dinners. In fact, we often speak faster than we think, and as a result, conversation leads the speakers down the slope of the fable, of the pitch... of the lie. Judgment lags behind; the mouth takes control and spouts off anything.

Less prestigious than novelistic invention, ordinary conversation produces fables of limited use, but it offers a den of lies and perverse pleasures. Rousseau gives a striking example that confronts him with a sadistic interlocutor. In the beginning, the anodyne scene mixes pain and pleasure and uncovers a new status and practice of lying, unthinkable in terms of morality. Jean-Jacques is having dinner with a few friends, including a young pregnant woman, a figure who no doubt reminds him of his mother, who died in childbirth, and Thérèse, five times pregnant. The woman then asks, looking him straight in the eyes, if he has ever had children. Jean-Jacques answers in the negative. He thus lies. He blushes. But the most interesting thing is that this young woman and the guests at the meal already know the truth. And Jean-Jacques knows that they know. At the moment, he cannot speak frankly and chooses to lie, with no possible gain since there is no point in hiding his crime. His mouth moved too quickly, and spontaneity, supposedly favoring the transparent truth, led him to lie! He writes that he would have sent back to the young woman her impertinence and malignity if he had had more time. He would have defended himself, not with a justification of his behavior, but with a verbal joust. Jean-Jacques finally gave up on telling the truth once for all because he did not hope to be understood.

What feelings animate this scene of false dupes? At the same time, Rousseau seems both to suffer and enjoy the humiliation linked to the practice of lying. He would not have escaped shame by publicly confessing his crime, but he redoubles it with another fault, the denial. He tells the truth in the form of a negation, and above all, he surrenders to the wickedness of the one who tyrannizes him. He submits to an all-powerful will that knows his crime and humiliates him by observing his cowardice. "I have only ever lied out of timidity,"[17] he claims; however, his masochism appears with the argument of weakness. He accepts his mistreatment and degrades himself in the lie conceded to the one who enjoys it sadistically. Without any symmetry and in the unequal sharing of a consented cruelty, Jean-Jacques and the young girl play at lying. A consensual and perverse practice of lying takes shape here, one that confounds its traditional definition: it does not hide the truth; it does not deceive anyone. According to a tacit agreement between the interlocutors, animated

____

17. Rousseau, Jean-Jacques. *Reveries of the Solitary Walker. op. cit.*, p. 44.

by good and bad intentions, a liar can thus disguise the truth to give himself up to obscure passions. Rousseau, the singer of truth, will have known the twists and turns of a denial princeps, which is composed as much of passions as of reasons. His reflections on lies say a lot, in retrospect, say much about his hymns to the truth.

From Rousseau's circumlocutions, we could draw a moralist's lesson, in the sense of the psychologists of the classical age: a thinker who talks about lying talks about his own lies. He translates his lies into general reasoning in order to justify his offenses, to make them acceptable to reason and morality. He can also invent a theory of truth, which is itself a lie defending a thesis opposed to what he practices, a theory that plays the role of a virtuous or philosophical screen in order to better hide unbearable lies. Although this lesson may seem too severe and systematic, it nevertheless suggests remaining wary of the great speeches on truth. The crystalline beauty of a theory of truth or of a profession of sincerity cannot make us forget the art of the crystal cutter. The purity of intentions... is a fable, and the one who claims transparency is undoubtedly the most opaque: the dupe of others and, first of all, of himself.

Being attentive to the modes of declaration of the truth supposes an approach both discursive and psychological, which does not take great assertions at face value. Figures, situations, and affects invested in the expression of the truth can be read and heard as the signals of a psychic work, made of energy and twists by which an assertor at once reveals and hides something. Despite what one might profess, the truth can never be revealed in the authenticity of an enunciation. The protocols of expression, the addressees of the words or the text, the opacity of the intentions... all these elements break the naivety of reading at face value, which would cling to the content of a stated truth, even if it were a confession accompanied by the most eloquent guarantees of sincerity. The word "truth" itself, in spite of its conceptual strength, is subject to permeable definitions whose differences in meaning are masked by the philosophical and moral aura of the concept.

The prestige of truth, an ideal of thought and conduct—what could be more noble than to live in the truth?—obscures the shifts in meaning and psychic investments at work in this word. A philosopher particularly attentive to discourse, Michel Foucault, studied the notion of truth according to the protocols of *veridiction*. His reflection is an important reference here for at least two reasons. Firstly, because Foucault analyzes ancient thinkers in their conduct and lifestyle, thus breaking with a "history of philosophy," that is only interested in doctrines. Secondly, because he subtly analyzes discursive practices and, more precisely, forms of truth-telling and the institutional situations where one is compelled to tell the truth, such as judicial confession or religious confession. However, we will turn to Foucault less for his model of analysis than for his personal use of the word truth. Indeed, the last seminar he held at the University of California, Berkeley and then at the Collège de France is entitled *Le Courage de la vérité*. Although it follows a series of studies on self-government, it marks a shift in the philosopher-historian's thinking. The existential context gives this seminar a special status: Foucault delivered it while dying of AIDS. Its success beyond an academic audience, also testifies to a discrepancy in the usage of the word truth, suddenly adorned with a moral prestige that is hardly in keeping with Foucault's intellectual positioning. Paradoxically, the analyst of veridical procedures could not avoid being caught in the trap of truth and investing in it as a final lie.

The Courage of the Lie: Foucault

If there are scenes of truth that have been glorified in the history of philosophy, the most famous one is pedagogical: the lesson given just before death. *The Apology of Socrates* has thus provided the model of an exemplary philosophical attitude, even of "the" philosophy as discourse and a spectacle, for a performance that exposes and *realizes* the truth itself. This scene haunts and dramatizes any reflection on death when, at the moment of leaving life, there is the question of finding a discourse commensurate with an existence suspended at its disappearance. The moment of death summons the truth and calls for a speech that subsumes the facticity of the world. According to Schopenhauer, philosophical discourse finds its source there: "Death is the true inspiring genius, or musaget, of philosophy."[18] Freud took up this comment, underlining anguish and enjoyment of thought: the desire

____

18. Arthur Schopenhauer, *Die Welt als Wille und Vorstellung*. My translation.

for philosophy aims to ward off the fear of dying with the omnipotence of the mind.[19] In a slightly aggressive way, but by trying to question the psychic function of this speech, the psychoanalyst brought philosophical address closer to animism. Exorcising the non-knowledge, arresting the unthinkable, wanting to give a sense to all things... according to Freud, these attitudes come from the idea of death, which arouses myriad representations of souls. We can hear the sublime speech of Socrates in *The Phaedo*—taking his disciples as witnesses and proposing a final lesson on the inessential character of the body and the liberation of the soul—in the light of this conjuring truth.

Foucault's last seminar is interesting in more than one way for the *truth just before death* and the convocation to philosophical discourse: it produces both analysis and practice of this concept by associating to it a virtue, "courage," and affects that can be shared by its listeners and readers. This evocation of courage calls for enthusiasm, admiration, respect, and imitation. The seminar's audience is solicited beyond the subject of study—the lifestyles embodied by the ancient philosophers. Yet who is invited to courage? Those facing a difficult trial, no doubt. Does the speaker address the exhortation to himself? But what truth is it about? An attentive investigation of the tensions of the discourse beneath the conceptual presentation proves necessary. It must track down the uses of the word truth, its declaration, its investment, its circumventions.

---

19. Sigmund Freud, *Totem und Tabu*. My translation.

When Foucault began to work on the notion of truth, Deleuze was worried: how could his friend take up such an outdated word, an "old moon"? Certainly, Foucault's last seminars at the Collège de France took a turn in the early 1980s, and this word truth resonated in a strange way for a generation of philosophers who had gathered around Nietzsche to pursue the denunciation or deconstruction of metaphysics. French philosophy then experienced a great Nietzschean moment, the crystallization of which was the 1972 Cerisy colloquium that brought together Derrida, Deleuze, Lyotard, Kofman, and Nancy, among others, was the crystallization. Foucault himself was part of a movement to reread Nietzsche by taking up his notion of genealogy. Deleuze's concern was undoubtedly unjustified, for Foucault had not, at first sight, sought to rehabilitate any metaphysical truth or any Platonic dualism. He was interested in the telling of truth, i.e., in the procedures of "veridiction" by which power exercises control.

However, the meaning of the word truth and the assignment of moral values to this word changed during the seminars. Foucault moved from a biopolitical analysis of the government of others to an ethical approach to the government of the self. In the spring of 1984, a few months before his death, his last seminar testifies to an inflection point. *The Courage of Truth* has a special status, not only because it corresponds to the philosopher's last public speech but also because it introduces a form of *pathos* into the course of expression: a *pathos of truth* that presupposes an uncommon adhesion, unusual for the philosopher-historian, who until then had adopted a cold and impeccable style and compared his analyses of madness or prison to autopsies.

The success of these reflections upon publication comes partly from a valorization of the philosophical figures who courageously spoke the truth *in* the face of society and tyrannical powers. In a more subterranean way, this seminar builds a small theater where Foucault enacts, on several levels, the death of Socrates. Another reading than the exegetical one, more precisely another "listening," dissociates the seminar's thesis and the role that underlies or covers it, allowing us to hear a voice with a double effect. Foucault speaks of others, now dead, but he also speaks through these others because he fears that his death is near.

Replicating the courage of truth, as embodied by Socrates, requires a reorganization, a new staging. Foucault cannot re-enact the Socratic lesson in the amphitheater of the Collège de France—one can hardly imagine him exposing his body in agony to show his public the assumption of his soul towards the heaven of pure ideas! He does not believe in it; this truth can only be a parody. Unless—such is our hypothesis—the reference to truth and courage comes from a tension between telling the truth and the impossibility of saying it, between a verbal protocol and a psychic repression. What if Foucault was trying to say something that he could not bring himself to say because he could not formulate it in terms of a confession, a confession whose standards and duplicities he knows so well? He knows he is ill and fears that he has only a short time to live. He does not want to talk about AIDS. Even the association between homosexuality and AIDS seems to him a monstrous and caricatural trap, so much so that he laughs when someone mentions a disease that would only affect homosexuals, a "gay cancer."

An analysis of the tone of the last seminar reveals this tension between a denial of and a paean to the truth. Foucault has entered into a strategy of secrecy, seeking to hide his illness, and at the same time he deploys a beautiful and powerful discourse on the courage of truth. Contradiction, weakness, distress... these are only circumstantial explanations, and we would like to detect in this twist a more fundamental trait of the theoretical discourse: one of the psychic functions of the philosophical language aims at shielding the lived experience of the subject, even exposing and affirming the opposite of what the speaker lives. It is in no way a question of denouncing a moral lie but of observing the fruitful production of a "speculative lie."

In *The Courage of Truth*, two temporalities are superimposed. One, historiographical, explores the lives of ancient thinkers; the other, enunciative, reflects Foucault's present life in that of the former, as a mirror, a screen. There is nothing extraordinary about this; the commentary of a philosopher on other philosophers often proceeds from appropriations and transfers. However, Foucault's present life goes against his stated thesis. He does not seem to have had "the courage of truth." This observation goes beyond a moral judgment and presents a paradox: Foucault tells the truth in the form of a lie. This lie is a metamorphosis of the truth heard through a conceptual hyperbole.

Before the enunciation, let us first distinguish the statement first: Foucault announces that his subject is based on "truth-telling" or "straight talk." He crosses a long philosophical tradition that has questioned sincerity, authenticity, and transparency, but he remains faithful to his analysis of the procedures of veridiction, the protocols by which an individual is led to speak the truth. "The subject *manifests* himself when speaking the truth, by which I mean, thinks of himself and is recognized by others as speaking the truth."[20] Foucault thus analyzes the production of a truth and the performative act by which it is realized by being addressed to listeners. He then justifies his method, explaining his path. He declares that he is interested not only in the truth proclaimed about a subject (such as the diagnosis of madmen or delinquents) but also in the truth that the subject himself formulates (through the confession, the examination of conscience). From the outset, the seminar listener finds the approach that the philosopher-historian had already experimented with in studying the institutionalization of religious and judicial confessions.

However, the word "courage" singularly inflects the enterprise. It is used here in a declarative way that exempts Foucault from philosophical analysis. Its definition, little

---

20. Foucault, Michel, *The Courage of Truth (The Government of Self and Others II) : Lectures at the Collège de France, 1983-1984*. Translated by Graham Burchell. Macmillan, 2011, pp. 2-3.

The Pathos of Truth

questioned, gives free rein to admiration. But is courage a virtue, a character trait, a natural quality? Is it a matter of rational consciousness or passion and affect? What will or what situation triggers it? Are all individuals equal before courage? Are we free to have courage, responsible for showing it or not? Foucault does not deal with these questions and prefers to show examples of courageous philosophers, such as the Stoic in front of the tyrant, to analyze the courage their attitude toward power represents. We are then entitled to ask ourselves if the one who speaks of courage in this way is himself courageous.

Truth is embodied here by individuals who take center stage in antiquity and whom the philosopher-historian presents favorably to his audience. Foucault singularizes his approach to the telling of the truth to highlight not only speeches but also personalities, Socrates, in the first place. He explains that he first spoke of *parrhesia*, the courage to tell the truth, as a political discourse and then gradually moved closer to the discourse about oneself. He distinguishes several actors of truth-telling: the prophet, the wise man, the professor, and the technician, according to whether they speak for themselves or for a principle that exceeds them. Then, he evaluates their degree of "courage" according to the danger they run. On this scale, the technician seems the least virtuous since he takes no risk in telling the truth of his knowledge.

Among the technicians Foucault places the figure of the doctor, far from insignificant because it brings in the figure of his father, his brother, and the doctors he deals with, as we shall see later. At first glance, this reference is only cited to highlight, by contrast, the *parrhesiastes* who, for their part, take the risk of cutting themselves off from their interlocutors by assuming the truth, sometimes to the point of death, like Socrates, who combines all the functions of truth-telling: he makes death an experience and an exhibition of the truth. At the same time, Foucault is aware that the courage to speak the truth does not have the same value in a society governed by a tyrant, where speech is censored, and in a democracy, where any discourse is allowed. However, in the form of a paradox, he suggests that *parrhesia* is the most difficult to practice in a democracy precisely because it confronts the subject with oneself, in the face of others' indifference. Foucault thus evolves in his definition of *parrhesia* to think of it as the fulfillment of an *ethos* and an individual *psyche.*

The choice to privilege Socrates against the doctors of the body, however surprising it may seem coming from a reader of Nietzsche and the *Twilight of the Idols*, signals how much Foucault finally assumes a philosophical tradition. He now declares himself a philosopher, whereas before he had kept this term at a distance. Above all, he takes up an exemplary dramaturgy, the death of Socrates, the symbol of a truth that clashes with democracy, ignorance, and the injustice of a law based on numbers. "Truth" is thus the name by which Foucault defines his ultimate identity and inscribes himself in a tradition whose genealogy he had until now drawn up. Here, he no longer deals with politics; he is interested in virtue and how a man behaves as a *parrhesiaste,* choosing his death and refusing subterfuge.

Foucault undoubtedly re-enacts this Socratic figure in the freedom he himself claims in front of the doctor: the latter, in the name of his technical knowledge, can impose the truth on him ("I'll be frank, you're going to die in a few months") but courage is not in this frankness of telling the truth to others, it is rather in the way on assumes it for oneself, exposing it all the more valiantly in its involvement of life and death.

In order to evaluate the gaps between speech and experience, it is necessary to show figures other than those proposed by the speaker, who reflects himself in the glorious examples of philosophy. We will produce several of them, the first of whom is a friend of Foucault's, a witness who is as much narrator as informer. Hervé Guibert has reported in several texts, the most famous being *À l'ami qui ne m'a pas sauvé la vie (To the Friend Who Didn't Save My Life)*, those dramatic moments when truth takes on the guise of a lie. The status of "testimony" remains ambiguous for such a book, as the author is a writer, not a historian, and he is involved in this story in the first place, as he has contracted AIDS and is considering the agony of his philosopher friend as a rehearsal of what he will live through next. The position of enunciation that Hervé Guibert embodies is that of a witness who testifies both for the memory of Foucault and for himself, doomed to die of the same disease. Despite these methodological reservations, it is revealing to see how much Guibert's speech about his AIDS is the opposite of that adopted by Foucault: six years after the philosopher's death, Guibert has exposed his illness in his books, visual work, and the media. It is certainly important to recall the social and medical context of the 1980s when AIDS was not a clearly identified disease, and all sorts of conjectures were circulating. The first cases appeared in 1981, and the retrovirus was isolated in 1983. Foucault's concern with secrecy was not out of the ordinary, and the questions raised by such a denial come mainly from its concomitance with a seminar on the courage of truth.

A disciple who is both faithful and unfaithful, Hervé Guibert adopts an inverted mirror posture: out of fidelity to the philosophy of truth-telling, he reveals his illness and that of his master, and thus he is faithful out of infidelity to Foucault, who extolled the courage of the truth but hid what he was living. He breaks the code of silence of his friends and disciples; he unpacks the truth, which becomes a revelation, notwithstanding the unwillingness of the dead. Since this publication, those close to the philosopher have justified their silence, some to affirm that despite his health problems, Foucault had no idea that he would die soon nor that the interruption of his courses in March would be definitive. A letter to Maurice Pinguet in January 1984 permits this hypothesis: "I thought I had AIDS, but a vigorous treatment put me back on my feet."

But was Foucault speaking the "dire-vrai" then? The man who was to die six months later was perhaps lying to his friend, or even to himself when he was very ill and could not begin his courses. According to his companion, Daniel Defert, Foucault's concern for was knowing how long he had to live. Hervé Guibert, close to death, had no qualms about "throwing out" truths about Foucault's

The Pathos of Truth

sexuality—his bag full of whips, leather hoods, leashes, bits, and handcuffs—as well as about his hidden agony. Guibert said he wrote "as close to death as possible" and trampled the "bourgeois" modesty of his friends. His readers recognized Foucault under the name of the character Muzil, whose attitude is the exact opposite of what the philosopher professed at the Collège de France.

In contrast to the philosophical lesson presented, courage no longer consists in telling the truth but, on the contrary, in hiding it: "Like Muzil, I would have liked to have had the strength, the insane pride, as well as the generosity, to tell no one, allowing friendships to live as lightly as air, carefree and eternal,"[21] writes Guibert. The Kantian ethics is reversed here because the respect of close relations differs from the respect of a universal moral law. Others must be protected from a truth that would spoil their lives and, above all, that would deprive them of an authentic relationship with the one holding the truth. Imposing knowledge of the illness on them would lead them to adopt consoling attitudes towards the sick person in the name of friendship when they could not share the unbearable truth. Not forcing others, not putting them in an impossible position, not placing them in painful moral situations... such concerns result from a generosity that passes through secrecy and denial. The word "lie" then seems hardly adequate: keeping secrets is not lying but keeping certain truths unspoken. As Benjamin Constant

---

21. Guibert, Hervé. *To the Friend Who Did Not Save My Life*. Translated by Linda Coverdale. Cambridge: Semiotexte/Smart Art, 2020, p. 21.

observed, the obligation to tell everything would imply an abusive right of others to know everything. Against the injunction to confess, one must claim the right to secrecy! However, Guibert's remark also suggests a perverse pleasure of secrecy, close to the one that Rousseau evoked about the lie shared in shame, associating sadism and masochism. The contagious individual suspends the truth of infamy, of sharing a shameful disease, known only by the contaminated ones who keep for their lovers the freedom to say it or not.

A secret of this nature, a mixture of hidden truth, cunning, and shame, is erected as an inverted ethic: it proposes a model contrary to that embodied by Sartre and Beauvoir, who, in *Adieux: A Farewell to Sartre*, had described, four years before Guibert's book, Sartre's agony over unsavory details of his physical decline. The truth lived and suggested by Guibert, in the shadow of Foucault, becomes, instead of an ideal of transparency proposed to all, an exclusive enjoyment shared in the secrecy of some. It draws a relationship of friendship based on a reserved, recluse, unexposed truth. The truth is no longer universal anymore: in particular, it is shared not in order to obey a duty of sincerity but to enlarge the privileged circle of enlightened people. The community of secrecy has the beauty of a society of the cursed: "It seems to me that my relationships with people are no longer interesting unless they know the truth,"[22] admits Guibert.

____

22. *Ibid*, p. 22.

Secrets, denials, and lies oppose the ethics of telling the truth. Foucault told Guibert he knew the danger of AIDS, which had become an obsessive subject of conversation in the saunas. While he professed the truth, the philosopher meticulously organized his secrecy: the head of the clinic where he was treated quickly had the means to diagnose his illness, and he set up, according to the wishes of the patient, the means to preserve his anonymity through camouflage and censorship. Foucault left this lie as a legacy, to the point that his friends continued to keep his secret, and the cause of death will be erased from the hospital form. It took "courage," that is to say, heart, to keep the secret, even if it meant lying to the public, denouncing rumors, and spreading untruths. One can thus lie out of duty, out of loyalty to the master's lie, which leads to another version of fidelity. But this courage has nothing moral about it; it is based on love, the affection of friends or lovers. Concealing the truth becomes a way of honoring it, unless it is a question of blocking access to knowledge in order to better appropriate it post-mortem. The possessor of the secret is positioned as the chosen one; he knows and has the right and the duty to lie. As an inheritor of knowledge, a virtuous disciple is the most faithful liar.

This scenario of the lying legacy joins a long history of family secrets, kept from generation to generation until the day when an heir interprets fidelity differently and twists it according to his desires and traumas. Guibert betrays while revealing the truth. He forces us to consider a new adjustment between the philosopher's life and his word. He provides us with terms and images to weigh the hesitations of the one who wants to decide on the right moment to tell the truth. Guibert thus reports his conversation with Foucault on the truth that circulates between patient and doctor. The philosopher explains to him that the doctor should offer access to the truth. According to Guibert, Foucault does not ignore anything but allows himself to hide and lie in the face of a demand for transparency. He knows he will die of AIDS soon, and he is tempted to go and die at the end of the world with a humanitarian association. Supreme frankness or ultimate betrayal, Hervé Guibert writes: "I knew that Muzil would have been so hurt if he'd known I was writing reports of everything like a spy, like an adversary, all those degrading little things, in my diary, which was perhaps destined (that was the worst of it) to survive him, and to bear witness to a truth he would have liked to erase around the periphery of his life, to leave only the wellpolished bare bones enclosing the black diamond— gleaming and impenetrable, closely guarding its secrets— that seemed destined to form his biography, a real conundrum chock-full of errors from end to end."[23]

Without providing a definitive truth, Guibert's revelations bring out a new ability to listen to Foucault's last seminar with differently tuned ears. The circumstances of his speech become important: from the very first session, Foucault begins by apologizing and rectifying a rumor; he wants to denounce a lie! He did not start his lecture on time because he was ill, he admits, and not because he wanted to get rid of a part of his audience. He exposes his tired

---

23. *Ibid*, pp. 96-97.

The Pathos of Truth

body; he evokes an illness without revealing it. He displays himself to better hide himself, like the stolen letter, present in front of the viewer but invisible. "I have been sick," he confides, and the audience can assume he is now cured. "It's true," he has to say to be believed before beginning his seminar on straight talk.

Some sessions were longer than others, particularly the one in which Foucault concluded on courage in the face of death, then apologizing for having kept the audience too long. At the end of the seminar, he declares: "There you are, listen, I had things to say to you about the general framework of these analyses. But, well, it is too late. So, thank you."[24] And among the notes to which he alludes to specify what he will not have had time to say, to show, *parrhesia* is defined as "the courage to manifest the truth about oneself, to show oneself as one is, in the face of all opposition."[25] A philosopher to the end, Foucault assumed a discourse on death before death. And who could lecture him on the right way to talk—or not talk—about AIDS, or not, about "his" AIDS? Nevertheless, his last seminar can be heard and understood by reintegrating it into its context, all the more so since it plays out a classic scene in philosophical history.

To be heard in its strength and complexity, the word of truth that is uttered before dying must be considered with all the afflictions of discourse, its detours and false

---

24. Foucault, Michel. *The Courage of Truth, op. cit.*, p. 338.
25. *Ibid*, p.339

pretenses, its lively lies. It is naïve to take this speech as sincere and true, when the speaker who is going to die resorts to language for motivations that he himself does not know. This so-called speech of truth plays multiple functions, unknowable and unmastered. In order to measure what it can entail in terms of traps and lures, the comparison of Foucault's seminar with a general public version of the "last speech" before death can shed light on this entanglement of truth and lies. The *ante mortem* lecture of an American academic offers a second mirror to the *Courage of Truth*.

What meaning can be given to a speech when it is presented as "the last"? The American university Carnegie Mellon regularly organizes lectures that it calls *last lectures*, delivered as a final speech that gives the distillment of one's knowledge or a thought. The university had invited the professor Randy Pausch, who learned he had pancreatic cancer and was destined to die a few months later. He took on this invitation wholeheartedly and embodied it as it was the last great speech of his life. His lecture, given in 2007, attracted hundreds of people and has since been viewed by millions of Internet users. The morbid voyeurism that it may have attracted does not prevent us from questioning this philosophical posture of a lesson given on the eve of death, according to the tradition of Socrates, in the *Phaedo*, who offered his friends a last thought *in vivo* on the immortality of the soul.

Randy Pausch, more of a computer scientist than a metaphysician, nonetheless reflected on the meaning of life and entitled his talk "Really making your childhood dreams come true." Following the university tradition, the lecture was structured with diagrams and illustrations, and with an American concern for keeping the audience's attention for seventy-five minutes with twists and jokes. Whereas Socrates appealed to *logos* to overcome emotion, Pausch used humor and sensitive complicity to accompany his departure. He recounted his life's journey, his hopes, the obstacles he encountered, and the lessons he learned. The moral of being *positive* conjures up fate and confirms that life remains worthy of being lived, whether or not our dreams are realized.

The death of Socrates allowed us to think about the inessential status of life and of the body, a simple envelope to be unempathetically despised. Don't mourn my disappearance, requested the philosopher; don't trust this last twitch on my face, which will only reveal the exit of my soul towards the heaven of ideas. The body's prison (*soma*) is already a sign (*sema*) towards the beyond. But for Randy Pausch, death is no longer the soul's deliverance. What is it then? The computer scientist could not say. Because he does not approach this question, his *ante mortem* lesson turns into a media spectacle. His humor about his imminent death provokes laughter and tears from the audience. His father, mother, students, and colleagues are summoned to the stage for the parade of relatable memories, then his wife for a *happy birthday*. A universal lesson on death has been transformed into an exhibition of a singular and ordinary life, like a *reality show*. As attendees, we indeed face a situation full of emotions, which imposes some minimal respect for the pain he experiences, whatever its mode of expression. However, it is not a question here of judging people but of analyzing protocols of speech. Randy Pausch could have talked about the dream of being immortal, but he preferred to share some good truths about the happiness of American life. He played the game wholeheartedly and "performed" this *last reading* to the letter, setting his end of life in the standard of a masterful speech. He brilliantly followed the protocol of a good academic and telegenic host.

Randy Pausch's lesson confronts us with the theater of farewell. The professor played *Socrates goes to Hollywood*. Other roles haunted the performance, such as the lay televangelist, so much so that *The last lecture* also resonates with Jesus' last speech, *The Last Supper*. Is it appropriate to mock the rituals of others? We each make do with our anxieties and solutions, large or small, to ward off the unthinkable. The sun and death cannot look each other in the face, warned La Rochefoucauld. What happened during this man's last moments, as for any person, at the moment of death? No one can say, and this intimacy escapes the spectacle and the speakable. However, there remains the observation that the last word authorizes itself with the truth while working with the lies of social life, those that a speaker formulates towards others and himself in order to avoid the impossible. No thinker is safe from the fictions of truth to which they resort before death. And the tension between their words and their lives, in these moments so little controllable, produces a number of figures, arguments, and concepts. A philosophical lesson can be transmitted and commented on while ignoring these affects, but they nevertheless impact linguistic forms and theoretical constructions. By considering them, readers and listeners access this entanglement of the universal and the singular, where truth and falsehood become inseparable.

The discourse chosen before impending death cannot be heard with the same ear as the one that listens rationally to theoretical propositions free of personal context. The recourse to philosophy then reveals its psychic motivation. It can assume several functions—control, illusion, intoxication, ataraxia, relief... In the 6th century, Boethius, a senator tortured and executed on the orders of an Ostrogoth king, wrote *The Consolation of Philosophy* before his death. In it, he recounts an encounter that was decisive for his appeasement. Whereas the Muses seduced him with their poetic speeches, Philosophy comes to dialogue with him and convinces him that he is sick because he stopped knowing who he is. He complains of suffering injustice, of being dispossessed of his goods, but he has forgotten the true meaning of life. Philosophy then shows him the way to wisdom and overcoming of death: "In thy true judgment concerning the world's government, in that thou believest it subject, not to the random drift of chance, but to divine reason, we have the divine spark from which thy recovery may be hoped. Have, then, no fear; from these weak embers the vital heat shall once more be kindled within thee."[26]

---

26. Boethius, *The Consolation of Philosophy*. Translated by H. R. (Henry Rosher) James. Auckland, N.Z: Floating Press, 2009, p. 36.

The true, the good, and the One are the concepts that allow the condemned man to overcome his anguish by restoring the health of his mind. This Socratic dialogue, imagined by Boethius in his prison, can be read as a reflection on wisdom, distinguishing between essence and illusion, and as a recourse to abstract expedients intended to convert misfortune into a secondary evil. The specter of death thus modifies the meaning of philosophical discourse, and its enunciation resounds with the psychic afflictions of a subject who affirms all the more his confidence in the truth because he doubts the meaning of his existence.

Hearing a philosophical conference knowing that its author is facing his imminent death modifies the meaning of his words. Take the last speeches of Jacques Derrida: as early as 2003, many of his close friends knew that he had pancreatic cancer, and, for them, his various reflections took on a spectral meaning, whether he spoke of genealogy, heritage, or the future. The melancholy tone that had already characterized his thinking was imbued with tragic intensity as if he were "realizing" the farewell speech he had given so many times before for others. From his lecture on the archives of Hélène Cixous[27], during which he spoke of the dreams that had escaped among the manuscripts left by the author, to his quasi-testamentary interview entitled *Learning to Finally*[28], each intervention could be heard as a *last reading*, a vertiginous mirror of

---

27. Jacques Derrida, *Genesis, Genealogy, Genres and Genius. The secret of the archive. Translated by Beverly Bie Brahic, New York, Columbia University Press,* 2006.
28. *Learning to Live Finally. The Last Interview with Jacques Derrida.* Translated by Pascale-Anne Brault and Michael Naas, Chicago, Kavi Gupta edition, 2011.

the many funeral tributes he had already written for his departed friends.

In this funereal specter, we heard truth as the desperate effort to hold onto a voice, to ward off the cry of madness. To gain this artificial assurance, one has to tell oneself many stories and follow many scores, audible in the language of meaning. Some thinkers have more talent than others to thwart the funeral music of the last speeches. However, the truth holds less in content than it vibrates in a voice close to death, even when it takes on the assured tone of one giving a lesson. Still, one must hear the air of the lie to perceive the speaker's cracked timbre and not let the noise of the affirmation deafen oneself. Above all, in such circumstances, the word of the doctor, authorizing a distance from oneself, is heard as *the lie of truth*. The most outstanding efforts at mastery do not prevent the specter of doubt from creeping over the most formal farewells: voice and meaning no longer move at the same pace. The truth is no more than a word that crumbles in the whispers, the sighs, and the silences of the avower.

Continuing the disharmonious history of the "last speeches before death," Foucault's last seminar is not only the completion of a philosophical reflection on truth. It is also part of an enunciative standard that transforms this masterly speech into a performance—in the dramaturgical sense—of an exemplary scene of philosophy. These two levels of discourse oppose and disturb each other instead of providing wise counterpoints. The imaginary scenography provokes clashes in the philosophical argumentation, enhancing a character such as Socrates, who was previously kept aside. Under the auspices of Nietzsche, Foucault was indeed reluctant to value the holder of the backworlds and the truth behind appearances. Nietzschean criticism had attacked head-on the foundations of a philosophical dramaturgy first acted out in the West by Socrates. In a kind of counter-apology, Nietzsche made Socrates the promoter of a poor and practical philosophy where life is directed by morality. In *Twilight of the Idols*, he thus demystified the all-too-famous death of Socrates: according to Nietzsche, the latter had always known that the tribunal of the City would condemn him, and he did not prepare his defense. He thought the time had come for him to die, happy to leave because he considered his existence a disease. This resentment of life was manifested in his philosophy, the *universal lie* that imposes the idea of a necessary "cure" by persuading humans that they are sick. Nietzsche, in *Gay Science*, nevertheless recognized a certain greatness in the death of Socrates, but he would have liked him to stop speaking at the moment of his death! The Greek philosopher would then have belonged to a higher order of minds.

Unexpectedly, Foucault re-actualizes Socrates's scenario against Nietzsche, but without explicitly stating it. He valorizes the idea of *healing* and accredits the Platonic version of the final lesson on death. He focuses on the sacrifice of a rooster to Aesculapius, the god of medicine, which Socrates recommended to his disciples. Instead of seeing this as a supreme irony regarding the care of bodies, Foucault defends the idea of "cure" as healing from a spiritual ailment: According to Foucault, philosophy means the struggle against false ideas, the need to cure people of ignorance and false beliefs. By embracing this classical interpretation, Foucault, who devoted his life to deciphering the construction of the figures of the sick, the madman, and the delinquent, in order to expose the social logic of control and correction of populations, now legitimizes the representation of the cure, based on the Socratic idea of a sick existence. He requires a narrative, and Nietzsche no longer provides a suitable one.

Healing, the cure, is linguistically laden with pathology, and even though Foucault is discussing medicine for the souls, he cannot neglect the proper medical meaning of these words while he is undergoing treatment in the hospital. His long-standing reflection on the clinic is now intertwined with a biographical history. Coming from a family of doctors and being the son of a surgeon who considers words as vain, Foucault understands the epistemological stakes of the medical language from which he intended to distance himself. In *Le Beau Danger*, Foucault critiques the concise diagnosis and therapy prescribed by doctors who "speak only to utter the truth, briefly, and prescribe medicine."[29] Simultaneously, the philosopher speaks endlessly of those departed. Analyzing the profound relationship between writing and death, he confides: "In one sense, I'm speaking over the corpse of the others."[30]

---

29. Foucault, Michel, in conversation with Claude Bonnefoy. *Speech Begins after Death*. Translated by Robert Bononno. Minneapolis: University of Minnesota Press, 2013, p. 35.
30. *Ibid.*, p. 40.

As a historian, he performs a kind of autopsy to "discover both the truth of their life and their death, the sickly secret that explains the passage from their life to their death." In his final seminar, Foucault involuntarily becomes his own anatomist, and the ancient figures passing under his scalpel substitute for his own body laid bare.

As a pedagogy of truth, nudity and the exposure of bodies to the point of scandal are at the center of Foucault's reading of the Cynics. He dedicates part of his seminar to them and discusses their way of life. He then presents them as a model of courage that is possible and desirable. However, Foucault himself cannot hold such a truth or display such audacity. Nevertheless, he discovers in them a potentiality for disgrace, the naked existence of the animal, which resembles the condition of a sick and vulnerable man. The cynics present themselves as doctors of truth, guiding the "know thyself" towards life, the *bios*, and an aesthetic of existence. Diogenes masturbating in the public square, argues that he also eats in public and that these are entirely natural functions for all to see. Foucault describes the attitude of these unclean men as half-naked, unkempt, and vociferating, imposing their "animal truth." In doing so, he lends credence to the cliché that animals embody truth because they cannot lie, feel shame, or engage mimicry. Without questioning these assuppositions, Foucault links this exhibition of "naked" nature to the presentation of truth.

While he is discreet about his body and illness, Foucault highlights those animalistic thinkers who impose their truths onto others. In describing them, he plays on a *pathos* of truth, that is found in many ancient philosophers. Freud identified this pathos of *logos as* a symptom of the philosophical systems. According to the psychoanalyst, the specular function of the spirit nourishes itself on the production and the exhibition of truths in which the spirit admires its own power. During his conference "*On a Weltanschauung,*" Freud identified the staging of truth as a narcissistic activity that is even more pleasurable for the subject, enunciating it while ignorant of his true motivations. Truth produces *jouissance* to the extent of its imagined and supposed effects on others and on the world. Cynical philosophers enjoy shocking the public because they firmly believe in the heuristic and pedagogical value of their exhibition. The truth they present does not require discussion or nuance; it feeds on its display. It functions as a linguistic fetish that originates from overestimating the magic of concepts. Hence, the nerve of the exhibitionists of the truth stems from a narcissistic illusion of having the power to impress others through signs.

The prestige of the word "courage" perhaps stems less from its moral intention than from the effects it produces. "Courage" is the command to give strength to those who lack it. But does it require courage to speak the truth? If this truth is valid for all and reveals the meaning of things, it is sufficient to utter it effortlessly. Its authority is easily imposed. The schoolmaster or the priest says, "You must tell the truth." On the other hand, if the truth concerns the one who speaks it, it encounters the opacity of expression, which is less transparent than the straightforwardness of universal truths. This truth cannot simply proclaim itself under the moral command because its motives are obscure. The only *courage* would be to confess the lie, as suggested by Nietzsche in *Beyond Good and Evil*. Once the lie is acknowledged as such and escapes from the binary opposition with the truth, the true and the untrue coexist.

The courage of truth is no longer understood as the exemplary attitude of ancient thinkers. Neither does it constitute the ethical horizon of a lifestyle. It is an expression suspended from the impossibility of stating the truth once and for all and from the deceptive tricks speakers employ for others and themselves. Foucault's seminar on the courage of truth is characterized by a tension between a methodically maintained secrecy and praise for the "telling-true"; this contradictory spring does not detract from the speculative power of this reflection or the beauty of its linguistic elaboration. It rather "encourages" the unwillingness of its author to move away from a didactic reading and observe the psychic functioning of the philosophical discourse. The singular enunciation of his last seminar brought Foucault to a theater where he reenacts the original philosophy scene. This diverted apology offers the Truth as a spectacle. Neither betrayal nor parody, it shows, at the heart of a masterful discourse, the pathos-filled invention of a "lying-true."

Upon rereading this singular seminar on the courage of truth, we understand that the possibility of delivering a true discourse before dying gives rise to as many scenarios as philosophical "lessons." Without a possible truth about death, the philosopher constructs an imaginary truth nourished by affects. It no longer highlights a superterrestrial world but incorporates the absurdity of existence in order to overcome doubts and inconsistencies. It provides the opportunity to take a final bow and invent the signature of a courageous self, despite what destabilizes and destitutes it, and despite the fear and ignorance of what is to come. The apparent timelessness of discourses on death or on knowing how to die is erased at this moment when the proximity of the end intensifies the need to find a reason. Truth is one of those fabulous reasons that become concepts and define a suprasensible afterlife or a way of dying. And the faith—heart and courage—in this truth provides the affect that enchants the fables.

After listening with a psychological ear to the affirmative speech of Truth, we should always doubt an individual who begins by saying, "sincerely...", "frankly...", "I will be frank with you..." Any speech delivered or written with the assurance, the sonic, textual, or rhetorical amplitude, of one who speaks "truthfully" conceals a concern. Why would a truth need to be supported by its name? The need for support indicates a fragility that should make us suspicious and disregard the all-powerful speech. This suspicion leads us to suspend the meaning of a statement, reflect on the psychic investment of concepts, and listen to the voice that underlies the affirmation of an idea and the affirmation of oneself in this idea. The need to speak, the recourse to grand rhetoric, to the authority of the universal, allows us to perceive tensions, straining, and escapes.

By invoking the affirmative pathos of straight talk, we also uncover the tricks and the speculative power of the lie that takes on the guise of truth. These lies cannot be reduced to error or falsity, which are just negations of truth. Conversely, denial, secrecy, and fabrication provide fertile ground for prodigious inventions. The term "fable" exceeds the realm of literature: fiction is not the exclusive realm of the "lying-true," and philosophy contests this claim, but according to another regime. The concept itself finds ways to mask its constitutive imaginaries and the affects that animate it. The tension between the secret and the "telling-true" summons a multitude of voices that intertwine, mingle, and clash. It is now time to analyze works of fabrication, which are beautiful and powerful theoretical machines that are argued, debated, and scrutinized through the lens of reason even while they originate in a hidden lie. These conceptual systems theorize the opposite of what their theorists experience, and their purpose is precisely to contemplate and affirm the opposite of lived reality.

Theory Versus Life

A thinker praises marriage despite never being able to marry, another known for his boastfulness writes a treatise on humility, a philosopher of altruism focuses his life on himself, a denouncer of capitalism hoards relentlessly, a promoter of travel is an inveterate sedentary. Presented in this way, the discrepancies between speech and life are surprising and shocking, to the point that the moral reaction detects hypocrisy. However, these "contradictions" can be seen as something other than an insincere attitudes or denials of thought. An a-moral approach to lying allows us to discover a complex relationship between what is said and what is lived. The investment of the self in theory involves compensations, tricks, and combinations, through which a subject tries on multiple personalities.

Dreaming the Life of Philosophers: Hadot

The focus on the arguments of a theorist distracts us from the understanding of their concepts. Consequently, the biographies of the thinkers often rely on an idealistic version where their thought evolves as if it were a living organism, progressing naturally through different stages. Any other consideration is reduced to a mere curiosity for anecdotes. The contempt that Heidegger displayed for Aristotle's life, reducing it to a concise "he was born, he worked, he died" in order to better focus on his philosophy, testifies to a resistance to connecting life and thought. However, this resistance seems to be a form a repression of which Heidegger himself was accused, to the point that the reading of his own texts suffers from his compromises with the Nazi regime.

The weakness of the biographical perspective lies in its focus on a "life" consisting of the ordinary events that one assumes compose it. Relating the existence of thinkers to that of everyone else is of little interest. Knowing Hegel's favorite foods or Wittgenstein's sexual preferences does not add much to the understanding of their work. And while some writers enjoyed creating surprising portraits of the philosophers' lives, such as Thomas de Quincey describing Kant's routine existence, this information is only used for amusement, sometimes even mockery. The purpose of these trivialities is to bring the great idols down from their pedestals and depict them as ordinary people. Despite their brilliance, they appear "like us" and are sometimes ridiculous, allowing the readers to feel as if they are getting a glimpse into the intimate life of great minds. These "truths" revealed about the "lives" of thinkers are presented as objective facts: opposing a supposedly ordinary life with its mundane realities to a spiritual and ethereal life. But such "lives" do not exist, and these truths are exaggerated representations.

However, another more productive approach consists of finding the connections between a thought and its conditions of production, not only socio-historical but also psychological. The biographer can then observe potential contradictions between the life and the theory of a thinker. These contradictions do not invalidate the claims of the thought, but they provide another key to interpretation, another understanding of the theory. Under this condition, the knowledge of certain "truths" of life becomes parts of the thought process and allows access to the complex entanglements—imaginings, affects, opportunities—that manifest themselves within the apparent distortions. Knowing that Sartre became incontinent and soiled his clothes at the end of his life does not contribute anything to the understanding of his work or even his existence. However, discovering that he experienced bouts of melancholy, contrary to the official image of the committed thinker, suggests alternative readings of his texts on dreams, imagination, and literature. The fact that this hyperactive man, who was involved on all fronts in international politics, dedicated hours every day to playing Chopin provides insight into an idea of passivity, which was certainly rejected but which was at the core of his thinking. Secrecy, the unspoken, and the clandestine activities open the door to psychic processes at work in theoretical constructions rather than encouraging the voyeurism of supposed intimacy with a thinker.

Leading a life contrary to one's professed beliefs, or constructing a theory that praises the opposite of what one lives—such behaviors provoke thought, not only morals. The frequency of such deviations suggests different postures of the self through deviation and reversal. An anthropological and "psychological" approach allows access to this paradoxical intelligence, which does not solely rely on circumstantial or accidental contradiction. However, in order to re-engage with the word psychology, it is necessary to specify its meaning, especially since philosophers and literary scholars alike disdain "psychologism." In fact, psychology, as it was transmitted in the 19th century, with its various theses on personal characters, presupposed an individual ego that "expressed itself" in intellectual productions. The deconstruction of the notions of human and author in the 1970s allowed for a different perspective on the production of texts and discourses, departing from structures that intersect the thinking and speaking subjects. The return, today, to a notion like the *self* must not overlook this theoretical dismantling of the duality between life and work that supposed a harmonious relationship between the two. The famous "end of the author" advocated by Barthes and the thinkers of New Criticism declared, was indeed a means to liberate the criticism from old psychological biases regarding biographical motivation of works. However, this *theoretical move did* not definitively eliminate the questioning of the subject who writes and the projections, divisions, and transformations at the heart of his writing.

Psychology, in this sense, maintains its legitimacy when it is inspired by the moralists of the 17th century or by Nietzsche, who claimed that it is considered the queen of sciences, the one that leads to fundamental problems. It does not allow itself to be blinded by the fiction of an all-powerful self and constantly searches for pretenses in order to try to understand the metamorphoses of an elusive self. When Nietzsche writes that " what every great philosophy to date has been: the personal confession of its author,[31]" he certainly does not mean the biographical substance of the thought, in the same way Sainte-Beuve saw the reflection of authors' lives in their works. Precisely, he does not believe in the "ego," nor in the "self," nor in the "I"—words that he analyzes as effects of grammar. A sentence such as "I think" certainly requires a grammatical subject but it does not imply a thinking subject, master of its ideas. Several souls or several consciousnesses pass through an "I" that says "I am," "I want," "I decide," Something is thinking, Nietzsche prefers to say, and this "something" still represents too much and distorts the process of the thought process that arises from multiple forces. These authors, these all-powerful "I's," who assert great principles, eternal truths, and explain the first causes of the world, are liars playing a role. Nietzsche does not position himself on the side of absolute clarity that would allow him to expose the lies of great theorists. Instead, he points out the malice and the masquerades employed by the philosophers, often without their awareness.

---

31. Nietzsche, Friedrich, *Beyond Good and Evil : Prelude to a Philosophy of the Future*. Translated by Marion. Faber and Robert C. Holub. Oxford: Oxford University Press USA—OSO, 2009, p. 44.

The arguments of authority and the theoretical arsenal of the philosophers prevent the reader from understanding the psychic motivations behind their thought. The most significant criticism of Nietzsche is undoubtedly his genealogy of philosophers and their systems. Rejecting the belief in a purely rational construction, he uncovers the interests, affects, and fantasies at work in conceptual production. Philosophers "act as if they had discovered and acquired what are actually their opinions through the independent unravelling of a cold, pure, divinely unhampered dialectic [...], basically, however, they are using reasons sought after the fact to defend a pre-existing tenet, a sudden idea, a 'brainstorm', or, in most cases, a rarefied and abstract version of their heart's desire. They are all of them advocates who refuse the name, that is in most cases wily spokesmen for their prejudices, which they dub 'truths'[32]; [they are very far from that heroism of the conscience which admits to itself its own lie[33]]." Nietzsche continued to employ this warlike psychology against the great idols of philosophy. He thus legitimized thus "biographical" readings without resorting to the illusions of the thinker's self, whether displayed by the thinkers themselves or presupposed by their commentators.

If Nietzsche's suggestions received little echo in his time, interest in the biography of philosophers has been revived in recent decades, both in the media and academia. However, this interest is fraught with ambiguity

---

32. *Ibid*, p. 44.
33. My translation.

regarding the use of the word "life." On the side of the public success of philosophy in certain social circles, the idea of a philosophical life corresponds to a pedagogical version of thought: the contents presented under the name of philosophy are supposed to provide recipes for living well, encourage individual wisdom, or foster worldly dialogue. The interest in the life of the philosophers and their theses, generally summarized in a few concepts or homogeneous theories, exposes blocks of content. Plato, the Stoics, Descartes, or Sartre... all provide coherent narratives that contribute to contemporary debates for readers who are "in search of meaning." Drawings, photographs, or statues of the thinkers are associated with sentences of profound style. Life is then reduced to biographical standards, to the conventional accounts of scholastic hagiography, accompanied by anecdotes and quotations—Diogenes with his lamp, Descartes in his study, Sartre on his barrel... Embellished with what is supposed to be a biography, it brings to life the knowledge of ideas and confirms the patrimonial status of authors whose challenging works seem accessible.

The cultural evolution of philosophers' figures is ambivalently consonant with a theoretical revival of "philosophical lives," of which the thinkers of antiquity are examples. This academic revival has been based in part on the studies of Pierre Hadot and Michel Foucault, who have reintegrated significant figures such as Socrates into the social practices of the Greek and Roman worlds. Pierre Hadot's seminal work represents a turning point in rehabilitating the "philosophical life." This approach does not embody psychologism; rather, it treats philosophy as a way of life and approaches ancient personalities as embodiments of thought. To assess Hadot's contribution as well as also his ambiguities, it is essential to first underline his critical dimension: the valorization of "philosophical lives" aims to challenge the privilege of the so-called pure theory that university teaching has long supported, at least in its "continental" version.

Hadot stigmatizes the opposition between philosophy as discourse and philosophy as way of life. He contests the hypertrophy of language, which, according to him, stems from the philosophers' pleasure of speaking and their tendency towards linguistic self-satisfaction. Rhetorical and demonstrative beauty fills them to the point that they forget that at its foundation, philosophy is, first and foremost, an exercise of life. "It is all philosophy that is an exercise, as well the teaching discourse as the interior discourse that orients our action.[34]" Against the oblivion or devaluation of the philosophical life, Hadot observes that the "first" philosopher neither taught nor wrote. Socrates indeed considered speech as practice and not as a text. Furthermore, in ancient Greece, speculative language always had an existential aim. The reversal proposed by Hadot consists in seeing philosophical exercise not as the application of an abstract discourse but as its constitution. A great connoisseur of ancient thinkers, he reminds us that even abstraction was a "practice" and that Aristotle,

---

34. Pierre Hadot, *La Philosophie comme manière de vivre*, Le Livre de Poche, 2001, p. 145. My translation.

when dealing with physics, thought about the movement of things to better conceive of the place of each one in a Whole. The theory of nature also implied a reflection on the self, its becoming, and its moral orientation. Thus, the "search for the truth," this hallmark of philosophy, would belong to a spiritual exercise, and philosophical doctrines would have always aimed at educating the spirit and the body.

The lives of philosophers, then, if they can be classified as "philosophical lives" at all, go beyond mere biographical anecdotes. Still, it is important to define this qualification as the practice of spiritual exercises is not exclusive to philosophy and also concerns religions. Hadot includes personalities such as Dion of Syracuse or Cato among the ancient philosophers who were content to live according to a particular lifestyle that led to peace of mind. No doubt such a broad vision has legitimacy, as it brings together practices such as self-control, concentration on the present, and wonder in the face of existence, all under the name of philosophy... However, these examples from different historical contexts are challenging to identify beyond their specific time period, despite their echo in modern life. Many ancient ideas seem to us similar or even foundational to the contemporary world, when they, in fact, originated from heterogeneous mentalities and distinct cultural contexts. Which figures of philosophers today could correspond to these ancient notions? Some play the role of theorists, while others may be seen as sages, teachers, prophets, intellectuals, or advisors. Their functions—learning, enlightening, questioning, setting examples, worrying, engaging—remain influenced by the times, and the reference to ancient models serves as a retrospective justification.

The central ambiguity that affects the rehabilitation of life under the expression of "philosophical life" has to do with the exemplarity of the philosopher's existence. Specifically, the "example" is presented in the form of a life story, to the extent that it has become a rhetorical genre. It offers a model of behavior through a unified and meaningful trajectory. The "life" is situated in a coherent path that establishes the identity and the meaning of a person who has lived in the truth of his existence, combining theory and practice, speech and action in harmony. But the exemplarity of this life stems above all from its narrative, as it achieves its unity through the linear structure of a story.

After all, to justify such a conception of philosophical lives, one could say that ordinary existence with its banality, contigency, and baseness, is not important; the essential should lie in the adequacy of a discourse and a practice. However, this account of a philosophical life is based on several presuppositions: the will, unity, and continuity of the self. The consequence of such a unifying approach is unfortunate because it refrains from questioning the psychic motivations of philosophical discourse and the possible distortion between discourse and life under the misleading appearance of exemplarity. Foucault, at once prudent and audacious, preferred to speak about "subjectivization" through the choice of behavior. Rather than an inner self, unified or reunified through spiritual exercises, he analyzed how a thinking being manifests a "souci de soi" and engages in subjectivity.

Rehabilitating the notion of life in the study of philosophical texts by considering theoretical or abstract discourse as one of its "expressions" or consequences is thus a decisive and groundbreaking proposition, but one that requires not representing life as a unified self. The biographical and exemplary narrative gives a misleading image of the link between the self and its discourses that must be articulated or disarticulated anew. What do we know about the motives of the Stoics to assert the empire of reason and to extol self-control? Beneath the glorious attitude of the wise man opposing the tyrant's violence or showing his disdain for the imminence of death, what non-rational motivations—fears, interests, self-love, fanaticism—are acting without the philosophers' knowledge? The skeptic Sextus Empiricus, in *Against the Professors*, already suspected that theoretical choices might result from personal passions, excessive pride, or singular tastes masked by high virtues and reasons. Thus, it would be necessary to systematically question the motives, the interests at work in the practice of such spiritual exercise, and even the choice of such philosophical discourse.

The history of the criticism of texts and discourses testifies that the deconstruction of the author's self has been more prevalent in literature than in philosophy. Proust's *Contre Sainte-Beuve* marked this departure from monistic psychology in literary criticism by urging the distinction of the author's different *selves*. Conversely, historians of philosophy, often confined to an instrumental view of theoretical language, are less inclined to question the thinking subject or the originator of concepts. However, in the very fabric of philosophical writing, it would be appropriate to inquire about the identity of the speaker, the meaning of the collective "we", or the impersonal figure who, under the name of the universal, claims certain truths. Examining the discursive stakes of philosophical prose, often undervalued or dismissed as "literary, " brings to light multiple enunciators manipulating linguistic conventions. The authority of philosophical discourse stems from how the writing subject is inscribed within verbal forms—treatises, essays, dialogues—each of which corresponds to distinct role played by a philosophical author. Who stands behind or within these roles? The emphasis on autonomous thought, master of itself, causes us to overlook the various *selves*, and even the anonymous forces that nourish the production of ideas.

Rather than seeking harmony between a unified life and coherent discourses, it is more fruitful to understand both the process of thinking and the commitment of a subject in a conceptual work. This involves analyzing how a self is constructed, transformed, acted out, saved, and invented by conceiving theses, writing treatises, and speaking publicly. Literary works, because they often rely on imagination, are the place of a recomposition of the self, the writer forging phantasmatic scenes and exploring possibilities that he lives out vicariously. But philosophical texts also allow for such reconfigurations, albeit in a different and otherwise complex way. The unifying function of writing or the construction of thought should not make us forget that this unification is a choice, voluntary or not, and a projection of the self that constitutes itself as a thinking subject. The identification of a thinker with his theses is a self-presentation, all the more powerful when it is asserted through appeals to truth and the use of a universal language. The shift towards anonymity that occurs through the use of this language obscures the personal investment of the subjects, transforming them into abstract producers of impersonal ideas.

The mask of generality dissuades the reader from questioning the existential relation of the author to his discourse. However, philosophizing is also a way of defining and transforming oneself, as thinkers such as Montaigne, Nietzsche, Kierkegaard, Sartre, and Foucault have recognized. By entitling one of his texts *Ecce Homo*, Nietzsche emphasized the psychic and physiological ground of his thoughts, evoking his illuminations and his internal revolutions. All the same, these confessions are not proof of transparency; far from it. They do, however, recognize that philosophical activity involves a construction of oneself and not solely a pure will to attain the truth.

Once the psychic and self-constitutive dimension of philosophy is acknowledged, it becomes legitimate to involve the thinking subject in his discourses and to question his division. The gaps between his life and his theories are not judged as contradictions, weaknesses, or insignificant anecdotes. Instead, they provide insight into the intimate manufacture of the self in the linguistic and social representation that the publishing—in writing or speeches—of a so-called philosophical thought entails. The word "lie," despite its moral and pejorative connotation, refers to the various postures, solutions, and tensions that connect a behavior and a discourse that seem to contradict each other. The theory does not always reflect the lived experience upstream nor guide the existence downstream. It can also foster within thought a process of negation, the repression of a lived truth that it denies and transforms.

The lie, when analyzed as a psychological combination, no longer points to the hypocrisy of a discourse that does not align with life. This new approach designates the connection between lived experiences—identified by moments, emotions, tendencies—and verbal expressions. The discourse should not be immediately labeled as "lying" because one could argue that sometimes it is life itself that deceives while the discourse presents a tangible truth. This life, viewed through the lens of biographical and social norms, may lack authenticity; its coherence and meaning may be false, shaped by an illusory self. Lives are fragmented, composed of disruptions, fragile and unspeakable moments, even unrepresentable. The study of philosophical works does not focus solely on the cohesive arguments of abstract theses. It pays attention to everything that influences them: affinities, friendships, and opportunities that determine, more than conceptual considerations, the direction taken by a philosopher. These agreements and disagreements, often unseen, play their part, just like the personal struggles faced by a vulnerable individual. The absences, the depressions, the interruptions, and the daydreams without images also contribute to the complex nature of existence. They can have a productive role in thought, just as much as the intense moments highlighted in biographies.

Now, let us analyze these connections concretely to understand the role of theory in cases where there is a stark division between a behavior and a discourse. The hypothesis of a lie fueling the energy behind passionate assertions must be supported by evidence, and we will begin by examining two instances of theories developed in apparent contradiction with the lived experience: Rousseau's theory of education and Sartre's theory of commitment.

The Lie Produces a Masterpiece: *Emile*.

No one has been as sincere as Rousseau; no one has pursued truth as diligently, yet the world has accused him! We have already heard Rousseau's statements and his desperate efforts to conceal or explain his crime, the abandonment of his children. The pathos of truth is a symptom of the lie we commit towards others and ourselves. However, the energy expended in creating an idealized image of oneself can also contribute to theoretical constructions. This is the power of the lie. With Rousseau, the fruit of such a tension between the feeling of guilt and a *pro domo* plea results in a book that is both clear and incongruous: *Emile, or on Education.* Its clarity stems from its significant place in the history of philosophy and pedagogy. Rousseau's analyses and proposals continue to be discussed today and shape theoretical stances on education. On the other hand, its incongruity arises from its inconsistent writing and chaotic composition. Rousseau appears to have wavered between various styles and genres, ultimately producing a voluminous treatise that contains conflicting forces. The most intriguing aspect is a generous theory of education by an author who did not desire to educate his own children. Criticizing this stance would miss the point, as this text reveals a multiplicity of Rousseau's *selves* that is more intricate than what is apparent in the explicit theses.

Emile's case could be summarized as follows: Rousseau wrote a treatise on education even though he had abandoned his children. However, we should suggest another formulation: Rousseau wrote a treatise on education *because* he abandoned his children. Each ""although", wrote Proust "is invariably an unrecognized "because".[35]" Nonetheless, we must avoid from the outset the somewhat simplistic hypothesis of compensation from the beginning, as if Rousseau had wanted to redeem himself by contributing, through a text, to the welfare of the children to be educated. Causality only becomes interesting when it implements a deceptive strategy, whether conscious or not. The development of a theory corresponds to the strength of the denial that the theorist

---

35. Proust, Marcel. *In the Shadow of Young Girls in Flower*. Edited by William C. Carter. Translated by C. K. (Charles Kenneth) Scott-Moncrieff. New Haven: Yale University Press, 2015, p. 10.

exercises. The more he conceals educational truths, the more he masks his educational defect. The frenzied energy he devotes to writing his treatise, resulting in a hyperbolic and never-ended demonstration, stems from the desire to hide the truth about abandonment. We have observed this hypertrophy of discourse, which reveals an internal tension and a blatant lie. The denial here is not limited here to the ruse of a schoolboy who wants to conceal a fault; it testifies to a complete mobilization of the mind in favor of a false truth, which becomes the driving force behind intellectual productions. The recourse to philosophy then combines the lie with a universal language and deploys it in an endless rhetoric. Theoretical prose is the place, the scene, the substance of this deceit, allowing the author to assert his innocence, goodness, transparency, and absence of remorse, while concealing an irreparable fault.

Constructing a theoretical work that contradicts the life led by its author leaves traces of this tension in his writing. These traces form scars that an attentive reader can detect in the text by identifying oddities or suspicious perfection. The lie proceeds by seams that demonstrate to a problematic connection between truths and falsehoods. Sometimes, these seams, sewn into the fabric of the text, are invisible, so well has the covering of the wound been done, with bright affirmations masking the lie and its activity. The psychologist reader must then scrutinize all the tricks employed within language: the overpowering dominance of a concept, the inflation of a demonstration, the repetitions or omissions, the excessive length of a sentence, the excessively complex nature of a thesis, the incompleteness or never-ending pursuit of an argument. The types of enunciation in which the author experiments with various "I"s also provide clues for uncovering the masks of a subject who uses different personal pronouns, "I," "we," "you," and resorts to the impersonal or the fictional. Examples, footnotes, illustrations, and all this supplementary material also contain traces to be examined. These are numerous figures, often overlooked because they fade into the background compared to the explicit meaning, which bears the stigma of the lie.

Rousseau's treatise on education contains many of these stigmata. Moreover, the writing itself constitutes the scar through which the author tries to conceal a wound that will forever remain open. The text is a lie, which does not diminish its theoretical relevance: the ideas are valid because a lie differs from an error. It is difficult to imagine that a lie can lead us to truths, but truth operates on a different level. It can be based on an insincere intention and still give rise to valid theses for a reason. It remains for us to embrace this idea contrary to the common morality: a truth can arise from a deceitful intention! The alignment between a self and its words must be relegated to the mythologies of unity.

Who speaks, says "I," thinks, and produces truths? The answer is never straightforward, to the extent that the commitment of an assertor in his statements remains problematic. Rousseau is aware of the ambiguous status of his treatise on education. He specifies to his publisher that it is not a manual of recipes for educating children, but a properly philosophical work reflecting the nature of man and his place in society. *Emile* is presented in the continuity with the preceding *Discourses* and is distinguished from works of fiction. However, Rousseau encountered difficulties of different kinds in writing it due to an accumulation of notes that exceeded his initial project, which was limited to a memoir of a few pages. After four years of work, the treatise became an enormous text, impossible to complete. The result is so diverse that it mixes thoughts on education with unrestricted considerations on travel, a criticism of the ecclesiastical institution, and a draft of a sentimental novel. The fourth book of the treatise contains a text that functions almost autonomously, "The Profession of Faith of the Savoyard Vicar," which became famous because it led to opposition against Rousseau from various churches. The fifth book recounts the meeting of Emile and Sophie, and their love life. This temptation to create a novel led Rousseau to write a sequel to his treatise, in the form of an unfinished epistolary novel, narrating Emile's misfortunes: deceived by Sophie, he leaves for Naples and is then captured by corsairs, continuing his journey in North Africa. Rousseau himself seems to have entered into adventures that he could not control and that went beyond his original intention. Therefore, he was very reluctant to publish the work, recognizing that he had intended to focus on a different topic than the ones that distracted him.

The reader of *Emile* can legitimately ask the question: What is the true purpose of this treatise on education? The length and heterogeneity of the treatise suggest a tension in its writing. Unlike aimless rambling, the theoretical framework enforces the repression of a truth that Rousseau contains and transforms. This truth occasionally emerges within an extensive discourse. The bubbling caused by internal currents requires the writer to disguise and sometimes acknowledge personal motives. In one instance, Rousseau cites the example of a woman of Sparta with five children, likening it to his own situation. The most poignant moment of this foam of truth is a paradoxical admission by Rousseau: "He who cannot fulfill the duties of a father has no right to be a father. Not poverty, nor severe labor, nor human respect can release him from the duty of supporting his children and of educating them himself. Readers, you may believe my words. I prophesy to any one who has natural feeling and neglects these sacred duties,—that he will long shed bitter tears over this fault, and that for those tears he will find no consolation.[36]" Who is addressing the readers here? Is it Rousseau, the philosopher of the *Discourses*, or Jean-Jacques, the private man? At this point, the author seems to confess his crime and express endless remorse. Guilt emerges as a key theme in this half-confession and throughout the text.

However, even if the treatise is filled with tearful writing, it is constructed using concepts and universal arguments. Rousseau presents himself as someone capable of offering strong ideas on education despite neglecting his duties as a father. Within a lengthy speech, this confession is indeed countered by a strong denial. Rousseau speaks as though

36. Rousseau, Jean Jacques. *Emile or Concerning Education.* Lanham: Start Publishing LLC, 2013, p. 23.

he understands what a child is and how they should be educated. He positions himself as the knowledgeable authority, attempting to replace the father's role with the educator's. His self-assuredness is only matched by his resignation. He asserts himself even more as he has tries to make readers forget his failure to fulfill his duties, the very duties he expects from all fathers. However, something remarkable happens when he rereads his treatise once it is completed: in *The Confessions*, Rousseau admits to feeling remorse upon discovering the ideas presented in *Emile*, as if he were not the author and the text was accidentally addressed to him. Clever excuses are immediately provided: the "almost [...] public confession[37]" within his treatise should dissuade any reader from blaming him for anything.

As proof of his redemption, Rousseau declares that he will cease all sexual relations with Thérèse. Abstinence is presented as a moral act, accompanied by more ordinary explanations such as the decline of desire in his companion or his health problems. However, Rousseau will not follow this resolution disguised as a moral pose and will find other justifications for his fault, which he assimilates into a mistake. Unfortunately for him, his enemies, and even some friends, will not forget. In 1764, Voltaire published *Le Sentiment des citoyens* in which he denounces Rousseau as a Tartuffe, a bad father and lousy husband who "drags with him from village to village, and from mountain to mountain, the unfortunate woman whose mother he made die, and whose children he exposed at the door

---

37. *Rousseau, Jean-Jacques, The Confessions, op. cit.* p. 594.

of a hospital[38]." Faced with such persecution, Rousseau multiplies the acts of repentance for several other faults, which should mask the greatest. In the *Dialogues*, he avoids the most bitter subject and practices self-criticism in a hysterical mode, while keeping control of the signs and stealing criticism from others. Excessive confession of sins is a way to deprive others of blaming you.

However, the tension between denial and confession finds a creative resolution through the alliance of reason and imagination. To expose his theory of education, Rousseau invents an imaginary pupil and thus mixes fiction with argumentation under the guise of applying his theses. *Emile, on Education* is the title of his treatise, proposing an equivocation: the book is about a character who embodies a theory. Is the character of Emile the illustration of the perfect education, or is education in the image of this child? Naming a treatise after a character is not obvious, and Rousseau thus inscribes his theoretical work in the continuity of the epistolary novel he wrote just before, *Julie; or, the New Heloise*. The emphasis on the child implies a singular status for the treatise, which oscillates between demonstration and novelistic construction. In fact, Rousseau, in order to elaborate a theory of education, devotes his writing to imagining this child and the stages of his development[39]. Of course, the point is to link theory

---

38. Voltaire, *Le Sentiment des citoyens*, in *Mélanges*, Gallimard, « Bibliothèque de la Pléiade », 1961, p. 717. My translation.
39. In a letter to Malesherbes, he describes his joy in imagining and populating nature with men worthy of living there (*Fragments autobiographiques*, in *Œuvres complètes*, t. I, *op. cit.*, p. 1140).

to practice. Still, the personality he describes directs the text towards the imagination of a life and relationships that could have existed between a child and an adult. The method chosen could be summarized as follows: Rousseau invents a student in order to invent himself as an educator. But behind such a demonstration suggests another formulation: Rousseau invents a son to invent himself as a father.

The lie goes beyond denial and acquires a creative power by becoming an affirmation through which the liar composes a new identity. Rousseau becomes a master educator, drawing his knowledge from a practice he never had. An interpreter of Emile could certainly observe that Rousseau, as a tutor, educated children other than his own. But the text belies this separation between educator and father, between teacher and parent. Rousseau constantly presents the education of a child as a duty incumbent upon the parent. He provides a wealth of details worthy of childcare to show the attention necessary from the first days of the newborn. Taking sides in the debates of the time about the restraint of children, he speaks out against the practice of swaddling. Then he advises against the use of a wet nurse; this "distorted" practice gives mercenary women the right to mistreat children by swaddling them in order not to have to watch them. An infant needs the breasts and the care of a real mother, Rousseau insists.

If the thought of education close to nature is the treatise's subject, the writing's purpose lies elsewhere, in constructing an imaginary kinship that masks and replaces the absent father. Rousseau navigates the currents of contradiction, projecting his own history into the educational theses. A quirk emerges in the argument mixed with the narrative: the reader learns that Emile is an orphan and needs a wet nurse. Rousseau's imaginary child had no parents because they were dead, whereas his real children were abandoned by their parents. The operation of substitution aims to absolve the biological father and even to reincarnate him as a generous educator. Emile indeed resembles what a young Rousseau might have been. And his imaginary father seems to draw a meticulous portrait of his care. Concerned about feeding the child well, he studied the quality of the milk of the wet nurses according to their geographical origins. Rousseau wanted country girls whose milk would be healthy, like that provided by herbivorous females. "No porridge but dried fruits!" the substitute father still recommends, following the diet of his pseudo-offspring with the concern of a dietician.

The author proposing the theory of education in *Emile* is a fictionalized version of Rousseau, the opposite of another self whose identity we do not necessarily know better, but of whom we at least know that he has abandoned his children. This. This fictional "I," who speaks under Rousseau's name, is a subject that authorizes itself through the language of general truth. However, this "I" is a fiction. In *Emile,* the "I" presents itself as a perfect educator and constructs a lie to hide the responsibility of another "I," the absent father. Through this "I," various contradictory emotions are expressed, such as shame and pride, loss and omnipotence. The author is lost, but assumes the position of someone who knows and asserts. The author's distress is palpable when addressing a "you" that no longer targets the reader but instead tries to reach the imagined child. The child is described as if he truly existed: "I see him", he writes, [...] I contemplate him as a child, and he pleases me; I imagine him as a man, and he pleases me more; his ardent blood seems to warm mine; I think I live by his life, and his vivacity rejuvenates me.[40]" The "I" in the writing hopes to be reborn by accompanying his philosophical and novelistic creation. This shift in the character's status becomes evident when Rousseau calls him, assuring him of the best preceptors: "O you who have nothing like this to fear, you for whom no time in life is a time of discomfort and boredom [...] *come*. He comes, and I feel at his approach a movement of joy that I see him share [...]. We are not with anyone as well as we are together.[41]" The style sometimes resembles prosopopoeia, as if the author is reviving and giving voice to a lost child. The philosophical essay on education thus transforms into an internal theater where the author confronts his specters.

Who speaks when a philosopher speaks? This incongruous, peculiar question raises doubts about the intentions of philosophical writing. Within the realm of theory, various characters take center stage—the author of a thesis, the audience, and the enigmatic figures lurking in the background of his thoughts. While the philosopher, through his chosen written form, assumes the role of a

---

40. Jean-Jacques Rousseau, *Émile ou De l'éducation, op. cit.* p. 419. My translation.
41. *Id.*

universal subject, he also explores clandestine roles within his concepts. Emile is a treatise teeming with diverse personas, as the writing subject reinvents, experiences, and transforms himself. Rousseau writes, "None of us is philosopher enough to know how to put himself in the place of a child[42]," a sentence that resounds with depth. It addresses a significant but often overlooked question in philosophy: the status of the child, whom thinkers have typically regarded as an adult in the making, as someone to be molded. By focusing his reflections on childhood itself—its joys and imaginations—Rousseau challenges the infantilization of the child, emphasizing its unique qualities. He recognizes the importance of educating the child based on their inherent nature, no longer viewing them as malleable objects shaped by society.

If a philosophy could truly tap into the essence of childhood, it would ascend to a higher plane by embracing the world of the child. However, Rousseau's sentence sounds peculiar due to its use of "we," including the author in his struggle to put himself in the perspective of a child. Implicitly, he acknowledges the contradiction inherent in his theoretical endeavor: he meticulously observes the child's development, working on this new philosophy, yet recognizes that he remains on the periphery of the child's world. Furthermore, the phrase "to put oneself in the place" remains ambiguous, as it can both grant a voice to someone typically silenced and take their place. Rousseau adopts the position of the child through empathy and

____

42. *Ibid,* p. 355.

projection. It has been suggested that he created an imaginary child to envision himself as a father, and it is also plausible that he crafted the child he could have been.

The invention of a child to be educated, for the sake of a theory of education, could be that of the author who is remaking his childhood. Emile is the lost child that Rousseau would like to find again under the auspices of substitute parenthood. Father and son simultaneously, reversing the roles, he constantly splits himself in the mirror of the theory. Through a narrative interlocking, Rousseau imagines his childhood as the child he could have raised. Doesn't he say one must look for "the child in the child[43]?" Of course, he challenges the pedagogy that aims to find the adult in the child, but he was indeed, like Emile, deprived of a mother and abandoned by his father. Rousseau gives himself, through his character, a childhood and an education that he did not have, led by a paternal protector. He invents a child who is none other than himself, thanks to the writing of the treaty. Doesn't he advise the tutor to play with this child, to share his amusements as if he were his little companion? In the fifth book, Rousseau imagines the young Sophie but destines her to "the work of her gender," especially sewing, reserving her education for her future husband. He dedicates the woman to procreation and the service of the man, as he asks of Thérèse, whom he wants to be simple and docile. Rousseau thus composes the family roles and, in an address to his readers, expresses the retrospective wish to have had loving parents who

---

43. *Ibid*, p. 242.

devote themselves to their child in this way: "As soon as he is born, take hold of him, and do not leave him until he is a man: you will never succeed without this. As the actual nurse is the mother, the proper tutor is the father[44]." The supplication is understood as a request to imaginary parents by an old child who would like to return to the beginning of his life, in the vain hope of a rebirth.

The philosophical construction serves a surprising function here, allowing for a genealogical recomposition of the writing subject. The conceptual character, Emile, who aims to practically present a theory of education, is adopted by its inventor. He reincarnates the child abandoned by Rousseau, who calls him, makes him live, and speaks to him. The author projects himself onto this philosophical creation, creating a double where he reinvents his own childhood. Through this surrogate pupil and son, he conceives his own education, fulfilling a desire for a new beginning. This desire is further emphasized by other genealogical shifts, such as the famous appellation of "Mama" given to Mme de Warens, as well as the designation of Thérèse, the mother of his children, as his aunt or sister. While there may be differing psychoanalytical interpretations, it is clear that the theoretical language is influenced by the writer's personal struggles.

This phantasmagoria in such a serious philosophical work raises questions about the relationship between life and discourse, between personal falsehoods and universal

---

44. *Ibid*, p. 261.

truth. The reader of *Emile* can choose to firmly separate the author from the text, a stance commonly taken, which allows for commentary and discussion on this significant contribution to educational thought. However, it is important to acknowledge that the theoretical arguments are not without contradictions rooted in the author's psyche. To truly understand these arguments, we must not ignore the inner conflicts of the different *selves* within the writing subject. One example is Rousseau's thesis on the relationship between a nature-based education and its role in shaping good citizens. The lie supports his argument: Rousseau criticizes neglectful parents on the dual grounds that they ruin their child's life and fail to foster a concern for the public good. "Children who are far away, dispersed in boarding schools, in convents, in colleges, will carry elsewhere the love of their father's house, or, to put it better, they will bring back the habit of not being attached to anything.[45]" Perhaps Rousseau is recalling Aristotle's views in *Politics*, wherein he emphasizes the importance of connecting children to their parents who are responsible for their care. Nature, particularly through physical resemblance, designates offspring to their parents. From a political perspective, it is crucial that adults take on the responsibility of educating children. Parents feel this duty, while an anonymous educator will never feel such a natural bond. Aristotle argued against Plato's utopian vision of a city without family ties, where children would be educated solely by the City. In his work *Emile*, Rousseau adopts an Aristotelian perspective, shamelessly

---

45. *Ibid*, p. 262.

proclaiming that "Nature made children to be loved and cared for." Rousseau argues that when children are raised by their parents, it strengthens the marital bond, as nature assumes that husbands and wives will become fathers and mothers. The treatise concludes that Emile's existential goal is to become a father and educate his child. By being educated by their parents, children develop a sense of responsibility towards others and a concern for social ties. The good father, Rousseau argues, shapes a good citizen because "through the small country, which is the family, that the heart becomes attached to the great![46]" Natural bonds serve as the foundation for conventional bonds.

However, there is another side to Rousseau's theories on education. He must justify the abandonment of children by their parents, a belief he shared with Mme de Francueil and later discussed in *The Confessions*. In this context, he draws inspiration from Plato's pedagogy in *The Republic*, which argues that children are better raised by public institutions. Rousseau adapts this idea to his own situation, suggesting that in the absence of a suitable family, children become better citizens by disregarding their family ties. This contradicts the thesis presented in *Emile*, where Rousseau emphasizes the importance of a child being raised by their parents. Thus, Rousseau finds himself contradicting his own beliefs and constructing a theory that stands in opposition to his own life and words.

---

46. *Ibid., p.*700.

Sometimes speaking is doing, but speaking is just as much not doing. Rousseau, a virtual educator and a theoretical father, replaced action with writing. "I will not put my hand to the work, but to the pen, and instead of doing what is necessary, I will try to say it,[47]" he concedes. However, the deceptive energy works differently; writing does not replace anything; it does not replace practice; it invents a personality that draws its brilliance from the inversion of another. It is forged by denial and contrariety. Rousseau's extreme investment in the theory and description of an ideal education, the image of the overprotective father, does not mean he would have wanted to assume such a responsibility. He cared for his dog and his cat and was careful to keep them safe when he had to travel and to take them back when he returned. But he did not really try to find his children. Late in life, he asked the Duchess of Luxembourg to launch an investigation into his first daughter for the sake of Therese, but fearing a possible confrontation with this child. Did he even believe his imposing treatise could amount to a real education? In this same work, he paradoxically mocks the lack of interest in books in the face of an education close to nature. The energy he deploys in his writing is not compensatory; it proceeds from the crushing of the lived life. The more the author affirms, the more he lies, and the more he invents a self in the stature of a philosopher.

The construction of a theory thus plays a determining psychic role for Rousseau, who will gradually identify

____

47. *Ibid*, p. 264.

himself with this book. The power of denial and transformation that was implemented led him to think of his treatise as the completion of his thoughts, personality, and existence. The publication of *Emile* took time, and the hassles caused by the printing places and the betrayals he suspects are experienced in his flesh as if the health of his body was linked to this book. "Whilst my situation became worse the printing of *Emile* went on more slowly, and was at length suspended.[48]" Rousseau is terrified at not leaving this treatise to posterity because he must make it triumph against all the plots. He even states that he is waiting for this publication to retire. And if he writes great works afterwards, he will always want to be judged by this one. *The Confessions* exposes his intimate life to all eyes, but *The Emile* remains his most invested theoretical self-portrait.

The psychic function of philosophical writing is rarely thought of as the construction of a self-image, yet it plays this role in the same way as a literary work. Indeed, the verbal material used by philosophers differs from that of writers of novels or theater. But the circulation of the *selves* there does not leave fewer scenes, mirrors where the writing subject constitutes himself, gives himself to be read and seen by his readers. Such self-portraits come from rational thought and existential choices, conscious or not. They are elaborated according to the circumstances and the opportunities that allow one to transform oneself, to remake a personality, to recover the load of the past, and

---

48. Rousseau, Jean-Jacques, *The Confessions, op. cit.*, p. 662.

to rearrange it. The lie, understood as a discord between the lived experience and the discourse, can have a decisive part without obtruding the theoretical relevance. Philosophical work is also a "true novel". Without a doubt, thinkers who use both literary and philosophical writings give more support to this reading. However, fine attention to the composition of theoretical works allows us to guess this link between the speculative and the specular, even in the most "abstract" writings.

To Be What I Am Not: Sartre's Commitment

To view oneself as a martyr of truth, to see oneself as a stoic hero, or to imagine oneself as the sole inventor of a groundbreaking theory are roles presented by the conceptual theater. This self-staging in theoretical writing contradicts the authenticity of a thinker who is solely dedicated to ideas. It is a sham if it is only meant to showcase a powerful self to others. However, the emotional investment in these ideas is often directed toward oneself, without the subject always being aware of their self-representation. At times, the author suspects the presence of self-love in the development of their theses, or an evil genius, albeit not necessarily malignant, that influences them in certain directions. Sartre was undoubtedly one of the philosophers most wary of this kind of self-deception or self-delusion. He continuously sought out the presence of inauthenticity lurking within his writings and actions. His self-reflection can be observed in the notebooks he wrote as a soldier during the "phony war". Through rigorous self-criticism, he questions each of his moral attitudes or philosophical positions, suspecting them to be tactics aimed at presenting a favorable image of himself.

As an expert in self-criticism, Sartre acknowledges his pride, even in moments of humility or self-control. He analyzes everything; he refuses to be deceived, using his intelligence and rhetoric to filter reality. When he is unexpectedly deployed in 1940 and becomes a ordinary soldier, he attempts to adopt a stance of complete indifference towards his experiences, seeking solace once again in words. With a sense of distance, he recognizes that History has placed itself upon him, and that he can do nothing about it because one can only take responsibility for what is within their control. Without naivety concerning his decision to detach, he ironically refers to his thoughts as "the tribulations of a stoic." He dissects even the smallest of his ethical motivations with uncompromising clarity.

This systematic self-doubt, if it can have speculative benefits, as Descartes practiced it, is not without risk when it fails to lead to a minimal certainty and threatens the unity of the thinking individual. Self-criticism becomes a kind of aimless pursuit, the author becoming the object of his own destruction. In fact, Sartre undermines his moral theses as he develops them, gradually losing all confidence and assurance in himself. "I am at once the same and another," he observes. "I embody different possibilities depending on the circumstances, what I call the 'situation.'" This contemplation of the transformations of his ideas and his relationship to existence during wartime reignites the doubts he has always harbored about the reality of his own self. In a personal notebook, written at the age of 18, he confesses: "I have searched for my self; I have seen it manifest itself in the relationships with my friends, with nature, with the women I have loved. I found in myself a collective soul, a soul of the group, a soul of the earth, a soul of books. But my true self, outside of men and things, my true, unconditioned self, I did not find it.[49]" Certainly, an interpreter of Sartre would point out that the philosopher, in developing his theory of free consciousness, explores the mourning of the old self and the idea that consciousness is never what it is, no longer what it was, and not yet what it will become. Yet, within this thesis of a perpetually evolving consciousness, Sartre admits that he has never truly felt connected to himself.

Those who envision Sartre as a self-assured author who imparts political lessons might be surprised to discover his uncertainty and even his lightness. However, numerous writings testify to his doubts and his desire to embrace existence despite the impossibility of fully adhering to it and recognizing himself within it. "What I mean is that the personality must have a content. It must be made of clay, and I'm made of wind,[50]" he laments, while attempting to wear lead soles. Sartre is a man who floats, even though he

---

49. Jean-Paul Sartre, "Carnet Midy", in *Écrits de jeunesse*, Gallimard, «Blanche», 1990, p. 471-472. My translation.
50. Sartre, Jean-Paul. *War Diaries: Notebooks from a Phoney War*, November 1939-March 1940. Translated by Quentin Hoare, London: Verso, 1999. p. 294.

feels guilty for such inconsistency. Indeed, the question of responsibility, the corollary of a theory of freedom that compels individuals to define themselves solely through their choices, constitutes a moral obsession in Sartre's works. And while he may not exhibit the same paranoia as Rousseau, who suspects the whole world of accusing him, he nevertheless sets the stage for a perpetual court of judgment in his plays. From *The Flies* to *The Condemned of Altona*, his main characters are subjected to the judgments of others and are held accountable for the actions they have committed or, more often, the actions they should have taken. His most renowned play, *No Exit*, portrays the endless deliberation between three characters as they seek to justify their actions and inactions, a torture of sorts. The fact that this work was written at the end of the war and that the male character is a coward, entangled in his own lies, directs the audience not only to Sartre's ideas about others but also to the author himself and his situation in 1944.

The truth must be told: the characters in *No Exit* finally admit it, after having lied and cried about the miscarriage of justice that led them to hell. But what truth exactly? The truth of the facts is not enough. Sartre suggests that truth cannot be definitively established because it always remains suspended from consciousness and time: it must be lived as such by the one who utters it, and it requires a retrospective reflection on the past. Sartre wants to base truth and lies on a relationship with oneself, rather than on an assertion that would be objectively true or false. Like Rousseau, he continuously explores these notions and delves into the depths of his being to find the motivations for speaking truth or falsehood. In his work of philosophy, *Being and Nothingness*, published in 1943, while Sartre was teaching in Paris during the German occupation, he writes about lies. He proposes distinguishing intentional lying—the act of deceiving by someone who knows the truth—from lying to oneself, which he calls "bad faith." This famous thesis aims to define a behavior of consciousness that abandons its freedom to exist as an object. The individual in bad faith convinces themselves that they could not have acted differently due to circumstances or their supposed nature. Deceived by themselves, they use self-persuasion as a means to escape their responsibilities. Bad faith, therefore, is the attitude of a conscience tormented by a freedom it avoids. However, while Sartre condemns bad faith, he does not oppose it to "good faith" or sincerity, as Rousseau claimed, because he recognizes that they are equally deceptive. The examples Sartre proposes to illustrate the lie about oneself became famous figures, particularly that of the waiter who pretends to be a waiter by exaggerating the supposed gestures of his job. He adheres to himself; he sticks to his role. In this little philosophical theater, the waiter is next to a coquette who allows her hand to be touched while maintaining her air of a saintly nun, or to a homosexual who is pressured to confess to being a pederast by those who claim to champion the truth. Sartre draws his examples from "everyday life" and incorporates ordinary characters into his complex philosophical theses. He writes in a café, observing the waiters and stories of manners around him... in the year 1942. However, at the end of his demonstration, a doubt arises that sounds more historical: "not being cowardly," when I am so.[51]" The pronoun "I" is used here as a school subject, certainly, but we can surmise that it refers to the philosopher who puts himself in the shoes of a coward. Even though Sartre delights in creating concepts, as he expresses in a letter to Beauvoir, his philosophical essay is haunted, in subtext, by examining conscience and the perspective of judgment, which unfolds in the extensive chapters on the gaze of others. To the point that he questions himself as if speaking directly to himself: "How can we believe by bad faith in the concepts which we forge expressly to persuade ourselves?[52]"

Cowardly or brave, liar or sincere... what did the deserter of *No Exit* truly do? What did Sartre not do? The case is never closed because we can always revisit it, give it new meaning, as the philosopher of truths in progress observes. Past actions only acquire value through present actions, through their resumption in a new project of existence. Desertion can be seen as cowardice if it consists solely of preserving a life free of risk. Nevertheless, it becomes a courageous attitude if it is part of a project of contestation and commitment to change the world. An individual can, therefore, only be judged based on their actions once they are dead, when they can no longer return to their previous life to orient it from a new perspective.

---

51. Sartre, Jean-Paul, *Being and Nothingness : A Phenomenological Essay on Ontology.* Translated by Hazel E. Barnes. London: Routledge Classics, 2003, p. 89.
52. *Ibid.*, p. 91.

Truth is always in the process of being judged. Sartre developed this ontological and moral reflection during the war when his life was turned upside down. Mobilized, then taken prisoner, he returned to Paris, took up a teaching position, and wrote a lot: a diary, letters, novels, plays, philosophical essays, and screenplays for the cinema. Writing under the Occupation gives a solid meaning to texts caught in an exceptional historical situation during which every word has a political resonance. Sartre would encourage this type of reading by pointing out, after the war, the "responsibility of the writer," whether or not he wrote about his time. He affirmed that non-commitment is still a commitment for which everyone is accountable. Therefore, rereading Sartre's numerous texts in the light of his own "commitments" seems legitimate, even if their scope exceeds the context. What is at stake is an analysis of his intellectual production rather than a historicist reduction: the motor of conceptual reflection, which some would call his "genealogy," is essential to bring out.

The theory of bad faith introduces several concepts— truth, sincerity, authenticity—that Sartre revisits with heightened acuity, especially in 1942, 1943, and 1944. During these years, the philosopher-writer focused on his writing after abandoning his plan to join a resistance network. At the age of 25, Sartre had already written a text on truth, inspired by Nietzsche's questioning of eternal and universal truth. In *The Legend of the Truth*, in 1930, Sartre challenged both science and rational philosophy for claiming to reveal pre-established truths, emphasizing instead that these truths are constructed and shaped by history. Despite debunking the idea of truth as a legend, Sartre did not entirely abandon the notion. Instead, he anchored truth in the practice of verification. Empowered by this demystification, Sartre could criticize and theorize about the idea of a constantly evolving truth during times of war—a truth that is both compounded and completed over time. In 1948, in *Truth and Existence*, he further explores this idea, engaging with Heidegger's text on *The Essence of Truth*. Sartre argues that truth is not passive contemplation or mere disclosure, but rather an active process that is historically constructed by humans. He asserts, "All truth is lived as danger, effort, risk.[53]" Undecidable, the truth is a test, even if it is a lie to oneself.

Reading these continuous reflections on "experienced" truth, one cannot help but connect them to their author and how he lived the truth of his time. According to Sartre, choosing ignorance is a refusal to be free and take responsibility. He points out that those who refuse to acknowledge slaughterhouses while enjoying their meat are acting in bad faith. If one were to witness the slaughter of oxen, the beef they consume would no longer be an anonymous substance called "meat," but rather the dead flesh of an animal. We are tempted to ask Sartre what he wanted to know about life during the Occupation while he sipped coffee at Le Flore, taught at Lycée Condorcet, or rehearsed his plays at the Sarah Bernhardt theater (renamed Théâtre de la Cité). But can one truly "choose"

---

53. Sartre, Jean-Paul, *Truth and Existence*. Translated by Adrian Van den Hoven. Chicago: University of Chicago Press, 1992, p. 8.

not to see the backstage? Ethnic cleansing was pervasive. Thus, when faced with the yellow star, Sartre pondered whether to confront it or ignore it. Supporting the individual wearing it would play into the hands of the Germans, who stigmatized a specific population. On the other hand, ignoring it risked indifference and acting as if everything was normal in occupied France.

In writing about lies and the reasons a subject gives himself for not seeing, assuming, or acting, Sartre is conducting his own examination of conscience. This is evident in the Notebooks, where he constantly tracks down his alibis and false justifications. How does he see himself in occupied Paris after the failure of "Socialisme et liberté," the resistance group he founded upon his return from the Stalag? By distributing leaflets, he took significant risks for minimal results. He did not have the physical build or the right networks like Jean Cavaillès to be a maquis fighter. However, he did contribute to the Resistance by writing books that could pass through the censors. Regardless of his motives, only the future can give meaning to his behavior. Past inaction can always be overridden by ongoing overactivity that will redefine his moral and political path. When Sartre's opponents accuse him of making errors of judgment regarding historical situations, he responds by saying that "truths have become[54]" and that only the accomplished path matters. This formula may sound somewhat Hegelian, but it mainly reflects Sartre's perception of his subjective involvement in History and

---

54. Jean-Paul Sartre, *Situations, X*, Gallimard, 1976, p. 183. My translation.

his encounters with collective determinations that eluded him in moments of action or inaction.

Contemplator of his own lies, Sartre regularly divorces from himself. He presents in stages the paradoxical self-portrait of a man who *does not adhere to what he is*, constantly transported beyond himself by the movement of his conscience and the course of history. Struggling but committed, he pursues the truth; he acknowledges his mistakes and incorporates them into a meaningful continuum. When he looks back, he dissects his life; he scrutinizes his past. As both object and subject, he engages in self-criticism and then reorganizes these layers from previous periods in an intellectual journey. The philosophical portrayal of his revolutions aims to reclaim the past, endowing it with a new truth. This retrospective representation of himself is a *theoretical autofiction*.

Self-criticism, now a method and a system, is a paradoxical mastery of truth: it disallows others from exercising criticism by preempting them. Would it be objected that Sartre's philosophy of freedom did not account for collective reality? The author himself rejected this misconception of a freedom divorced from interdependence, and he had already responded to these objections with a new theory. As a protean philosopher, Sartre assimilates references and contradictions that previously held him back. He engages with Husserl, Heidegger, and Marx, only to surpass and transcend them, leaving their interpreters to lament betrayal. Elusive, Sartre provides them with a map of his movements. He does not conform to himself and invents theoretical identities by surpassing and transforming.

The moment of the war is the one that Sartre dramatizes the most, marking the primary division of his life in two. There is a before and after that enables the writer-philosopher to categorize his works and interpret them in light of this transformation from individualism to socialism. He will paint a retrospective picture of it during interviews at the end of his life. However, at the very moment when he experiences this change and feels himself becoming someone else, he is already writing a novelistic continuation with a biographical nature. *Les Chemins de la liberté* depicts the journey of an individual who believes he is free because he rejects any form of commitment, but eventually realizes his failure. Mathieu Delarue, a replica of pre-war Sartre, will be surpassed and replaced by other characters in the third volume, concluding a dialectical journey that portrays a freedom engaged in history. While living through these personal changes, Sartre simultaneously theorizes them, categorizes them, and stages them as if he were writing History. However, this epistemological separation aims to detach the past from his personal existence. While mobilized and involuntarily involved in the war, Sartre writes: "The strongest or highest moments of my past life do not interest me anymore, as soon as they are past. My natural tendency will always be to belittle them since I believe I am better than the one I was. This solidarity with oneself, so touching in Stendhal, which prevents him from painting his best moments because he would depreciate them for himself by talking about them, is entirely lacking in me. This is partly the reason for the publicity of my life. Everything is detached from me, and I give everything to everyone because I am already detached from everything.[55]"

This division between life and its public representation—novel and theory—is both a result of extreme clarity and a distressing psychological instability of someone who no longer recognizes himself and believes he can rid himself of his past by leaving it to others. In any case, it highlights the role of theoretical autofiction: the categorization of an intellectual path and the dramatization of its intense moments do not follow the lived experience; they impose themselves and alter the meaning of the past in the present. The theory constructs the timeline more than it expresses it. It allows Sartre to invent an artificial continuity with which he does not fully identify, and to punctuate it with remarkable ruptures. The philosopher becomes the conceptual character that he manipulates on the stage of truth.

We know that this theoretical and fictitious representation is, to some extent, a lie. It is not a deception, but rather a need to find a psychic solution. Later, when he attempts to write the total biography of Flaubert, his antithetical double, Sartre will propose "solutions of continuity" between an individual and his time. However, he will always want to inscribe them in a dialectical relation,

---

55. Jean-Paul Sartre, *Carnets de la drôle de guerre, op. cit.* p. 127. My translation.

giving meaning to every small fact and attitude, wrapped in a totalization. These theoretical solutions hide the unspeakable but still experienced lived experience, such as weak times, side steps, tangents, and syncopations: the dreams, the melancholy, the depression, the sentimental adventures, the music, the travels... a multitude of other rhythms that are just as essential to life, but are left in the shade by theoretical hagiography. This distinction between strong and weak times is convenient but irrelevant because it maintains the illusion of a superior life, a reasoned existence, and an ordinary everyday life. Even the notion of contradiction cannot account for this dissociation between the lived experience and its intellectual representation. Instead, there are complex articulations woven with fictions—decoys, ruses, lies, denials, and inventions—that arrange the tensions between life and discourses. Sartre experienced the war as a series of ruptures that he had to integrate into a scenario. The most improbable and fascinating scenario is undoubtedly the one he constructed at the end of the war—his theory of commitment—to which he remained loyal until the end of his life, even if it meant betraying it clandestinely.

In 1944, as the war was coming to an end, Sartre had to give meaning to the aftermath. He had showed *Huis clos* in May, Paris was liberated in August, and he wrote in *Lettres françaises*, the journal of the National Committee of Writers. In his articles, he wanted to reflect on the temporal break and the new perspectives for humanity. A year later, he launched his journal, *Les Temps modernes*, and became the leading figure of the committed intellectual for a long time. He occupied the political field with unwavering ardor, adopting the cause of all the oppressed of the earth, starting in 1945. Perhaps the most striking article that marked this conversion to politics was the one entitled "The Republic of Silence," which appeared on September 9, 1944, on the front page of the first issue of *Lettres françaises* that emerged from hiding. It begins with a formula as famous as it is misunderstood: "Never have we been so free as under the German occupation." The philosopher promotes his conception of freedom based on choice. Oppression gave more weight and authenticity to the actions taken by some and others, risking death in defying the occupier. Unlike choices made during peacetime, which are often met with "yes but" or "no but," those made during the Occupation were life-affirming. The French were either collaborators or resistance fighters, with no room for half-measures. Sartre clarifies that he is referring to all French people who said "no" for four years, not just the resistance fighters who led armed struggles. He idealizes this Republic of silence and darkness, where every Frenchman, regardless of their condition, chose their own freedom and that of all others by refusing Nazism. Sartre's text is lyrical, driven by the euphoria of the liberation of Paris. Keeping only the first sentence is a misunderstanding, as it would imply that Sartre endorsed collaboration. But we may also be mistaken in accepting his portrayal of a dualistic world. Numerous behaviors during the Occupation, including the most common ones, did not fit into the clear-cut categories of resistance and collaboration. Action or inaction, speech or silence could be interpreted as either objective complicity or passive resistance. Sartre himself did not face the risk of death in the activities he engaged in for four years. Nevertheless, he speaks on behalf of everyone in this text, which constructs the myth of a universally resistant France. It is not sufficiently surprising that he uses "we" to describe freedom under German occupation. What is this "we" referring to? Is it the "we" of the Resistance fighters, the "we" of the Parisians, or the "we" of the French? Sartre inserts his own "I" into this "we" that is clad in the garments of martyrdom—"we were deported en masse, as workers, as Jews, as political prisoners..."—even though he does not fit into any of these categories. To speak for others is to assume their position through either generosity or an abuse of language. In this text, Sartre fabricates an image of a resistance fighter, and his inaugural text of his future commitments is a lie.

Once again, the word "lie" must be clarified in an amoral sense: our astonishment at the text Sartre wrote in 1944 does not stem from the hypocrisy of a last-minute Resistance fighter, as there were many. Instead, it prompts us to understand the disconnect between a discordant discourse and lived experience. What role does this text play in shaping Sartre's representation of himself and his past? How does the theory of commitment that followed stem from a denial of reality, from a reconfiguration of identity in the form of a circumvented confession? Sartre acknowledges that he was mistaken in his pre-war notions of solitary freedom and recounts his theoretical transformation that occurred during his captivity in 1940. He then presents an intellectual rendering of his journey that retroactively justifies his investment in political philosophy and action. However, this self-narrative does not align with the philosopher's actual experience, as we can discern from other texts or testimonies.

The tragedy of existence that Sartre describes—the death that constantly stalks the streets and heads, the awareness of extreme responsibility towards others, the absolute rejection of the Occupation, the panic-inducing fear, the prison, the torture, the deportation—this was not his fate, let alone his destiny. Sartre was not unhappy during his time as a prisoner in Germany; in fact, he even confided in Simone de Beauvoir in a letter dated December 10, 1940, that he had "never felt so free." While in Paris, he spent his days at the café and was passionately pursuing his new career as a playwright and screenwriter. He was delighted to find broadcasts for Simone de Beauvoir at the Radiodiffusion Nationale in Vichy and eagerly anticipated her return with a tan from winter sports at the end of 1943. Sartre's correspondence from that period often reveals him as a happy and cheerful individual, despite the worries that pervaded everyone's lives during wartime.

Undoubtedly, it is necessary to address the contentious issue of certain French writers and artists' behavior under the Occupation, which has been the subject of malicious polemics. However, it is crucial to refute the hypothesis that Sartre was complicit with the occupying forces. By reading his texts, even those approved by German and French censors, it is evident that Sartre was a Resistance fighter at heart from the start of the Occupation. Testimonies also support his unwavering determination to fight against Nazism upon his release from captivity. Rejecting this baseless accusation, however, does not automatically transform Sartre into a hero of the Resistance. It appears that Sartre, like many intellectual petty bourgeois individuals, adopted a more ambivalent stance, participating in a relatively thriving cultural scene in the theater and cinema during the Occupation while still hoping for the victory of the Resistance. Our aim is not to reopen this controversial topic or participate in any moral and political judgement. Rather, we wish to explore the following questions on different levels: How can one claim to write in the name of the Resistance when one has not actively fought as a Resistance fighter? How can one base a theory of freedom on a situation that one knows to be false? How does one assume the role of a moral critic while being aware of one's own guilt?

The posing of these questions should not prompt moral judgments. Otherwise, the individual asking them would falsely assume a position of moral righteousness and be exempt from accountability. It is more nuanced to view such "contradictions" as integral to a psychological framework and a philosophical resource. Sartre does not develop his theory of commitment "despite" his actions during the Occupation; rather, it is born "from" his experiences. Paradoxically, the radicality he advocates after the war finds its origins in his history of compromises and half-measures. Similarly to Rousseau's paradoxes, the notion of compensation is insufficient. It was suggested by Vladimir Jankélévitch, who sought to evaluate French philosophers based on their conduct during the war. Recognizing the avoidant approach of intellectual and artistic elites regarding this contentious question, Jankélévitch analyzes the strategies employed by those who navigated the Occupation without hindrance and continued their careers. Rather than portraying Sartre as a cynic or opportunist, Jankélévitch proposes that Sartre's commitment to morality became more extreme as a result of his guilt, stemming from his sense of inadequacy in the face of genuine resistance. Sartre's political engagement after the war, advocating for the marginalized and oppressed, can be seen as a plea for forgiveness for his own shortcomings, including cowardice and compromises.

Bad conscience can serve as a driving force not only for morality, but also for theory. However, a mere psychological explanation is insufficient to demonstrate the speculative and theoretical power of denial or lies. The stakes, both psychologically and philosophically, of reversing one's beliefs and theorizing the opposite of one's lived experiences require a transformative shift in one's discourse. Utilizing language with a universal purpose, employing a speech that aims to erase the "I" that speaks and writes, signifies a takeover and mutation. Sartre's personal and political engagement, which he positioned himself as the champion of, must be understood in light of this conversion that seemingly contradicts his life and theory. The text he wrote for *Lettres françaises* marks the beginning of this transformation whereby a singular and uncertain "I," that of Sartre questioning his nature, changes, and lightness, transforms into a collective "we"— the French oppressed by German occupation, the victims of Nazism, the tortured resistance fighters. More than a mere facade through which Sartre asserts his dominance over the intellectual landscape of the post-war era, this text inaugurates a new self: Sartre constructs his identity through this "we," which subsequently becomes the pronoun that embodies all calls to resist.

The rhetorical and philosophical construction of the lie surpasses the defect's transformation into excess. It is precisely this excess that reveals an unresolved tension, an obsessive insistence on affirming a thesis or displaying a behavior that suggests a desire to conceal. In his interviews reflecting on his life, Sartre only mentions feeling guilty about the Spanish Republicans of 1936, for whom he had sympathy but no consequences. On the other hand, he says very little about his life during the Occupation, and only his correspondence offers insight into his schedule and interests. However, one text, written in December 1944, shows embarrassment and self-justification. Addressing English and American readers, he could not confidently sing the tune of a unanimous and resistant France. In "Paris under the Occupation," Sartre alleges the "feeling" of the French, which was not necessarily expressed in action. He emphasizes the mixed feelings, such as hatred and embarrassment, anger and reason, toward the German occupier or the Allied bombardments. Unlike the text intended for the French, this one highlights the "ambiguities" of life under German control while defending the idea that "the Occupation was often more terrible than the war." Words and gestures can be interpreted in many ways. This contrasts with the lyrical tone Sartre adopted at the same time when addressing the French public, stating, "Each word became precious as a declaration of principle since we were being hunted down, each of our gestures weighted a commitment." Thus, with a clear understanding of the facts, Sartre erases past ambiguities to affirm the absolute necessity of engagement. As an activist in the strictest sense, he will go to extremes, fascinated by the violence he will support in the name of counter-violence, adopting the revolutionary rhetoric of the new man who must destroy his oppressors to be reborn. Sartre's radicalization and maximalism became a trademark of the philosopher, mobilizing his existence for revolutionary causes.

However, this coherence of thought and action results from self-representation and remains the result of denial. The theory of commitment was built on a lack of commitment. Indeed, the famous manifesto of *Les Temps Modernes* finds a perfect place in post-war France by calling for the "responsibility of the writer"; it breaks with the disillusioned insouciance of the 1930s and the contempt of bourgeois humanism. But when reading Sartre's comminatory sentences, written in 1945, the reader may wonder about the exemplarity of an author who institutes a "tribunal of letters", undoubtedly in the continuity of the trials of the Liberation, and extends it to previous centuries. Thus, in the "Presentation des Temps Modernes," Sartre holds Flaubert and Goncourt "responsible for the repression that followed the Commune because they did not write a line to prevent it.[56]"

------

56. Jean-Paul Sartre, *Situations, II*, Gallimard, 1948, p. 13. My translation.

Would Sartre also hold responsible for the Vél' d'Hiv roundup a writer who, in 1942, did not write a single line in support of the Jews or to condemn the participation of the French State in their deportation? Yet his *Reflections on the Jewish Question* attests that he was very sensitive to their situation. Sartre's aplomb and energy in writing his manifesto overwhelmed doubts about his past. The subject writing in 1945 has taken on the authority of a writer who affirms the "truth" of literature and embodies a sense of responsibility by denouncing irresponsible authors. The stigmatization of a defect is undoubtedly the sign of an unavowed guilt. The denunciation of Flaubert's irresponsibility sounds here like an alert, even a confession. Sartre's reversals highlight the psychological dissonance between a philosophical construct and the lived experience from which it stems. The theses of *Being and Nothingness*, which establish responsibility by starting with the concept of situated freedom, choice, and action, possess an independent speculative power. However, they are influenced by the philosopher's personal experiences, as seen in his use of pronouns such as "we" and "I," which subjectively implicate him in his aspiration to develop a universal and shareable thought. Consequently, he explores the notion of responsibility in relation to war, both as something endured and consciously chosen. Sartre attempts to explain that he, along with his contemporaries and all individuals at war, bears responsibility for the ongoing conflict, even if it is not their desire. He states, "There can be no question of considering it as "four years of vacation" or as a "reprieve," as a "recess," the essential part of my responsibilities being elsewhere in my married, family, or professional life. In this war which I have chosen I choose myself from day to day, and I make it mine by making myself. If it is going to be four empty years, then it is I who bear the responsibility for this.[57]" The ambiguity of the philosophical discourse enables the audience to perceive both Sartre's reflections as he wrote in 1943 and a paradigmatic scenario wherein temporality fluctuates, allowing individuals to ponder responsibility, even in times of peace.

A Sartre specialist may observe that these theses on responsibility lay the groundwork for the philosopher's moral and political stance following the war, with his writings on committed literature serving as the prologue. However, this idealistic interpretation presupposes that lived experience follows a philosophical decision: Sartre supposedly reflected on responsibility, and only then did he assume responsibility. Nevertheless, we must question the timing of thought, its context, its narration, the experiences that inform it, and the transformations it provokes to comprehend the interplay between language and an individual's journey. While authoring his thesis on responsibility, Sartre envisions, dreams, and invents identities. Through characters at the heart of the discussions of *Being and Nothingness*, he assumes various roles and embodies conceptual personas. He plays the part of the man peering through a keyhole and the man being observed, the sadist and the masochist,

---

57. Sartre, Jean-Paul, *Being and Nothingness : A Phenomenological Essay on Ontology. op. cit.,* p. 575.

the man of bad faith and the responsible one. By writing his "essay on phenomenological ontology," Sartre not only shines as a distinguished successor to Husserl and Heidegger but also strives towards personal reinvention through these roles. He projects himself into philosophical speculations, be they abstract or tangible, akin to the child he once was, constructing chivalrous characters to defend innocent victims.

At the end of the war, Sartre set himself a course of action: to be a responsible and committed writer until the end of his days. He believed in this mission and dedicated his life to the causes it required. He continued to establish the philosophical legitimacy of this intellectual figure through his theoretical essays and relevant articles. The individual who had been floating, disconnected from himself and his time, has now immersed himself in the whirlpools of his time. "We live in history like fish in water,[58]" he declared in 1945. He reflected on and incorporated the meaning of his past into a comprehensive project; his irresponsibility was just a moment in the journey toward responsibility. However, even the committed intellectual cannot prevent an individual from having unexpected escapades or unacknowledged anachronisms. Above all, the grand theory of commitment carries a force of conviction and self-conviction that corresponds to the denial from which it arises: it was forged by an experience of impotence, inaction, and compromise.

---

58. Jean-Paul Sartre, *Situations, II, op. cit.* p. 41. My translation.

Did Sartre lie about his behavior during the Occupation? Certainly not, as he always practiced "transparency" and did not hide anything to deceive. He even admits to usurping his reputation as a Resistance fighter during his conversations with Beauvoir in 1974. He mentions the lousy trick of a friend who wanted to award him the Legion of Honor against his will at the Liberation. And he cites an Italian prize received as a "Resistant intellectual," an expression that Beauvoir uses unabashedly and that Sartre downplays: "It was a prize connected with the Resistance. I had it—though God knows that my Resistance. . . I was a resister, and I knew resisters, but I never suffered much for it. [...] So I looked upon myself not as personally worthy of this distinction, but worthy insofar as other writers might, like me, have had the award."[59] Once again, Sartre speaks less in his own name than in that of others, hence the use of the "we" into which he blends from his articles at the end of 1944.

However, lying can take different forms, especially when dressed up as truth and sincerity. To deceive oneself and transform one's self-image is a different kind of deception than intentional dishonesty. The claim of transparency is therefore not contradictory or hypocritical. In fact, someone who lies to themselves exposes all their reasons, even their doubts. They don't risk much because they are the ones who put themselves on stage and know everything that can be seen. To reveal oneself without pretense is a recurring

---

59. Beauvoir, Simone de, and Jean-Paul Sartre. *Adieux: A Farewell to Sartre.* Translated by Patrick O'Brian. New York: Pantheon Books, 1984, pp. 250-251.

theme in autobiography. Rousseau already criticized Montaigne, who was quick to expose his weaknesses, for only presenting amiable defects[60]. However, Sartre wasn't seeking the affection of his readers, and his morality of transparency goes beyond a commitment to honesty. He integrated it into the way he lived his life and the ultimate purpose of human existence. The most well-known example of this visibility is his relationship with Simone de Beauvoir, as the couple denounced the bourgeois model of married life and its sexual lies. By allowing each other the freedom to engage in so-called contingent love and remaining transparent to each other, they invented a new kind of fidelity, where the sharing of truth outweighed any suffering it might cause. This love pact, often discussed in the sentimental sphere, went far beyond the bounds of marriage. In the ideal of Sartre and Beauvoir, transparency had to be public and concern not only the major aspects of life, but also the most minor ones, both social and intimate. The life stories, diaries, and correspondence that they published testify to their desire to be transparent not only to each other but also to everyone else. At the end of his life, Sartre still expressed hope for a society where lies would disappear: "I imagine quite well the day when two men will have no more secrets for each other because they will have none for anybody, because the subjective life, as well as the objective life, will be totally offered, given.[61]"

---

60. "I put Montaigne at the head of those false sincerers who want to deceive by telling the truth. He shows himself with faults, but he only gives pleasant ones [...] Montaigne paints himself as being similar, but in profile" (Rousseau, Jean-Jacques, *Les Confessions, op. cit.,* p. 1150).
61. Jean-Paul Sartre, *Situations, X, op. cit.* p. 142. My translation.

Transparency is connected to the eschatological project of humanity overcoming Evil and freeing itself from lies. Sartre appears to maintain an almost naive faith, perhaps even a demiurgic one, in the revolution that would enable this abolition. Like Nizan, Sartre's friend from youth who believed that the USSR would eliminate the fear of death by involving each person in the grand communist project, Sartre imagines this truth being saved in the form of a translucent society where everyone would be transparent with one another.

However, while the abolishment of lies belongs to the realm of the future, the present remains opaque, and Sartre admits that he has not achieved his ideal of transparency. He acknowledges that he has not lied, but rather told half-truths or quarter-truths. This division of the truth allows him to avoid being accused of lying. Sartre admits to concealing certain aspects of his life, as he declares to his interlocutor, Michel Contat, in his "Self-Portrait at Seventy Years": "I try to be the clearest and the truest possible, to deliver entirely, or to try to deliver entirely, my subjectivity. In fact, I don't give it to you, I don't give it to anyone, because there are still things that, even to me, refuse to be said, that I can say to myself but that refuse to me to be said to the other. Like everyone, I have a dark background that refuses to be said.[62]" If he cannot be as transparent as he would like, it is not so much due to modesty, particularly regarding his sexuality, but because of the impossibility of being completely honest

____

62. *Ibid*, p. 143.

with himself. "Even to me," the truths cannot emerge! This is at the core of our investigation: it focuses less on lies by deliberate intention than on the obscure self-deception, which even affects the most intellectually astute, those theoretical and philosophical affirmers.

Sartre's admission of an irreducible opacity compromises his ideal of transparency and truth and also aligns with his quest for authenticity and self-reflection. He is determined not to deceive himself and engages in a rigorous examination of conscience, even if it means confronting the uncomfortable aspects of his own identity. While he acknowledges the limitations of achieving complete authenticity and transparency, he openly acknowledges his efforts to strive for them. Despite the challenges, he remains steadfast in his belief in self-knowledge. Although he rejects Freud's notion of the unconscious, he expresses a willingness to undergo analysis. But he conceives this experience on the mode of knowledge: he hopes that psychoanalysis will be able to teach him about himself, like other forms of knowledge. He sees it only as a question of method and not as abandoning himself to uncontrolled speech. J.B. Pontalis, whom Sartre approached for analysis out of intellectual curiosity, notes the misinterpretation of Sartre's motives.

Sartre would like to preserve the two positions of self-knowledge, that of object and subject. He allows himself to be observed and plays the game, but he wants to interpret what is happening. As a young man, he was preparing for a degree in the study of imagination and wanted to experiment with hallucinatory phenomena. So he injected himself with mescaline to study hallucinations from the inside, as if he could, even while hallucinating, maintain control of himself and describe the distortion of mental images. He multiplies this desire for ubiquity by making himself the object of various forms of knowledge, analyzing himself through sociology, history... many ways of distancing himself under the watchful eye of a superior self that defines the field of vision. What could remain in the shadows amidst so much illumination? Even the obscure is known to the knowing subject. Sartre admits that he has established a system and that he cannot—does not—want to escape from it: "Since I was the one who made this system, there was a good chance that I would fall back into it, and consequently, this would have proved that truth, for me, cannot be conceived outside this system. But it could also have meant that this system remains valid, at some level, even if it does not reach the deep truth.[63]" In contrast to this explanation, an analyst would hear that the system is precisely set up to guard against the emergence of truth. This truth only emerges once the alleged reasons have been silenced, when a subject manages to remain silent, to no longer speak or write.

Writing hides and reveals by hiding, through over-invested assertions. It displays a truth while striving to keep it concealed. Which kind of writing is more inclined towards this twist: literary fiction or philosophical speculation? Literature, with the imagination it demands

---

63. *Ibid*, p. 148.

and the stylistic tricks it encourages, is more conducive to such games between truth and falsehood. How a writer stages their life with more or fewer masks generates multiple tricks that shape an image of oneself through these arrangements. Thus, autobiography and its pact of truth only engage credulous readers. In *Les Mots*, Sartre can describe his break with faith as a sudden decision, while in his diary, he confides how gradual the path to atheism was. Despite these tricks, Sartre suggests that literary fiction is more suitable for expressing the truth. He specifies that his novels provide a much closer picture of his thoughts, doubts, and emotions than the universal and abstract speeches he could deliver. Truth does not exist without implying the subject who proclaims it; it cannot completely erase it under a veneer of universality: "One can arrive at objective truths without thinking one's truth, says Sartre. But, if it is a question of speaking at the same time of the objectivity that one is, and of the subjectivity which is behind this objectivity, and which is part of the man in the same way as his objectivity, at this moment, it is necessary to write: "Me, Sartre." And, as this is not possible at the present time because we do not know ourselves sufficiently, the detour by the fiction allows us to approach better this totality objectivity-subjectivity.[64]"

The possibility of reaching the truth and understanding oneself is postponed. It is still attainable, but with our current knowledge, it remains out of reach. Writing, therefore, encounters obstacles such as opacity, secrecy,

---

64. *Ibid*, pp. 145-146.

and deceit. It can either choose to dwell in the realm of ambiguity or seek a glimmer of light. Sartre acknowledges that screens, mirrors, and decoys are sometimes necessary to uncover hidden truths. He often expresses his frustration through the works of Baudelaire, Genet, Tintoret, or Flaubert, even though he despised Flaubert, as it helped him understand his own experiences at the time. Fiction can convey truth when it becomes a "true novel."

Philosophy claims to pursue a different truth from the self and its subjective reflections. However, despite the denials of its authors, it also relies on fiction. Fiction extends beyond using everyday examples to illustrate theses or conceptual characters that symbolize moral dilemmas. It is embedded within the discourse as a subjective investment in general assertions. The use of pronouns, rhetorical devices, the structure of treatises, the organization of sentences, the manner of affirming, reasoning, and the choice of verbs and nouns all go beyond mere rhetorical conventions and involve the writing subject. While literature produces fictional stories, philosophy presents "fictional truths." Here, fiction takes on a different meaning from its literary connotation. It embraces various speech strategies tied to the aspiration of discovering truths, intertwined with psychological investments that empower the writing subject to compose and transform their representation of themselves through language, suspending their subjective burden and allowing for a fictional reconfiguration.

A psychologist reader will therefore be wary of a philosopher subject's desire for transparency. As powerful as Sartre's reflections on freedom, choice, and responsibility are, they are not any less inspired by a psychic operation in which a subject invests abstract language of ontology, morality, and politics to project their life into another life and draw a horizon of existence which tears them away from doubts and weaknesses. The eschatology of transparency is also a theater where virtuous affirmations bring salvation. Focusing on concepts makes us forget the long path leading to their exhibition. Once they enter intellectual and academic history, these notions hide the process that gave birth to them and the transformations they underwent. Why did a philosopher identify himself with a particular concept? The answer is uncertain and often surprising, as it clashes with our idea of coherence between life and thought.

The Fetishism of the Concept

A thinker's imprint on a concept ensures their place in the history of ideas. Linking an author's name to a word or a formula provides visibility, even if not intelligibility, to a specific thought, even if it means reducing it to "arguments". Disciples, interpreters, and pedagogues quickly highlight "key concepts", words that transform the work into a safe whose locks they like to open. Philosophers are expected to forge notions through their work on an abstract language, notions that they either invent or update. These emblems find a place in contemporary discourse through concepts, figures, sentence segments, or new compounds. Old words gain topicality (*conatus, ethos, aura...*), while others become philosophical nouns (the other, the event, the difference, the community...), and sometimes prefixes, prepositions, or adverbs are used to compose a notion (the post-human, the being-with, the not-all...).

These markers of thought catalyze the interest of commentators, transmitters, and repeaters who circulate them in various fields of knowledge and opinion. Such extensions often result from an assumed "bricolage"; this word has lost its pejorative connotation with the use of works of the mind as toolboxes allowing unbridled services. The key concepts free themselves from their authors and run through the syntax of the day—a borrowed syntactic form repeated over and over again in distinct disciplines ("Ça fait symptôme", "penser à nouveaux frais", "de quoi x est-il le nom"...). The shaper of expressions does not hold the patent but thus becomes the creditor of a theoretical language whose legitimacy he guarantees upstream, with users referring to their authority.

Magic and Denial of the Concept: Freud

All philosophical uses cannot be summarized in words and can be characterized by rigorous analysis, a critical attitude, free meditation, or other approaches to reality, language, and ideas. However, intellectual historiography indexes thinkers through a term or thesis that serves to classify them almost like a trademark. This overvaluation of certain words goes beyond the necessary publicity to disseminate a thought. It is also part of the psychological investment that thinkers make, granting uncommon importance to these words. Under the influence of trends that lead to the symbolic language of a master thinker and their interpretations, the belief in the power of words characterizes a specific use of philosophy. Freud ironically noted that philosophers overestimate the magic of words and abstract constructions. They believe "that real events in the world take the course which our thinking seeks to impose on them.[65]" However, psychoanalysts should not dismiss the influential role that certain words play for a subject who not only builds a speculative system but also constructs a representation of themselves through it.

What is the relationship of authors to a notion over which they have acquired "authority"? When an author immediately experiences the power of their word, even though they may fear its misinterpretation, they recognize themselves in the act of naming, which becomes an extension of themselves. The work of defining returns to them in the form of a reflection, sometimes distorted by uncontrolled applications, but which still carries the author's performance and continues it. Despite the assertion of universality and anonymity of concepts, their inventor defines and composes themselves through them. However, it is necessary to explain this relationship between an "author" and their word, which is not simply a sign resulting from their interior thought. The myth surrounding "great thoughts" portrays exceptional beings from whom great ideas "come out," symbolized by words like seeds of truth that they have the privilege to bring forth and enlighten ignorant humanity. As custodians of universal and eternal ideas, they "deliver" concepts. While this is the role they play in intellectual history, the effectiveness of their thoughts is rarely realized contemporarily and is often evaluated retrospectively.

---

65. Freud, Sigmund, *New Introductory Lectures on Psychoanalysis*. Translated by James Strachey. New York, N.Y: Norton, 1965, p. 146.

However, as suggested by hagiography, portraying a thinker as a mere conveyor of ideas obscures the underlying processes involved in constructing intellectual systems. In fact, we can overlook this aspect and instead focus on the personal motives that drive a thinker to propose concepts, theses, or systems, considering them to be insignificant. Subjectivity is relegated to the background in favor of what it produces, and the person behind the work becomes a symbol: Plato becomes synonymous with the embodiment of truth, the republic, and metaphysics. The interest in understanding the subjective investment of a thinker in their ideas and words is of a different nature. It does not compete with the historiography of thought, whether it be based on idealistic criteria of listing the significant authors or more structurally oriented to studying the intellectual contexts of an era. Nonetheless, the psychological analysis of intellectual productions, although pursued for different purposes, does not challenge the idea of transparency between a thinker and their thoughts.

The public image of a thinker, often accompanied by the emblem of their school, also implies a flip side in the process of their thinking, so that this flip side represents more of an active counterpart rather than a hidden essence. This duality creates a zone of tension where the author's psyche invests itself in elaborating a concept. Acknowledging such a psychic complexity at play in the formation of ideas blurs the transparency and presumed unambiguity between the thinker and their thoughts. A simplistic approach to intellectual production presents concepts as pure expressions of essence or existence.

However, "expression" can involve trickery, lies, and various forms of deliberate deception through which a thinking subject invents, observes, and transforms themselves through theoretical fetishes. "Expressing oneself" does not simply involve bringing forth a thought from the depths of one's interior that language then reveals. Expression occurs concurrently with linguistic conventions and rhetorical devices through which a subject consciously or unconsciously articulates ideas, emotions, and images with intended meanings.

The valorization of a word, which then becomes the focal point of a thought, can be understood as the use of a *fetish*. This term carries a long history of interpretations, which we do not interpret solely through the lens of ethnology or psychoanalysis. Instead, we retain two aspects: *magical power* and *denial*.

The first feature highlights how certain objects are adorned with virtues that go beyond their basic function. For example, a figurine in a religious ritual transcends its literal meaning to evoke emotions and inspire multiple interpretations. This is the enchantment that surrounds many expressions or concepts, which immediately become infused with values and emotions when uttered. It is not often that such power of words is emphasized in philosophical language. However, a high level of abstraction allows for a greater emotional investment, as it conceals the concrete associations that motivate it. Words such as "loyalty," "fraternity," "spirit," and "justice" possess tremendous evocative force and can elicit a powerful enthusiasm that should not be simply attributed to the subjective circumstances that prompted an individual to repeat and revere them. These fetish-words assume a magical quality, becoming synonymous with the moral ideal and draped in seemingly unconditional legitimacy. They carry hidden influences within clandestine realms and cannot be easily dismissed, as they form the foundation for all the principles, like a heart from which the arteries of thought flow and give meaning. The fetish-word contains a charge of emotions that makes it universally relatable, despite the individual interpretations we may give it. We can raise a glass in celebration of freedom, and we may even be willing to take risks to defend it when it is under threat. However, the strength of this cherished idea may stem from a political experience for one person, a family memory for another, or a professional situation for a third. The communion surrounding a fetish-word is based on a multitude of representations and emotions, which reasoning tries to consolidate.

The most exciting thing about the fetish is undoubtedly its second feature: the denial it entails. Psychoanalysis has noted its sexual nature, manifesting as an excessive attachment to a body part or garment that operates through negation and substitution. We won't delve into the theory that the fetish is a substitute for the maternal phallus. Instead, we'll focus on the connection to denial, which we've already discussed in relation to self-deception. Freud used the Chinese fetishization of bound female feet as an example of denial. Despite the painful deformation caused by traditional binding from childhood, the Chinese hold a fetishistic reverence for the foot. Unlike repression, fetishism doesn't involve blindness or forgetting but rather maintains reality by reversing its value. The tortured and stunted foot is now idolized and revered. The fetish-word serves a similar purpose: it denies the wrong committed against its referent and replaces it with adulation. Moreover, the fetish-word conceals the crime by completely reversing the value assigned to the referent, transforming hostility into adoration. For instance, someone may vocally declare their veneration for freedom and their willingness to sacrifice everything for it, yet they constantly fear making choices and live with minimal freedom. By uttering, writing, repeating, and expanding upon the word, they go to great lengths to refuse the reality it represents. The fetish employs denial to create an illusory sign that shields the subject from anxiety and provides a comforting substitute. Fear no longer exists; now they possess a word they can toy with, repeat, adore, and use to articulate their thoughts and arguments about freedom. They may even criticize those who don't value this cardinal virtue enough. Their actions don't actually reflect their proclaimed love for freedom because they incessantly talk about it, convincing themselves that they ardently serve it. The fetish constructs a fortress that lures others in, precisely because it transforms a secret into a grandiose spectacle. Paradoxically, it safeguards the secret by presenting it with the most misleading advertisement. "Look, I am a free person," says the indecisive individual who endlessly pontificates about the merits of emancipation. They no longer need to be free in reality because they possess the word "freedom." However, they must constantly utter it, cherish it, and display it, or else face the return of the distressing demand to act freely.

On many occasions, the invention or use of a concept becomes a means of self-adjustment, simultaneously working with and against oneself. A word-idea, functioning as a concept, symbol, or image, can become a distorted representation of the author's true self due to its repetitive nature. The philosopher's *conceptual face* cannot be summarized by its truth alone; it serves as a mask by which the self can be hidden, worked on, and transformed. Philosophers often have a penchant for creating abstract terms, multifaceted concepts, and expressions that become infused with imagery. Deleuze justified this practice by characterizing philosophy as "the invention of concepts." His collaboration with Guattari led to the creation of numerous ideas that contributed to their success, to the extent that their terminology crossed over into various non-philosophical domains. Examples such as fold, rhizome, deterritorialization, plane of consistency, striated spaces, and body without organ became almost fetishized, as they provided a framework for artists, critics, and political scientists to articulate their thoughts and identities.

Does a thinker *expose* himself through his concepts? Although thinkers is supposedly hidden behind their concepts, they assert their personal brand in an ambivalent manner. They present themselves and cloak themselves in abstract words, which act as a second skin. They recognize their own identity in these concepts, yet they stand out even more because others comment on and appropriate them. The relationship between thinkers and the labels associated with them needs further clarification. They may reject these labels to avoid oversimplification, but often accept them because they contribute to their notoriety. For example, Sartre initially rejected the words "Existentialism" and "Humanism," only to embrace them when his audience expanded after the Liberation. By surrendering partial ownership of the concepts they create, thinkers reserve a secret space where they preserve their intellectual craftsmanship. Dr. Jekyll does not consider himself fully responsible for Mr. Hyde, even if it is indeed a part of himself. Of course, this Manichean view is too simplistic to analyze the psyche of a thinker, but it implies a certain division or detachment from the linguistic entities they have created. The creator of words may even take pleasure in seeing their creations proliferate beyond their control, as it provides an unexpected extension of their ideas. By identifying philosophy with the invention of concepts, Deleuze glorified their expansion through diverse encounters, resulting in grafts and surplus that transcend their authors' authority. Concepts flow freely among various languages, and as a result, their authors lose control while gaining new life. The word 'fetishes' indeed exerts an attraction on speakers who wield its power of magic and denial. They seize its condensed meaning and unleash it in their theoretical imaginations. Nomadism is the term that Deleuze and Guattari used to describe this joyful and creative circulation, of which they were both theorists and practitioners. Several related concepts, such as decoding, deterritorialization, and ritornello, contributed to the success of this metaphorical amplification. While Deleuze was careful to distinguish his conceptual inventions from "metaphors" due to the approximations of analogy, which is the foundation of meaning transfer through images, his concepts have indeed been used metaphorically in various disciplinary fields. The term "nomad" functions, from a linguistic perspective, as a metaphor due to its philosophical uses. It transforms an everyday notion—where nomadism signifies continual displacement among populations without permanent residence—into a philosophical principle, a catalyst for thought, and a resource for metaphorical expression. It can be employed to conceptualize artistic practices, schizophrenic behaviors, and political resistance. While Deleuze emphasized the active/passive relationship of thinkers toward their concepts, it is important to understand why this celebration of circulation is not limited to a philosophical truth but also becomes part of a psychic strategy that allows a thinker to conceal themselves and escape.

**Fleeing into His Concept:
Deleuze, a Nomad Who Stays Home**

How did the word "nomad" and the principle of nomadism become the identifying mark of a thinker like Deleuze? The answer lies in sociology and the history of ideas, but the connection between an author and their flagship word remains in question. The success of this principle owes something to this more or less opaque relationship. We focus on Deleuze, although he wrote with

Guattari, because his name, associated with academic philosophy, represents the unity of his work and an established coherence, whereas Guattari remains more untamed and uncategorizable. If Deleuze's persona raises a unique question about the notion of nomadism, it is due to the paradox of his life and his declarations about his hatred of travel. The question can be posed in a simple, perhaps even simplistic, way: how can a man who despises travel become the champion of nomadism? This question may seem irrelevant at first glance. After all, it does not matter if the personal behavior of a thinker who has produced such profound reflections disqualifies the anecdotal interest in their ordinary life. This argument is well-known, and we have already acknowledged both its legitimacy and its shortcomings. In fact, the biography of an author can be ignored without harming the reading of their work. However, the idea that the work is purely thought, both in its process and its results, rests on an illusion.

If we perceive a contradiction between the promotion of nomadism and an aversion to travel, it is crucial to understand the underlying psychology rather than detect hypocrisy. Behind words, multiple meanings can conceal themselves, and the term "travel" necessitates precision. It is possible to love travel and yet dislike certain forms, such as tourist travel. Claude Lévi-Strauss begins *Tristes Tropiques* with this paradox: "I hate travel and explorers, and here I am about to recount my expeditions." The anthropologist was thus targeting the travel accounts of those who smugly document their adventures. He mocked the conventional style, the shallow exoticism, and the idealized projections

The Fetishism of the Concept

that prevented the traveling dandies from truly discovering other cultures. Authentic travel is not measured by the number of miles traversed. Nevertheless, Lévi-Strauss journeyed through many territories, willingly embarking on trips during his ethnographic missions in Brazil or, out of necessity, during the war. Thus, the paradox of the traveler who loathes travel is developed and theorized to counteract a romanticized version of nomadism. Other thinkers who have experienced a life of travel and reflected on displacement can be distinguished from sedentary ones. Plato traveled by boat to Syracuse, Descartes rode through Europe on horseback, and Nietzsche wandered relentlessly between the Engadine and the Mediterranean. These nomadic lives influenced their thinking to varying degrees. Montaigne, too, found his traveling life to be a profitable exercise for his reflections. Inspired by his wanderings in Switzerland, Germany, and Italy, Montaigne wrote, "I do not know, I have often said, a better school wherein to model life than by incessantly exposing to it the diversity of so many other lives, fancies, and usances.[66]" But does Deleuze belong to this constellation of traveling thinkers? Indeed, yes, if we consider his praise of nomadic figures. However, his sedentary life and behavior suggest otherwise. Deleuze moved very little in his personal and professional life, despite being sought after by many foreign universities. One trip to New York sufficed for him, even though he became a prominent reference in French theory. He confided that traveling made him sick, and he

---

66. Montaigne, Michel de, *Essays*. Translated by Charles Cotton. Waiheke Island: Floating Press, 2009, pp.1704-1705.

preferred the Limousin countryside of Saint-Léonard-de-Noblat over far-off places.

Thinking or imagining a journey can dispense with the need to actually embark on it. This hypothesis supports a theory freed from experience. The trip can thus be exercised by proxy, whether through abstract reasoning or imaginary projection. Deleuze combines both approaches when he follows the extreme journeys of his conceptual characters. In his mind, the philosopher travels, dreams of exploring spaces and imaginary worlds, and fixates on the vertigo experienced by others to the point of insanity. Nietzsche, Artaud, Michaux, or Burroughs provide him with limitless experiences. These traveling thinkers lived through the dislocation of the self, the hatred of genealogy, and the schism of the bodies with radicality. They put themselves in danger, tasting hallucinogenic drugs such as peyote, ayahuasca, and mescaline, and traveled to distant lands in Latin America, Asia, and Africa. Deleuze does not put himself in danger, but he lives it through them in a way that is undoubtedly vital. His statements express his need to "breathe" thanks to these unlived experiences, as he captures their power in the form of inventive concepts. The thought of nomadism would be a nomadic thought. This argument stems from a change in meaning, allowing us to transform the object of thought into a qualifier of this thought as if the qualities of an object of study were reflected on the author. However, would we say that a thinker of freedom is a free being? The confusion about nomadism arises from the ambiguity of such a word, which the philosopher uses both literally (referring to the way an individual or population moves) and figuratively (referring to independence from codes). Before writing a treatise on "nomadology," Deleuze had already formulated the concept of "nomadic thought." He drew inspiration from the life and work of Nietzsche, whose dreams, madness, and writings cannot be confined to a singular interpretation as he defies all codifications. According to Deleuze, when one reads Nietzsche, "we embark, then, in a kind of raft of the Medusa; bombs fall all around the raft as it drifts toward icy subterranean streams-or toward torrid rivers, the Orinoco, the Amazon; the passengers row together.[67]" Deleuze embraces the wandering imagination to illustrate that the shadowless traveler exemplifies "deterritorialization." As he reads Nietzsche, Deleuze envisions himself sailing on the rivers of South America, experiencing conditions worthy of an adventure novel. While Nietzsche did not physically cross the Atlantic, he did indeed move from boarding house to boarding house, drifting irreversibly and never able to return to his university chair in Basel. Therefore, Nietzsche's nomadism is intertwined with his physical displacements and his irreversible wandering.

The contradiction between the praise of nomadism and the hatred of physical displacement could evaporate in metaphorical expressions. Still, Deleuze did not miss it; he proposed its resolution through a paradox. The nomad, he affirmed, does not need to move! The history

---

67. Deleuze, Gilles. *Nomad Thought*. Translated by David. B Allison, in *The New Nietzsche : Contemporary Styles of Interpretation*. New York : A Delta Book, 1977, p. 144.

of philosophy could provide him with logical paradoxes about movement and displacement, such as the one of Zeno of Elea demonstrating the immobility of a flying arrow. However, Deleuze wanted to base his paradox on an anthropological definition of nomadism. And he hammered home, to the point of obsession, in his writings and interviews, not only that the nomad doesn't move but that he refuses to leave: "Some voyages take place in situ, are trips in intensity. Even historically, nomads are not necessarily those who move about like migrants. On the contrary, they do not move; nomads, they nevertheless stay in the same place and continually evade the codes of settled people.[68]" Deleuze forces the paradox to strengthen his argument and uses his formula to side with the nomads, despite his dislike of travel. The contradiction is evident, and readers who still support it would be accused of not understanding Deleuze's thought since the definition of nomadism implies a refusal to move.

Through repetition and deployment, the paradox acquires a force of evidence because it constructs a definition more than it presents an argument. The nomad becomes a figure of immobility to the point where Deleuze opposes him, in a binary manner, not to the sedentary but to the migrant. The one who constantly moves and doesn't live in any territory, this person travels for the sake of travel, in the manner of Baudelaire, who wrote: "[...] the real travelers are those only who leave/For leaving's sake [...]" On the other hand, the nomad moves only

____

68. *Ibid*, p. 149.

because he is obliged to, against his will because he lives in a "form," while the migrant leaves only amorphous territories. Deleuze continues with metaphors and ethno-geographical descriptions to create landscapes. The nomad clings to a smooth space, the steppe or the desert. And when he moves, he is immobile, like "the Bedouin galloping, knees on the saddle.[69]" He escapes the striated spaces, the vertical ones of the forests, the square ones of the cultivated fields. Deleuze, who has hardly traveled, draws maps, imagines vegetation, and observes climates. He places characters on them and moves them around his symbolic territories. In this geography that replaces historical temporality, he constructs a small philosophical theater, putting nomadic thinkers in his smooth spaces: Nietzsche, Epicurus, and Spinoza. On the opposite side, in the camp of the sedentary, he targets the philosopher of the forest, Heidegger, whom he also calls the "Nazi druid."

Thus, the paradox is supported by symbolic cartography and the imaginary journeys it enables without movement. These antitouristic journeys authorize Deleuze's self-portrait as a nomadic thinker. Inventive as well as argumentative, his theoretical prose is infused with projections of himself through doubles and philosophical characters immersed in the nomadic flow. Deleuze could have simply critiqued travel and argued that an experience of the distant must be abstracted from the reality of travel. Tourism often caricatures actual discovery or experience

---

69. Deleuze, Gilles, and Félix Guattari. *A Thousand Plateaus : Capitalism and Schizophrenia*. Translated by Brian Massumi. Minneapolis: University of Minnesota Press, 1987, p. 381.

of the unknown. The paradox would then have highlighted the figure of the homely nomad, as Pierre Bayard expressed it with sedentary travelers[70]. But Deleuze radicalized the paradox to the point of making it a philosophical marker. The immobile individual becomes the most liberated being of the territories, whereas the migrant remains somewhat enslaved to them. In his *Abécédaire*, Deleuze once again justifies himself for not traveling, despite becoming the thinker of nomadism, and he begins by disparaging travelers and the cheap escapes that travel offers. Instead of citing personal reasons, such as his respiratory illness, he applies his theses on nomadism to himself: he does not travel in principle. He was able to enjoy walking in Beirut, but that chapter is closed. He does not have the desire to go anywhere; he does not feel the need to move; he lives through immobile intensities; in short, he is a "nomad."

Deleuze's focus on the word nomad and its extension in the form of a thesis on nomadism shows how a philosopher invests a part of himself in a concept, a notion, a figure, or a metaphor. This word can become the pivot of all his reasoning, like a guiding framework that allows him to link together various subjects that may not necessarily have a common point. It configures a philosophical, psychic, and political attitude: " To make thought a nomadic power is not necessarily to move, but it is to shake the model of the state apparatus, the idol or image which weighs down

----

70. Pierre Bayard, *Comment parler des lieux où l'on n'a pas été,* Minuit, «Paradoxe», 2012.

The Fetishism of the Concept

thought, the monster squatting on it,"[71] writes Deleuze in his Dialogues with Claire Parnet. The "char nomade" becomes for him the embodiment of struggle against the state apparatus, and he builds his political hope on "imaginary nomadic units."

Other nomads, however, call upon the philosopher of nomadism to justify his paradox. When the philosopher intervenes in the social and political sphere, he encounters actors who use concepts with pre-established meanings. He is no longer addressing only students or peers, and his words become part of different grammars. The logical paradox is then once again seen as a "contradiction" that he must legitimize in the eyes of those who understand concepts within the context of their own practices. The philosopher often finds himself in a position where he must compete and claim a concept or doctrine, as if he has to live up to the image others have of him and not disappoint their expectations. He must assert even more strongly his commitment to the idea he represents. The concept then settles on a *horizon of expectation.*

Given that historiography focuses primarily on political questions, we often remember the one-upmanship and loud declarations of a thinker, even if it means forgetting about his silences or his "disengagements." This was the case with Sartre, who became known as the leading proponent of commitment, overshadowing the

---

71. Deleuze, Gilles, and Parnet, Claire. *Dialogues.* Translated by Hugh Tomlinson and Barbara Habberjam. New York: Columbia University Press, 1987, p 32.

philosopher and writer that he was before and continued to be secretly. Deleuze also didn't engage with politics until later in life. As a high school student during the Occupation, he was close to Guy Môquet in his senior year. However, he did not feel personally involved in the political struggle, unlike his brother, who joined the Resistance and died in deportation. Even during May 68, while Deleuze sympathized with the student movements while teaching in Lyon, he spent his summer completing his thesis. His main concern was finding a position and settling in a university: "Il faut que je me case, à Vincennes or in Nanterre[72]," he wrote to François Châtelet. It's true that he suffered from a lung disease and needed to rest, despite his enthusiasm for student mobilization. However, his political radicalization primarily came from personal encounters rather than from a political theory: most notably, his friendship with Guattari led him to engage in various "causes" such as prisons, mental illness, and Palestine. Later on, the desire to connect his early works with his later positions and to demonstrate their political nature will contribute to a retrospective interpretation that his revolutionary friends, like Toni Negri, will support.

How and when does a concept become prominent in the author's thought and its dissemination? Historical conditions determine the success of a discourse embedded in the language and imagination of its time. Understanding this current state involves combining an

---

72. Gilles Deleuze, «letter to François Châtelet «, 1969, Châtelet IMEC collection, quoted by François Dosse in *Gilles Deleuze Félix Guattari. Biographie croisée*, La Découverte, 2007, p. 218.

individual's singular production with what their time expresses through them. The reception of ideas, concepts, and images eludes the author, even if they are the initiator. The author often finds themselves chasing after their concepts, disseminating them and then pursuing them in a frantic race to catch up. Sometimes, these concepts come back and demand recognition, reminding the author of their attachment to them. The interest in political analysis and theory leads thinkers into the public arena, where they are confronted with this pursuit of their concepts. For example, philosophers take up, modify, and dispute words like people, community, biopolitics, and multitudes, which are then relayed by multiple commentators and disciples. Moreover, the theoretical stakes, crucial for shedding light on and potentially transforming society, overshadow the personal investment of theorists who knit together these notions with their own lives and construct their intellectual coherence.

The moment when a thinker embraces the political dimension of their writings, closely linked to the historical situation, is also the moment of a psychic projection into a presumed horizon of expectation. This explains their more assertive address, directed towards enemies or an audience to be mobilized. The first book that Deleuze considers as his foray into politics is *L'Anti-Œdipe*, written with Guattari. The philosopher's tone undergoes a radical change. The philosophical impertinence and bellicose attack against psychoanalysis reveal a Deleuze in conflict with norms. It is nothing less than contesting Freudian psychoanalysis and substituting it with a "schizo-analysis" that draws on

Marxism to restore revolutionary power to desire. This work brings about an exceptional theoretical rupture that will have a lasting impact on the debate surrounding the unconscious, as well as psychoanalytical and psychiatric practices. This impact emerges not only due to its critical intensity but also through the creation of numerous alternative notions, such as desiring machines, flow, and molar and molecular. Primarily, its target is familialism, in which the Oedipus figure and its theoretical manifestations serve as the conduit for genealogical normativity.

By exposing himself to such a declaration of war, Deleuze not only encounters intellectual opposition but also has to justify the conformity of his way of life to his political injunctions. One of his former students, Michel Cressole, pointed out his contradictions. This homosexual activist, who died of AIDS, denounced the discrepancy between the philosopher's ideas and his peaceful existence: the critic of familialism married religiously and lived with his children according to a classic Oedipal model. He only mimics the psychic rupture of schizo-phrenics, like a lyrical star. Mocking the nomadism of the one who stays in place, he compares him to " those opera battalions that repeat 'let's march' without moving from their place, creating only the illusion of a movement[73]". Beyond the punitive tone of the polemics of this time, we must reflect on the link that a thinker establishes between a speculative discourse and a lived experience, between a performed truth and a psychic investment.

---

73. Michel Cressole, *Deleuze*, Éditions universitaires, 1973, p. 91.

Far from wanting to revive any trial, let us examine Deleuze's understanding of truth and falsehood in order to respond to the accusations and engage in philosophical reflection. When confronted with the contradictions between his theories and his way of life, Deleuze responded with insightful observations about the underlying assumptions of such accusations. He was at liberty to bring the debate to a theoretical level and assert that the issue of Oedipus is not restricted to one's personal family history, nor is it necessary to be unmarried, childless, and homosexual in order to conceive an escape from the Oedipal structure. It is worth acknowledging that discussing a problem does not require one to be directly involved in that problem, just as talking about China does not necessitate being Chinese or analyzing schizophrenia does not require being schizophrenic. However, there remains the question of "speaking for" or "speaking in the place of," which arises when considering Sartre and his use of the enunciating subject, the "we." This raises numerous ambiguities surrounding the status of the one speaking, encompassing both a universal and individual standpoint, as well as the potential for abusive positions.

Deleuze's orchestrated defense transforms the incoherence between life and theory into a fascinating reflection on truth and lies. Deleuze, rejecting the expectation to pledge his sincerity or political commitments, opposes the need for truth with "secrecy." This is not to suppress facts, but rather to assert the power of the false: what is claimed to be true may hold no value or relevance, while falsehood can generate practical validities.

Deleuze critiques narratives that testify "a lamentable faith in accuracy and truth.[74]" But what does the celebration of falsehood mean to him? His philosophical approach rejects the Platonic conception of truth and stands in opposition to the simulacra described by Lucretius or the masks examined by Nietzsche. Rejecting the dualistic notion of essence and appearance, Deleuze early on relinquishes the idea that truth is philosophy's objective. Metaphysics gives way to a realm of discourses, affects, and relations.

The suspicion surrounding the truth arises from the motivations behind seeking it. *Why do we desire the truth*? This initial question must be asked even before defining what truth entails. It is undeniable that the discovery of a lie, whether real or perceived, triggers both the quest for truth and the belief in an "attainable" reality. Essentially, and despite the evidence, it is advisable to *start from the lie in order to reach the truth*, or at the very least to comprehend the origins of our desire for truth. Rather than assuming a preexisting truth concealed or distorted by lies, it appears more prudent to demonstrate how the notion of truth arises from suspicion of falsehood. In his work *Proust et les signes*, Deleuze asserts that the object of the *Recherche* is more about truth than it is about lost time. He shows that the narrator and the characters are adept at unraveling lies. Through their uncertainties and actions, he implies that the desire for truth always stems from a concrete situation and is never purely an act of will.

---

74. Deleuze, Gilles. *Negotiations*, 1972-1990. Translated bt Martin Joughin. New York: Columbia University Press, 1995, p. 11.

We do not seek THE truth, but rather A truth that is necessitated by specific circumstances. This is how jealousy emerges from mere suspicions and triggers the quest for truth. It is enough for someone to appear to be lying, by vehemently asserting a particular version of events or by stumbling over their explanations, for the impression to be formed that an alternative truth exists. The jealous individual then embarks on an investigation, following clues in the hopes of uncovering the truth by exposing the lie. This truth both exists and does not exist; it is both observed and constructed. Indeed, Odette de Crécy is cheating on Swann, leading him to doubt everything she says and imagine her infidelities. However, truth itself is not objectively defined. It is merely conveyed through a particular prism, in this case, love, which shapes its form. Swann constructs scenarios based on the unintentional signs Odette gives him, envisioning her with Forcheville or other lovers. If the unfaithful person avoids the truth, it is not solely to hide it, but rather because it can only be grasped through languages that produce partial and variable interpretations. Consequently, the more hesitant the loved one is to express themselves, the more the jealous individual suspects lies. His desire for truth is driven less by a thirst for knowledge and more by conflicting emotions such as rebellion, hatred, power, and vengeance.

The desire for truth is always underpinned by a more powerful affect than the will to know. It thrives on the protean power of lies, which multiply like tracks and virtual scenarios. Out of jealousy, Swann has fallen into a spiral of signs that serve as infinite clues to justify his suspicions.

Does he not already know that Odette is unfaithful? He searches for a truth that he is aware of but cannot end with a simple statement of facts. The story in which this truth will take shape is subject to scenarios in which the jealous man multiplies for his own misfortune. This sequence of fiction leads him back to other hidden truths, such as the nature of his love and the confusion about the object of his desire for a woman "who was not his type."

Deleuze, in this way, points his opponents back to their obscure *desire for truth*. He lectures them on the meaning of truth and liberates himself from their summons to appear. Questioning the desire for truth challenges the philosophical search for truth and presents a new understanding of lies. Deleuze rejects any general definition and aims to bring the search for truth back to a specific situation and an interaction that forces one to interpret signs. As a follower of Nietzsche, he asserts that this search is always self-serving and demonstrates a devious psyche, much like Socrates directing thought toward supposedly ulterior worlds because he cannot face the tragic forces of his own life. "The mistake of philosophy is to presuppose within us a benevolence of thought, a natural love of truth. Thus philosophy arrives at only abstract truths that compromise no one and do not disturb."[75] Logical or metaphysical truths stem from an idealism that conceals its psychological motivations. In contrast, Deleuze wants to present truth as a unique fiction that engages its creator. This truth

---

75. Deleuze, Gilles. *Proust and Signs*. Translated by Richard Howard. Minneapolis: University of Minnesota Press, 2000, p. 16.

arises from a violent encounter that compels the one who formulates it to compromise himself by committing entirely to a construction of truth and falsehood, much like any work of fiction, whose power is equal to that of ideal truth.

How does a designer of truths *compromise* himself in his concepts? What are these powerful truths, and what effects govern their desire? The question interests Deleuze, who tacitly answers it for himself. His statements are ambiguous, like many philosophers who assume and do not assume the authority of their theoretical creations. On the one hand, they claim a signature, a singular commitment to thought; on the other, they invest their ideas and concepts with autonomous power. By affirming that the quality of a concept comes from its "performance" more than its relevance in stating what is true, Deleuze underlines that he is the author of such performances but also that other thinkers and creators perform them by taking them back and expanding upon them.

In response to accusations about the gaps between his life and his thoughts, Deleuze describes his *ambivalent desire to appear and disappear in his concepts*. Drawing on the Nietzschean assertion that all philosophy is a biography of its author, he qualifies it by specifying that this biography is not narrative. Authors do not tell themselves in their abstract theses; they are made and unmade there. Thought has the effect of challenging the personality of thinkers; it decompresses their selves, makes them doubt, and sometimes pulverizes them. Sartre said that we always think against ourselves; otherwise, we remain in the bad faith of those who forge a satisfactory image of themselves through their thought. To break the bones of the skull is the image of the thinking head. Deleuze says it in revolutionary language: to do philosophy is to lead a guerrilla war, not only against powers but also with oneself. This destabilization of oneself leads to splitting, to multiplications in which each becomes several, metastable, unrecognizable.

Continuing with the thread of guerrilla warfare with oneself, Deleuze seems seduced by the idea of the thinker's *clandestinity*. Not being recognized, despite the name signing the books, not assuming the unity of a life that unfolds in a linear account, changing without moving, without others perceiving you... the philosopher is tempted by invisibility, effacement, and escape. "To be imperceptible among the imperceptible," says Deleuze several times. Combining the Nietzschean definition of life as a supra-individual power with his desire to escape the definition of an authorial self, he suggests the notion of *impersonal life*. Combinations, becomings, and intensities replace the unity of the person: Deleuze claims to always be elsewhere, even if he does not move, and thus does not have to answer for his life as we see it. How could he be accused since he does not answer for his person? He suggests, "I am not who you think I am," and no one corresponds to what he gives to see.

What remains is the name, the signature of the thinker, one might object, the one that allows an author to assert their mark on books, theses, ideas, and concepts! Here again, Deleuze attempts a reversal and dissociates the name and the person, even proposing a new paradox with the idea that the name comes from a process of depersonalization. "It's a strange business, speaking for yourself, in your own name", he writes, "because it doesn't at all come with seeing yourself as an ego or a person or a subject. Individuals find a real name for themselves, rather, only through the harshest exercise in depersonalization, by opening themselves up to the multiplicities everywhere within them, to the intensities running through them.[76]" Deleuze opposes this depersonalization to the one practiced by the traditional philosophical discourse where the impersonal gives access to the universal. This depersonalization was only of style, whereas the one advocated by Deleuze comes from a welcome to all that fragments, crosses, and transforms the self. Deleuze assumes his name of philosopher only to escape the unity of a philosophical thought better: this name is a bursting of singularities activated by encounters. Connections, bodies without organs, counter-currents, eddies... writing mixes with other flows: "of shit, sperm, words, action, eroticism, money, politics, and so on.[77]"

The question of the *name* by which a thinker signs his concepts is old, and Deleuze tackles it in the wake of many philosophers who have discussed the authority of thought. Montaigne already observed that a concept, an idea, or a thesis do not belong to anyone. When he took up

---

76. Deleuze, Gilles. *Negotiations*, 1972-1990, *op. cit.*, p. 6.
77. *Ibid*, p. 8.

an argument developed by Aristotle or another recognized thinker, he considered it his own because he had integrated it into his thinking. Montaigne used the metaphor of nutrition to describe this digestion of other thoughts: once ingested and not spat out as scholars do by using "authoritative" arguments, intellectual food feeds the mind, the nerves, and the blood of the person who ingests it. It is part of his body, and he does not need to quote its initiator. As Derrida will suggest, by counter-signature, a thinker affixes his name, signs with and against, and countersigns what has been thought before them. The association between concepts and names is a circumstantial relationship between a thinking subject, their culture, and its representations. Sometimes, this alliance has a limited duration. Thinkers have used multiple names and pseudonyms to express their ideas, marking their journey of reflection and life. Kierkegaard is a prime example of this, and we will soon analyze his enunciative strategies. There is a recurring question about the name of thought that accompanies philosophical paths. The notion of the author, which is highly problematic, is linked to different statuses based on historical conditions, presenting increased difficulties in philosophy. While the authority over a literary work may be similar to that over a painting or a musical piece, the authority of an idea is always complex and resistant to any definitive classification.

However, the "proper" name associated with a concept also reflects on the creative individual and his ambiguous relationship with the ideas he develops. When it comes to his creations, he does not always adhere to the model of a parent who has given birth to a being that eludes him. The creator of the concept can both glorify himself through his creations and hide behind them, deny them, and display them in order to detach himself, using more or less conscious strategies. These creations are like different faces, profiles, and appearances constructed by the author who presents them. Deleuze is not content with simply offering a new version of philosophical authority; he expresses *a desire to disappear*, to transcend the personal identity of the author. Going beyond a rejection of the traditional notion of the subject-self and personality, Deleuze aims to avoid the obligation of having to personally "answer" for his inventions. "Your secret can always be seen on your face and in your eyes. Lose your face,[78]" he urged in his *Dialogues*. In *Mille Plateaux*, he dismantles the concept of the face by expanding it to include multiple connections—animal, landscape, and musical—so that there is no longer a distinct face, but rather features that can intermingle and create new arrangements. This remarkable endeavor, which proposes new representations, pursues Deleuze's theoretical and subjective desire for disfigurement and depersonalization. The goal is to become unidentifiable, to become covert, to produce masks, to multiply and dissolve... The encounter with Guattari provided Deleuze with the opportunity for a dual and intentionally delirious writing that puts into motion this energy of escape, which the term "nomadism" grants its philosophical importance and public notoriety. The relation between a thinker and his concept or driving principle is ambivalent

---

78. Deleuze, Gilles, and Claire. Parnet. *Dialogues, op. cit.*, p. 47.

and dynamic. It continuously reconnects the subject to his theory, combining the projection of a divided self in abstract language with various figures that hold the symbol, the metonymy, the paradox, the oxymoron. This is all based on the gap between lived existence and professed theses. The thinking subject constructs, misunderstands, and transforms himself through the work of a word or a thesis. These become witnesses of his psychic investment in theoretical activity. This concept is the thinker, but not as an expression or representation. The "expression" assumes that the concept was already there and emerged from him, faithful and unambiguous, but it only represents him as a trademark. However, there is indeed an alliance formed between the thinker and his concept—both strategic, ensuring the continuity of thought, and psychic, as the thinker recognizes what he has produced as his own. A creator embraces his concept, supports its development and success, making it a key element in his conceptual framework. He often struggles to maintain control over his creation, to the point that abstract words become subject to theft and detour. However, this appropriation remains conventional and often conforms to the demands of communication. The thinker speaks on his own behalf for an audience, he claims to be writing without address. Thus, Deleuze seems caught up in his own game, pledging his notion of nomadism and using it to evaluate and articulate many objects of thought. He is carried along by the very power of his conceptual invention, regardless of his personal experiences, whether in a state of disconnection from what he theorizes or through paradoxical connections (such as immobility as a way of living nomadism). Regardless, he must still account for and redefine the terms.

At the same time that the power of his concepts empowers him, a thinker finds himself defined by his theoretical production. He is thus not only the owner of a concept but can also become its prisoner! The word or the thesis identifies him and prevents him from thinking and existing as he pleases. So, he sometimes tries to preserve his freedom of thought by freeing it from the concept that restricts him. The reflective energy often has to contend with the words that solidify and immobilize it. Thinkers thus assert their autonomy by modifying one of their central notions, sometimes by abandoning it, under the pretext of "going beyond" it. Sartre did not stop engaging with concepts (contingency, for-itself, being-for-death, consciousness, scarcity...) that he later rejected, declaring them outdated in favor of other ideas. He has absorbed the language of Husserl, Heidegger, and Marx: he has "exhausted" them, he has appropriated them by adapting them to his thought, and then he has discarded them for new ones, declaring that they had lost their relevance, as he himself had moved elsewhere.

Another way to free oneself from the concepts with which one has associated oneself and displayed oneself is to deny all authority and refuse any identification between them and oneself. Deleuze establishes this protocol by proclaiming himself as *multiple*. With the desire to remain undercover and free to engage with other languages, he liberates himself from the obligation to personally answer for a thesis or a contradiction. Only his name is committed, but this surname is not that of a father, he asserts; it is simply a circumstantial word behind which several singularities live and think. Reconnected to multiple networks or, according to his successful metaphor, to rhizomes, he promotes depersonalization through his fragmented plurality. He describes his collaborative writing with Guattari: "The two of us wrote Anti-Oedipus together. Since each of us was several, there was already quite a crowd."[79] This questioning of the unity of the thinking subject, writer, and thesis developer allows us to disrupt the superficial unity of the thinker with his thoughts. It dismantles the image of coherence in the living and writing self, an image that persists in philosophy and, more broadly, in theoretical discourses. In contrast, literature has abandoned it, readily accepting the distinction between author and narrator. The multiplicity championed by Deleuze contributes to distinguishing, in theoretical writing, the subject who thinks from the one who writes and even from the one who signs books. It fragments the notion of the author through its diffraction into multiplicities, with the person, the name, and the subject intersected by multiple flows in becoming.

As fruitful as it is, the depersonalization of the thinker remains ambiguous and raises many questions. An author who claims to be multiplied is also an author who hides himself. What solidarity exists between the various singularities that the thinker claims? If I am several, what is the

---

79. Deleuze, Gilles, and Félix Guattari. *A Thousand Plateaus : Capitalism and Schizophrenia*, op. cit., p. 3.

The Fetishism of the Concept

link between these "several"? The theoretical force of this discourse, which allows for a radical rethinking of philosophical notions such as self, consciousness, and subject, will enable us to question the reasons that support it. The energy of thought comes not only from the connections it establishes with heterogeneous elements, but also from singular affects. When Deleuze defends his conceptions with great vigor and attacks other philosophers, the intensity of his speeches suggests that he is over-invested in his theses as an author, denying others the intelligence to think. The anger, enthusiasm, vagueness, and pugnacity offer psychic springs at the heart of the concepts that are the object of such intense fights. It is not a question here of addressing Deleuze's "personal" reasons or those of any other philosopher. Instead, the highlighting of an equivocal relation between a thinker and his concepts aims to question the psychic materiality of the so-called works of the mind.

Why do such concepts take on significant importance for a thinker? How does a thinker build himself through their elaboration and diffusion? What complex relations unite him to these keywords that become symbols of himself? The gap between behaviors and theories suggests that thinking is wider than logical reasons. It also proceeds from a construction of oneself and a complex arrangement between desires, affects, and fears, where truth is mixed with lies. The abstract language of theory represses these internal battles that produced it, and at the same time, it carries a trace of them since it is composed of these unstable forces. Its greatness is such that it maintains balance and logical rigor while containing and repressing unavowable, chaotic, and uncontrolled motivations. Through a sublime lie, this language exalts truths as it represses their fraudulent reasons. There is no denunciation here: we can enjoy the power of thought without knowing the backstage of its making.

Blinding Oneself in a Concept:
Levinas and the Dazzling of the Other

The structural beauty of a philosophical system immediately earns admiration for it. For those who appreciate the complexity and coherence of thought, the effort to understand it brings intellectual enjoyment that can lead to empathy. One does not have to be a Spinozist to admire Spinoza's *Ethics*, nor does one have to believe in God to read Leibniz's *Monadology* with passion, nor does one have to become a Hegelian to be fascinated by the *Phenomenology of Spirit*. Philosophy lovers know the joy of discovering abstract constructions that go beyond mere intellectual agreement with the theses they promote. Entering into a language, accessing the internal logic of thought, and gradually mastering its machinery... these moments bring tremendous and lasting spiritual emotions. The concepts, propositions, and nuances that these works impose on our representations of the world and our use of certain words provide a musical score for those who embrace them. Of course, the comparison can be shocking if it underestimates the meaning of philoso-phical theses. Nonetheless, it holds true if we acknowledge that specific thoughts, with their language, accompany our existence and contribute to shaping how we perceive the world. It is rare to read a theoretical masterpiece without being impacted by it, even if we don't explicitly agree with its purpose.

Like any music in which we have invested ourselves intensely, specific abstract constructions sometimes lose their charm when they have been heard or analyzed too much. Some remain sublime to our ears, while others become clichés: they no longer manage to enchant our existence because their processes seem too obvious. Such a language has exerted a force of attraction that gradually fades away when its tricks appear only as processes. It is the same with certain old harmonies that touch us more or less: we listen to an unknown piece by Bach, and yet we can intuitively finish his phrases because we know the grammar. The experience is sometimes more bitter if the figures have been transformed into clichés or tics that some composers have overused.

Listening to an abstract language, when it has followed this path from solid empathy to a feeling of saturation, can lead to this kind of disappointment without invalidating the quality of a work. However, it does cause one to distance oneself from its meaning and gives rise to reservations about a thinker's speech or writing and their excessive reliance on certain words, metaphors, and situations. A "contradiction" that can be identified in thought, or between the author of an idea and the theses they profess, encourages one to step back and question the obsessive recurrence of a concept or figure. However, it is not always necessary to discover such a gap, and discourse analysis alone can be enough to detect what we have called a fetishism of the concept. To illustrate this, we will focus on a crucial notion of philosophy, the *other*, and its treatment by a philosopher whose work is closely associated with this term, Emmanuel Levinas. This time, we will not delve into the "life" of the thinker, disregarding biographical information about him or his commentators. On one hand, his existence does not seem to demonstrate any more or less vivid altruism than that of anyone else. On the other hand, we would like to concentrate on his discourse and, first and foremost, its use and the effects it has on his readers, who have become legion.

Read very late, Levinas emerged as a significant figure in 20th-century philosophy, inspiring numerous commentaries on the concepts of *other* and *otherness*. In the realm of philosophical exegesis, it is important to acknowledge Levinas's singular contribution in removing the notion of the *other* from traditional ontological frameworks. By granting the existence of others a dimension that cannot be reduced to the relation between subjectivities, he transforms it into an event. *The other person* escapes knowledge, the social game, and the struggle of consciousness; he establishes a separation that challenges the subject's mastery and provides access to infinity. The other does not merely exist as an other than myself; the other disrupts the identity of each individual within the human totality. By affirming the transcendence of others, Levinas reinstates them in metaphysics and transforms encounters with them into a pathway to the absolute. This coup de force alters the position of ethics within philosophy, elevating it to a primary concern and compelling the subject to immediately respond to others and their call for higher responsibility. The profound nature of this philosophy was not immediately recognized, nor was the turning point it signified within the current from which it originated, the phenomenology of Husserl and Heidegger. Initially, Levinas's seminars garnered little interest until other thinkers took up his theses and, like Derrida, offered commentary on his concepts of infinity, the face, and hospitality.

The recognition of Levinas at the end of the 20th century, despite his earlier writings dating back to 1930 and the publication of his major work, *Totality and Infinity*, in 1961, can be attributed, in an idealistic way, to the discovery of his philosophy. When analyzing the intellectual field sociologically, we can identify correlations with the zeitgeist, paradigm shifts, communities of interest, and representations. We will not here delve into historical reasons, but rather highlight the forces of attraction present in his discourse that promote readers' empathy *with philosophical texts*. The impact of adopting a particular concept goes beyond the psyche of the author; it also involves the participation of the audience in the success of certain words and ideas. The fervor with which a thinker constructs concepts and develops a body of work around them can be *contagious*. It may incite adhesion, and even a quasi-religious devotion, from those who embrace the language and navigate the conceptual landscapes that accompany it.

Understanding the psychic investment in concepts involves observing their *reception* as well as their *conception*. The power of thought does not solely lie in its argumentation but also in the seductive qualities of connoted words, associated emotions, and self-representations. These aspects simultaneously engage the reader's psyche and intellect. Some concepts, through extensive speculation, acquire substantial significance and become like mantras. Thus, the word *other* is endowed with a profound evocative power, surpassing its ordinary meaning due to exceptional elaboration. Those who employ this word within a theoretical framework inspire numerous arguments, extensions, and logical nodes related to the other, others, and otherness. This is unsurprising, as a concept does not merely exist as an object of study but also inhabits the thoughts and imaginations of its adherents. What is more mysterious, however, is when the success of a concept rests on a paradox and a misunderstanding of its application in real life. Here, we encounter a self-deception. Embracing such a concept or principle can manifest as a denial or even a discourse conflicting with lived experiences. To grasp this surprising paradox, abstract language must already possess a propensity for reversals.

In reexamining specific works, we have thus far pondered why and how a thinker could promote a concept that contradicts their own life. It was essential to examine their life or at least how it is interpreted. However, when analyzing *the diffusion of the paradox*, it becomes risky to rely solely on the lives of readers and disciples. Instead, it is more relevant to explore what aspects of the discourse encourage a propensity for a paradoxical psyche. This exploration invites one to consider notions and arguments that are reversible, dualistic, and conducive to duplicity, glorifying that which is denied. What could be more tempting than these figures of denial that allow one to exalt what they wish to abolish? By focusing on the notion of the *other*, we do not accuse its proponents of lying, but rather aim to reveal the inherent reversibility, within language itself, of a conceptual apology.

Frequently, philosophers take up concepts from the philosophical tradition to give them new meanings. Levinas reinvests the notion of the other and thus goes beyond redefinition of this concept; he absolutizes it. According to Levinas, the *other* is not just any "other" and even less an *alter ego*; it is otherness itself, the absolute other. This notion goes beyond comparison and relation; it becomes a transcendent principle. However, this radicalization creates an ambivalence. The notion is defined exceptionally by an absolute, incommensurable, and at the same time, it remains indefinable. *The Other* stands beyond any concrete reference; it remains unknowable, infinite, and unassignable to a social condition. Levinas defines the Other negatively to remove it from any ontological and worldly approach. "The Other, who is invisible, and of whom one awaits no fulfillment, would be the uncontainable, the nonthematizable—an infinite transcendence.[80]"

---

80. Levinas, Emmanuel. *God, Death, and Time*. Translated by Bettina Bergo. Stanford, CA: Stanford University Press, 2022, pp. 137-138.

The encounter with the other defies description and narration; it occurs before humanity, before Being, affirms Levinas, who always places it elsewhere, before or beyond... If we were to define or narrate it, we would immediately lose it. *Other* is a concept that eludes the concept itself, exceeding all rationality and even language. Levinas establishes a dissymmetry between myself and the other, preventing me from considering them as an interlocutor to engage in dialogue. Infinitely transcendent and foreign to human relations, the other does not belong to the same nature as me and invites me to transcend any common nature. The radical nature of this ethic, which sees others as exceptions to all criteria, leads us back to the approach of negative theology: *others*, like God, can only be conceived through the systematic negation of the qualities and definitions we usually attribute to them.

Beyond nature, concepts, and ontology, the notion of the *other* is based on the absence of a referent. It is pure yet vague, and its force of attraction comes from the figures that haunt this emptiness, swirling around without filling it. The term "other" allows the user to enjoy its transcendence while implicitly summoning "others," both present and denied. Levinas maintains this ambiguity between the impossible representation of the other and the multiplication of the names of the other. He draws from phenomenology the concern to start from the concrete and gives consistency to the other through an abundance of human prototypes, with biblical connotations: "The Other who dominates me in his transcendence is thus the stranger, the widow, and the orphan,[81]" he writes in *Totality and Infinity*.

The other is the first person to arrive, anyone, the weak person I meet on the corner of a street and who, according to this injunction to accept him, is different from all the others, always more than I think. Levinas can thus play, on the one hand, with the contingency, the concreteness of the encounter and, on the other hand, with the elevation, the abstraction that it is supposed to provoke. The other is the poor person who begs, and at the same time, he is "His Lordship." Such ambivalence leads to contradictory interpretations: on the one hand, Levinas's readers find in it an altruistic morality that commands welcoming the neighbor, whoever he may be, beyond any social identity; on the other hand, some commentators, challenging the preachiness that trivializes such a thought, defend a "high version," a theological one, of this encounter with the infinitely other. However, this equivocation lies at the heart of language, in the tension between a concept emptied of any referent and the diversity of figures it can evoke.

Conceptual fetishism also thrives on the compulsive use of a concept. A word thus becomes the core from which all the other terms are derived. It plays the role of a *hub*, which allows one to grasp all the philosophical questions. The word is invested with the power of articulation, which authorizes it to exert influence on language.

---

81. Levinas, Emmanuel. *Totality and Infinity: An Essay on Exteriority*. Translated by Alphonso Lingis. Dodrecht: Kluwer Academic Publishers, 1991, p. 215.

Used obsessively, it acquires a magical function that overshadows its speculative virtues. Enthralled by its rational logic and the arguments it enables, its users can explore various theoretical realms and expand the scope of their affirmative enjoyment. The Levinasian example demonstrates this multifunctional use of an abstract concept. The *Other* is the concept that reopens all philosophical questions: ethics, of course, time, God, Being, infinity, truth, religion, language, communication, society, peace and violence, sexual difference...

The Other is a versatile operator of reflection, thanks notably to argumentative scenarios duplicated in each theme. Thus, some of Levinas' assertions spread into significant territories of philosophy: metaphysics, the subject, and society. For the philosopher, the *other* is the elusive one that enraptures us so that time will be defined according to an identical scheme: "The future is what is not grasped, what befalls us and lays hold of us. The other is the future. The very relationship with the other is the relationship with the future.[82]" The *other* is the absolutely other who provides the key to all openings, that of the infinite whose idea comes to man because he has already welcomed the other, that of transcendence, of God. In concrete relations, the other gives language its philosophical definition: " To speak, at the same time as knowing the Other, is making oneself known to him. The Other is not only known, he is greeted [salué]. He is not only

<hr>

82. Levinas, Emmanuel, *Time and the Other and Additional Essays.* Translated by Richard A. Cohen. Pittsburgh, PA: Duquesne University Press, 1987, p. 77.

named, but also invoked. To put it in grammatical terms, the Other does not appear in the nominative, but in the vocative.[83]" When Levinas invests reflection on the social, his absolute definition of the *other* allows him to think of a society without violence: "The relation with the other as face heals allergy. It is desi re, teaching received, and the pacific opposition of discourse.[84]" The *other* absorbs all concepts and makes them shine in its light and luster.

The expansion of a fetish word, which philosophy sometimes refers to as a motor scheme, proceeds through structural analogies, metaphors, and metonymies. The word evolves by donning various "clothes" that allow it to assume multiple roles. It comes to life, it becomes tangible through avatars. Levinas's most renowned metonymy for showcasing the brilliance of the concept of the other is the face. Thus, it operates within his discourse, even though the philosopher refuses to reduce it to a mere figure of speech. The face is first redefined in accordance with the absolutization of the other: it is no longer just a face or a surface reflecting the self; it embodies the ethical imperative itself, the call to responsibility. Empowered by this idealization, it can concretely and abstractly demonstrate all the principles associated with encountering others. The face is not the assembly of a nose, a forehead, eyes, etc.," writes Levinas, "it is all of these things. Still, it takes on the significance of a face by the new dimension it opens up in

---

83. Levinas, Emmanuel. *Difficult Freedom : Essays on Judaism*. Translated by Sean Hand. Baltimore: Johns Hopkins University Press, 1990, p. 7.
84. *Levinas, Emmanuel, Totality and Infinity, op. cit.* p. 197.

the perspective of a being[85]." The thinker of otherness can then decline the Heideggerian metaphor of "openness," which has enjoyed a still undeniable success in European philosophy. The face is the "opening", the clearing, and, to give it the ethical dimension granted to *others*, Levinas sees in it the expression of a commandment, the "thou shalt not kill".

The face, a metonymy of the *other*, comes to life, speaks, commands, and becomes a hypotyposis, a figure of speech that allows for a realistic and striking description that gives the reader the impression of living a scene thanks to imagined representations. Levinas proposes several dramas of this in his books, mixing affirmations of general truths ("it is") with pathetic situations, as in this excerpt from *Totality and Infinity*: "This gaze that supplicates and demands, that can supplicate only because it demands, deprived of everything because entitled to everything, and which one recognizes in giving (as one "puts the things in question in giving")—this gaze is precisely the epiphany of the face as a face. The nakedness of the face is destituteness. To recognize the Other is to recognize a hunger. To recognize the Other is to give. But it is to give to the master, to the lord, to him whom one approaches as "You"" in a dimension of height.[86]" The redundancy of the terms, the parallelisms, the nominal chains... these stylistic effects install a scene of contemplation; they summon affects

---

85. Levinas, Emmanuel, *Difficult Freedom, op. cit.*, p. 20.
86. *Levinas, Emmanuel, Totality and Infinity, op. cit.* p. 75.

(emotions, pity, feeling of elevation) leading to empathy as much as to the conviction of the reader.

An affective connection between the thinker and his readers is established through the use of metonymies and the presentation of the concept. It should be noted that Levinas specifically engages in a debate on the status of the other, particularly focusing on the face and the gaze. Building on Hegelian reflections on the struggle for recognition between consciousnesses, Sartre, Merleau-Ponty, and Lacan have discussed consciousness in relation to the gaze of others. Among them, Sartre's ideas are the most influential in Levinas' reinterpretation of the relationship with the other. Levinas refers to Sartre's famous passages in *Being and Nothingness*, which describe how otherness emerges when someone directs their gaze towards another. However, Levinas rejects the notion of a conflict between two subjects, where one subject objectifies the other through their gaze, and instead affirms that the gaze of the other prohibits violence. Examining the gaze (which Sartre considers to be ontologically impossible) allows for the development of an ethics of responsibility towards others. Nevertheless, Levinas adopts Sartre's style and well-known examples, incorporating a minor dramaturgy into his philosophical prose. A comparison between the two philosophers reveals differences in how they use the concept: Sartre puts his figures on display and appeals to reason, while Levinas employs empathy and contemplation, creating a style that evokes rather than provokes.

The dramatization of the concepts entails distinct dramaturgies. Levinas' approach to drama includes tableaux and relies more on action scenes. Driven by a religious context, it offers moments of ecstasy, epiphanies, and announcements. The philosopher of the primary ethics warns that encounters with others are impossible to fully grasp, but nonetheless, they can be experienced through allegories. The other is the impoverished, the vulnerable, the hungry. The other is the master, the lord who summons and uplifts me. By blending emotion and injunction, Levinas incorporates pathos into his ethical philosophy, and he accomplishes this by employing various metaphors to describe the trauma caused by encounters with the other: "The passivity of wounds, the "hemorrhage" of the for-the-other, is the tearing away of the mouthful of bread from the mouth that tastes in full enjoyment.[87]" The biblical base—the Book of Isaiah—concurs implicitly to revive a common imagination that populates the philosophical text with characters, scenes, and familiar motives.

The charm of philosophical discourse is sometimes judged as superficial seduction that departs from expected conceptual rigor. However, it is an illusion to believe that it does not operate, even in the most austere texts that shy away from stylistic devices. Philosophical writings each have linguistic traits that make them similar to works of literature. Analyzing their singularities helps to understand

---

87. Levinas, Emmanuel. *Otherwise than Being or Beyond Essence.* Translated by Alphonso Lingis. Dordrecht: Springer Netherlands, 2010, p. 74.

both their speculative power and their attraction. Levinas' work mobilizes several styles around a key concept, and many of his texts testify to this rhetorical excitement around a word that is both argued and venerated. As the other remains an indefinable absolute, the discourse becomes a periphrase that revolves around the fetish for not seeing it, naming it, or meeting it. The merry-go-round of styles—Heideggerian metaphors, biblical psalms, phenomenological descriptions—produces remarkable deformities, oscillating between tautology ("You are you"), hyperbole, and long incantation. Once the obsessive turns of theoretical writing have been identified, it is essential to question their motivation to better understand their effects.

A scandalous paradox then arises from a suspicion: what if the hypertrophy of a concept were a means of abolishing the referent from which it originates? More precisely, would the construction of the word "other" not come from its negation, and would it not encourage its erasure? To make the other an absolute would be to no longer see them, to promote a blindness towards their concrete presence. In fact, Levinas insists on this exposure of a face from which nothing is perceived, neither the color of the eyes (observing it would mean the absence of an authentic relationship), nor the clothes (it is naked), nor the social status (whether they are a slave or a university professor, he says, I address them equally), nor the ethnic resemblance (it is through the accidental resemblance to a third party that they can appear). The epiphany of the other is less of an appearance than a disappearance of their reality. Out of all context, their face is finally obliterated in favor of an interlocution of which they are the intact word. By taking up the word "face" as a metaphor, according to an ancient philosophical usage (the face of God, of Being, of truth, of the self...), Levinas "loses" the personal face, but in a way that is the opposite of that of Deleuze, who connected it to other realities: by magnifying it and transforming it into a magical word, endowed with a strong power of evocation and incantation.

If the fetish word proceeds from a negation of its referent, the theory it founds is also suspected of promoting the opposite of what it affirms. By pushing the paradox even further, we can suggest that ethical radicalization reveals an impasse, even the impossibility of practicing it. No doubt, a moral ideal serves as a horizon towards which actions should tend, but they never reach this perfection. Most "morals" are based on unconditional principles. However, the insistence on the sublime of an attitude—in this case, total self-effacement before others and the dedication it requires—produces a secondary discourse that exceeds the rationality of the moral law. Through his hyperbolic propositions, Levinas affirms a duty of responsibility that puts the subject in perpetual default, insisting on their infinite and never paid debt. "A relationship that obsesses, one that is an obsession, for the other besieges me, to the point where he puts in question my for-me, my in-itself [en-soi]-to the point where he makes me a hostage.[88]" Throughout his texts, he explores the theme of the hostage, the subject forever imprisoned by others,

---

88. Levinas, Emmanuel, *God, Death, and Time, op. cit.*, p. 138.

constantly compelled to detach himself from his own self and even from what rightfully belongs to him or what he should give to others. Therefore, the act of eating a bite of bread cannot be performed without acknowledging that it has caused harm to others and that it is consumed selfishly, as it must ultimately be shared with others. Levinas constructs a concept to define infinite hospitality: "Being torn from oneself for another in giving to the other the bread from one's mouth.[89]" Radically alienated, with an unconditional passivity, the hostage subject welcomes another, his host, whoever he may be, and relinquishes all subjectivity before him.

The beauty of such proposals lies in the sublime nature of the moral relationship. It offers a glimpse of an ethical ideal where humanity is freed from the conflict of selfish interests. It calls us to share a faith that is all the more uplifting because it is demanding, combining rational argument and biblical narrative. Levinas often oscillates between his philosophical texts and his Talmudic commentaries. However, this beauty also stems from the speculative radicality that pushes an idea to the extreme, disregarding practical considerations. This hyperbolization becomes impervious to contradiction. Thus, the dialogue between Levinas and Philippe Nemo demonstrates an ethical overbidding that nullifies any objection due to its sheer excess. The philosopher first reiterates his thesis on responsibility for the other, independent of reciprocity or

---

89. Levinas, Emmanuel. *Otherwise than Being or Beyond Essence, op. cit.*, p. 79.

The Genius of Lies

any contract. He explains that we are responsible for the other, but we must never expect the other to be responsible for us. Then the interlocutor raises an objection, mentioning the role of the executioner in this moral realm.

Should the persecuted Jew feel responsible for the Nazi who sends him to the gas chamber, in the face of Humanity? Rather than providing nuance, Levinas asserts that each of us is accountable for the non-responsibility of others and declares: "I am responsible for the persecutions that I undergo.[90]" The formula does not exonerate the persecutors, but it places the subject in a moral bubble that tears him not only from himself but also from any psychological and political reality. It takes up an injunction present in *Autrement qu'être...*, Levinas's most radical book: "In the trauma of persecution it is to pass from the outrage undergone to the responsibility for the persecutor.[91]" Levinas goes beyond the already complex moral question of forgiveness and demands more, particularly in the ethical affirmation, by asking to take responsibility for the crimes committed by others. It is not our intention here to question Levinas's moral attitude towards the Nazis. However, by presenting a saint's perspective, he pushes the sublime consequences of his original ethics to superhuman limits.

---

90. Levinas, Emmanuel., and Philippe Nemo. *Ethics and Infinity.* Translated by Richard A. Cohen. Pittsburgh: Duquesne University Press, 1985, p. 99.
91. Levinas, Emmanuel. *Otherwise than Being or Beyond Essence, op. cit.,* p. 111.

While not disputing the value of such a thought, questioning its radicality and the attraction it exerts leads us to detect a power of denial within it. The maximum exposure of the subject to the other, as an exaggerated representation of all situations where individuals meet, leads to a photographic overexposure to an abstract discourse that erases the rough edges, contours, and contrasts of the other person. It becomes seductive to the extent that it erases ordinary emotions in favor of an idealized image of interpersonal relationships. It conceals the complexities of everyday situations where relating to another individual involves various factors such as differences, statuses, and circumstances. However, its greatest fascination arises from the reader's projection into this ethical imagination.

The absolute allows for escape from any condition and relativity; it authorizes the magic of a blank practice. The reader indulges in speculative empathy that leads them to enjoy an ethical posture where they do not cease to testify to their effacement, their sacrifice for the other. They can outbid through idealities to invest in the moral role of a superior altruist. They put themselves on stage thanks to a theoretical postulation and represent the debt, the infinite duty, without having to realize them, without even questioning the conditions of their practice. And we are tempted to say that it is precisely in order not to have to question their practice that they fervently adopt such an ethical ideal. The fact that this responsibility for the non-responsibility of others is unlivable and impracticable makes it all the more attractive. Hyperbole, the passage to the absolute, is a way of not assuming responsibility for the other because it becomes impossible to bring demands to this level. On the one hand, the reader clears themselves of any practice, this morality remaining unattainable; on the other hand, they represent themselves as supermoral beings endowed with a noble conscience of duty. The gain is double.

The abstract language can thus become an operator of lies, in the sense that a thinker—author or reader—lies to themselves through an exercise of self-deception. They represent themselves in an imaginary way, following ideas that propose a substitute existence, staked only on words and which allow them to live a double life. This type of mirage differs from the one produced by literature, theater, or cinema because its power of entrainment towards unreality is due to the language of the ideal, which obscures all subjectivity. With abstract language, the production of a universal truth authorizes this neutral splitting. Users adopt these fleshless words to disincarnate their existence. They do not project themselves into this or that character, as readers and viewers of fiction do, transferring their emotions through empathy. Instead, they live as pure idealities, subjects without subjectivity who conduct thought experiments and represent themselves under the guise of an ideal consciousness.

How can a conceptual truth promote a lie about itself? Philosophical truth is often inaccessible to proof and verification, even if expressed in the language of reason. It is adorned with systematicity, authority, or authenticity, exempting it from being held accountable to factual relevance. Thus, the Levinasian argument on the authenticity of the relation to others: by affirming that the ethical relation is primary, before any "interhuman" connection, it displaces the question of truth and falsehood and makes it secondary. His ethical affirmation is no longer indexed on verification. It is only presented as a revelation that he presents in the register of incantation, even if it has an argumentative appearance. Levinas writes thus: "deceit and veracity already presuppose the absolute authenticity of the face-the privileged case of a presentation of being foreign to the alternative of truth and non-truth, circumventing the ambiguity of the true and the false which every truth risks-an ambiguity, moreover, in which all values move. The presentation of being in the face does not have the status of a value. What we call the face is precisely this exceptional presentation of self by self, incommensurable with the presentation of realities simply given, always suspect of some swindle, always possibly dreamt up. To seek truth I have already established a relationship with a face which can guarantee itself, whose epiphany itself is somehow a word of honor.[92]" In attempting to conceptually reach this primary ethical moment, the philosopher directs his language toward a mode of expression that escapes proof and becomes self-referential. Like *others,* he must be taken at his word.

---

92. Levinas, Emmanuel. *Totality and Infinity: An Essay on Exteriority, op. cit.,* p. 202.

The functioning of abstract words, when they are used in a second language alongside the current language, can involve the suspension of ordinary meanings. These words become the focus of an imaginary investment that supports the self-representation of a thinking individual. Adorno criticized Heidegger's "jargon," highlighting this magical use of keywords (Stichworte). Beyond its controversial nature, he observed the ambiguity of philosophical language, which can both clarify and intoxicate. Adorno's ideological criticism is not our focus here; rather, we are concerned with the psychological impact of abstract discourse. However, his analysis of philosophical language sheds light on the fragmentation of one's identity caused by stylistic devices, particularly the enchantment of a concept. The construction of a word that encompasses all areas of thought creates an illusory power for readers who believe it provides a universal meaning to the world. The empirical language is manipulated so that the keyword radiates onto other words, transforming them into elements of another language of truth and revelation. While poetry often employs this approach, philosophical discourse rarely follows suit, instead employing language as a tool. Its second language is not an exercise in style, but a result of working through ideas, reflecting a classical and misleading dichotomy that many philosophers adhere to. It is through covert means that this second language constructs a constellation of words that resembles an ideal vault. This promotes a world of connections, allowing readers to experience a sense of community: they recognize certain words as fetishized within a specific language, and they recognize each other by sharing the aura of a language imbued with revelation.

The keyword has acquired a meaning beyond its original definition. It is not uncommon for words to take on a broader sense than their usual interpretation. However, when language is used fetishistically, it goes beyond a simple expansion of meaning. Philosophers who constantly strive to transcend the empirical significance of words can employ this technique in two ways. When constructing a technical language for precision, philosophy aims to clarify complex questions. On the other hand, when words escape debate and, through their intrinsic presence, become guarantors of a superior meaning, abstract discourse resorts to fetishistic language. Used in this manner, the keyword appears to reveal a truth, as if its revelation arises from an essential property and encapsulates a meaning that goes beyond its signification. It creates this illusion because it has become a fetish of a parasitic syntax that refers only to itself and requires the complicity of readers. The deviation of philosophical rationality, as decried by those who advocate for the rigorous use of rational language, stems from this departure from common understanding.

Through the fetishistic use of a concept, arguments derive their power from self-referential language and operate through a network of effects that captivate readers. Several stylistic techniques contribute to this shimmering of language, distancing the keywords from any form of debate, as they have become unquestionable, like fetishes. Elevated and multiplied through metonymies, they evoke the pathos of readers who participate in the adoration of these notions, blessed by thought. As a result, the distinction between true and false becomes less relevant, as the empirical referents have faded away in favor of a sublime linguistic and idealistic enjoyment. Despite the self-referential nature of abstract language, the referent has not completely disappeared; it persists as an illusory duplicate without substance. It has become an image ripe for simulations and metamorphoses.

Unsurprisingly, this conceptual avatar can provide reversals and trigger the deceptive power of fiction. This second language, observes Adorno, "unites the appearance of an absent concreteness with the ennobling of that concreteness.[93]" From then on, it becomes possible to valorize, and even to sacralize, the missing reference—be it an idea, a value, or a moral principle... It allows the reader to imagine themselves as one of its most fervent disciples. The servant of the word, for instance, envisions their relationship with others as the utmost devotion, the most significant responsibility; they perceive themselves at the pinnacle of this sublime idea by delivering a speech that combines demonstration, revelation, and creed. However, the primary function of the discourse is to eliminate the concrete other, of which only a mere semblance is retained, transformed into pure ideality. The more the fetishized word is an object of pleasure, the less it signifies its referent. Alternatively, one could say: the less bearable the concrete reality is, the more necessary it becomes to venerate its name in order to abolish it by idealizing it.

---

93. Adorno, Theodor W. *The Jargon of Authenticity*. Translated by Knut Tarnowski and Frederic Will. Evanston: Northwestern University Press, 1973, p. 81.

Aware of such ambivalence at the heart of the great abstract discourses, we might be tempted to avoid them by distrusting their deception or the lures they present. However, succumbing to such fear would be equivalent to believing that there exists, on the contrary, a pure, concrete, or rigorous language that would enable us to escape self-deception. Unfortunately—or fortunately—such a tongue does not exist, or at least its power of illusion is determined by its usage. On the contrary, a lucid approach to the linguistic tricks and the psychological investments that a speculative language provokes reveals the formidable dynamics generated by these abstract languages.

Observing the stylistic functioning of a concept does not aim to devalue it or underestimate its theoretical relevance. Instead, attention to the "language" of a philosopher reveals that style, far from being an ornament, is the verbal matter through which thought engages and reveals itself, with its effects and imaginings, while following a rational logic. Philosophers often resist such analyses because they perceive a disregard for the intentional meaning, which is of interest in speculative discourse. However, they overlook the fact that thought is entirely contained within its verb. The so-called stylistic study does not consist of enumerating formal features (such as metaphors, syntagms, and examples), but rather in seeking the forging of thought in a language that is as much expression as it is torsion and transformation of pensive energy, where the psyche of the writing subject composes with verbal sediments weighted with inherited and unstable representations.

Far from underestimating the power of philosophy and all speculative and abstract discourse, questioning the psychological investment of the subject who thinks, speaks, and writes in this language suggests a listening that is distinct from but complementary to the semantic study of texts. It addresses the eminently Nietzschean question posed on the authority of the self and the masks adopted by a thinker. Who writes such theory, who promotes such concepts, to what interest does the thinker adhere, and what does he desire through his thoughts? What face do we reveal when we speak in the language of abstraction and when we affirm ideas or promote specific figures of thought? So far, we have scratched away the rational veneer of conceptual language to detect contradictory forces that mobilize the psyche of authors and readers. It is now time to show the extraordinary power of personal recomposition offered by the recourse to abstract language, not to impose order on the chaos of the world, but to live multiple existences.

Multiple Personalities

To live opposite to what one writes or to write opposite to what one lives leads to questioning the functions of writing, especially theoretical prose. Undoubtedly, the division between "real life" and thought or imagination is questionable. "A book is, for me, a special way of living," explained Flaubert. So, how does one define this life in writing? Writers know how much literature contributes to experiencing imaginary existences and emotions, often more robust than ordinary "reality". Sartre had conceived of this as his greatest neurosis since childhood when he confused words with things and lived solely through books. Abstractionists admit it less willingly, yet the conception of abstract systems and the experience of thought bring as much joy as anguish, a feeling of power as abysmal vertigo.

The writing of treaties, essays, and theses is also a construction of oneself, not so much in the sense of an intellectual personality but rather as a psychic mobilization, through which an ideal self draws and represents itself in the features of an abstract language. This "construction" also involves disfiguration and transformation, as concepts intertwine with intimate affections, without truly knowing oneself, under the protection of the universal. It serves to exacerbate or oppose the self-image one has created. The affirmation of ideas allows for the manipulation and recomposition of a thinking self that invests its desires and fears, its pride and its shame in a speech of general scope. It is not easy to approach this psychic work, as abstract language does not produce images from the start like fiction does; it does not present a substitute portrait of the author; it masks its transfers with conceptual screens. However, asserting principles or arguments offers clues to a subjective exposition through complex verbal forms. The proponents of ideas always say something about themselves without necessarily being conscious of this reflexivity. And when a gap appears between their assertions and their existence, the function of abstract discourse emerges: it aims to elaborate a new self-image.

The various speeches whose "contradictions" with the life of the speaker we have already observed put us on the trail of the psychic functions of affirmation: the unification and the multiplication of the self. These two functions may seem opposed, but they are combined through a deliberate intention to deceive, a denial that allows one to articulate contradictory experiences. The lie, understood once again as a transformative fiction, offers the possibility of affirming a virtual personality in the words of theory ("I am the author of this thesis; I am the creator of this concept"). Positively, it facilitates a representation of oneself that is different from, or even opposite to, the thinker's mode of existence. It unifies through contrariety and unleashes a desire to potentially exist in reverse of lived reality. This unification could stem from unrestricted and inventive fiction. However, it remains directly driven by a practice of denial, more or less conscious. To illustrate the power and its tricks, we will analyze the remarkable case of Simone de Beauvoir, which is rich in lessons, as so much of her thoughts and writings bear witness to both a desire for transparency and a multiplication of the self that contradicts this claimed truth.

The Double Life of Theory: Beauvoir in America

Simone de Beauvoir's numerous writings allow us to connect the narrative and the theory that she practiced in parallel. On the one hand, she recounts her life in detail through memoirs and novels, and on the other hand, she reflects on her condition as a woman to construct a philosophy of emancipation. The narratives contribute to what Ricoeur has called a "narrative identity" that transforms the self into a plot. However, the theory is also a matter of such elaboration, without resorting to a mimetic projection of oneself onto characters and a story. As we will observe, it authorizes a personal fiction where contradictory lives, doubles, and multiple lives are experienced through the prism of abstraction. In this case, Beauvoir proposes a theoretical model that contradicts her own life, or, to put it the other way around, she lives in a way that is contrary to the principles she theorizes. This is not a value judgment on Beauvoir's overall behavior but a questioning of a specific moment in her life, and it is significant because it concerns the writing of her major philosophical work, *The Second Sex.*

While Beauvoir was writing the book that remains one of the fundamental texts of feminist thought, she was involved in a love affair with an American writer, Nelson Algren. This private affair does not contradict the philosopher's theses and narratives, especially since she recounted it in several of her stories, and it even seems to confirm the sentimental and sexual freedom that she always claimed. However, the posthumous publication of her correspondence with the writer was surprising because it revealed another personality distinct from the one she exposed in her novels. It should be noted from the start that no "truth" is discovered in these letters that would reveal the "real" Simone de Beauvoir. They mostly indicate that the author had contradictory experiences and that the portrayal of transparency functioned as a lure for readers who thought they knew everything about her life. This correspondence deviates from Beauvoir's self-portraits; above all, it points to behaviors, emotions, and ideals that are contrary to those advocated in her philosophical theses. We must carefully revisit this material, without making any moral judgments.

The letters written to Nelson Algren by the writer-philosopher were published in 1997, after Simone de Beauvoir's death in 1986. Despite being posthumous, they cannot be considered texts exclusively for private use, as their author intended for them to be published. In line with the ethics shared with Sartre, Beauvoir always insisted on the transparency of their respective lives. We must be cautious in not considering these letters as a secret that the author has hidden away. Instead, we should focus on the "contradictions" between writings, narratives, and ideas that interest us here, particularly the disharmony between the life expressed in the letters and the theory developed during the same period. However, the opposition between the two personalities, the lover and the theorist, is too simplistic. It is more fruitful to understand the psychological stakes of these experiences, simultaneously opposed and articulated in love and theory, developed in synchrony.

On the way to this double life and its narrative tensions, we can first observe some discrepancies between the versions given by Beauvoir and Sartre, who became the models or counter-models of the modern couple. Nelson Algren was represented as one of the lovers in the constellation of contingent loves, according to the contract established between the two existentialist philosophers who maintained their couple as the center around which satellite relationships were articulated. A first polemic preceded the publication of the letters to Nelson Algren when the correspondence between Sartre and Beauvoir was published and in which certain lovers recognized themselves. One of them, Bianca Bienenfeld, who became Bianca Lamblin, discovered the way the couple spoke of her under the name of Louise Védrine, and wrote *Les Mémoires d'une jeune fille dérangée*, a parody of one of Beauvoir's books, to denounce their version of sexual freedom. The existentialist couple more closely resembles the characters of Dangerous Liaisons than the heralds of a sexual morality based on truth. And those who were contemptuous of Sartre and Beauvoir took advantage of this breach to denounce their immorality. This ill-intentioned polemic, linked to the decline of libertarian ideals in the 1990s, nevertheless puts us on the track of a dissociation between ethical principles and passionate experience.

Readers familiar with Beauvoir are inclined to classify Nelson Algren as one of the lovers whose portraits are scattered throughout the Memoirs. This misleading vision gives the impression of a sexual freedom whose protocol, theorized by a pact between Sartre and Beauvoir, would have been perfectly mastered. The literary versions of these experiences testify rather to the difficulties of living situations where an ethics of freedom and contradictory emotions are mixed. In Sartre's *novel L'Âge de Raison* or Beauvoir's *L'Invitée,* one can sense the crises of jealousy and the little lies that punctuate the multiple relationships or the life with three. Freedom does not spare us from sad passions. On the other hand, the notion of a contract suggests a symmetry between the signatories, whereas the word sexuality encompasses distinct desires and practices for each individual. But beyond these clarifications, it is essential to understand why Beauvoir's relationship with Algren escapes the series of lovers. Reading the Memoirs, we could describe this intense relationship as exceptional compared to the other lovers, as Algren was the object of a formidable passion.

Simone de Beauvoir traveled to the United States in 1947, giving university lectures and writing an account of her journey that would be published under the title *L'Amérique au jour le jour*. She met Nelson Algren in Chicago, and as soon as she returned to California, she began to write to him and started a love affair that would last for seventeen years and include three hundred letters. The year 1948 was devoted to writing The Second Sex, her outstanding work, of which she spoke to Algren at the end of that year, announcing that her voluminous work was "full of amusing stories". She commented on the title and continued to talk about this work throughout 1949, referring to the second volume as her "second child". The moments of great love, as attested by the passionate letters, coincided with the theoretical endeavor leading to a "gigantic" book in terms of its size and philosophical power.

Indeed, the argumentation of the Second Sex combines an anti-naturalistic philosophy, a socio-historical analysis, and a politics of emancipation. It opposes, on the one hand, the freedom of the subject, her future open to all choices, and, on the other hand, the degradation of her existence under the effect of a sexual vocation that is imposed on her. As a faithful existentialist, Beauvoir affirms that nature and biology do not give the reason or the orientation of lives but that they remain the conditions from which all behaviors are possible. It is not because bodies have capacities—that of procreation, for example—that they are destined to function. The physiological body is only a contingent fact, available for all meaningful projects. From such a postulate, Beauvoir can show how sexual difference is based on a construction. As a precursor to gender studies, she emphasizes that sex is only a predicate: it becomes gender through the realized performance of a social role. According to existentialist philosophy, there is no female nature, just as no human nature exists. To be a woman is to choose to exist as a woman in the gaze of others and to undergo the petrification of one's alienated consciousness, lived not for oneself but for others.

The famous formula that signs the flagship book of feminism, "one is not born, but rather becomes, a woman," leads to a study of the cultural conditioning that makes a woman think of herself as a woman, born to "be" a woman according to the canons of sexual difference. Beauvoir thus leads a deconstruction of the supposedly feminine roles through the myths and education that destine women to secondary functions. Her analyses allow her to reach the concreteness of lived existence and not to remain at abstract statements. She thus deals with "situations," an existentialist term that defines the relation between a free consciousness and a given which conditions it. All freedom exists only in a situation and is defined by the way it lives this situation, whether it accepts it or not as its own. To describe the situated consciousness, Sartre insists on its place in human time and space; Beauvoir declines a series of concrete situations: marital, maternal, sexual, love, etc. Each time, she analyzes the woman's situation phenomenally and explores the ordinary experience, giving it an exceptional philosophical relief.

Among the situations in which Beauvoir proposes a phenomenological and critical description, household tasks offer an essential moment of psychic analysis. It is rare for a philosopher to be interested in tasks as ordinary as washing, ironing, or sweeping. Beauvoir knows how to detect the psyche that attaches to this type of work because it not only mobilizes the body, energy, and time of the worker, but it also implies a relationship to the world and to time. Performing tasks such as removing dust or washing clothes means an endless activity without the possibility of edification: the dirt returns, and the housework can only be seen when it is not done. The repetition of a task doomed to failure forbids the agent any transcendence, any possibility of imprinting a project of consciousness on reality, because this reality of domestic life remains frozen, with no prospect of change other than the return of the same constraints, the same dirt to be eliminated: "for in one movement time is created and destroyed; the housewife only grasps the negative aspect of it. Hers is the attitude of a Manichaean. The essence of Manichaeism is not only to recognize two principles, one good and one evil: it is also to posit that good is attained by the abolition of evil and not by a positive movement.[94]"

The housewife is thus condemned to live in a world of endless destruction without salvation: the house will always get dirty again, regardless of her efforts. The meals she prepares for the family are bound to be eaten up, and

---

94. Beauvoir, Simone de, *The Second Sex*. Translated by Constance Borde and Sheila Malovany-Chevallier. New York: Vintage, 2011, p. 541.

she will always have to start again. Even if she enjoyed satisfying the household's needs, she would still depend on a domestic system without transcendence and closed off by the opposition between production and destruction.

Beauvoir's analysis focuses on the conditions of domestic life and the psyche it shapes. However, the philosopher does not limit herself to the material situation of women; she also describes their dependence on emotional life. Among the significant theoretical moments of the Second Sex, the description of the feminine "prototypes" that culture has constructed gives rise to a gallery of philosophical and psychological portraits. We will especially emphasize that of the lover, in comparison to the versions of her sentimental life that Beauvoir presents elsewhere. She mainly emphasizes the dissymmetry between men and women, who do not experience love in the same way, not by nature but due to the roles assigned to them by culture. According to Beauvoir, the woman identifies herself with the beloved; she sees the world from the beloved's point of view and adopts his tastes, ideas, and friends. "The measure of values and the truth of the world are in his own consciousness [...]: the center of the world is no longer where she is but where the beloved is.[95]" Alienation in love thus forms an abdication since the woman finds justification for her existence only in the love of the other. She exists only in this "recognition", love granting her a place, certainly necessary but secondary. Contingency and freedom are erased in favor of a fusional

---

95. *Ibid,* p. 784

life that gives the woman the illusion of a "we", while the man continues to be a subject, an "I", while experiencing his love. "The woman in love experiences in her resignation the magnificent possession of the absolute.[96]"

The woman is immersed in the "we" of love and condemns herself to live through the gaze of the all-powerful beloved. An emblematic situation of this alienation in love is the waiting for the beloved. The woman who waits experiences anxiety, jealousy, and anguish as she imagines her death at the thought that her beloved will not return to her. Since she only exists through the love of the other, the possibility of abandonment annihilates her, depriving her of any justification for her existence. Beauvoir emphasizes the experience of absence as a form of betrayal. Why does Beauvoir associate absence and suspicion of infidelity to such an extent? In a broader sense, we can ask ourselves which sources the philosopher relies on to develop her case studies with such precision.

Philosophy books could be reexamined through their examples. Intended to illustrate ideas, they sometimes precede and determine theoretical choices. Beauvoir's examples embody her theses, and the phenomenological description leads her to simulate situations and theatrically portray roles to present her concepts. She creates multiple prototypical figures: the housewife, the lesbian, the prostitute, the young girl, the older woman, and the mystic. She immerses herself in the perspective of these characters,

---

96. *Ibid*, p. 785.

much like an author of a novel. However, as an analyst would present cases, she deciphers their gestures and thoughts, investing in them empathetically to better understand their attitudes and reveal their existential meanings. She stages them in her philosophical theater; she plays herself through them, giving them a great power of embodiment. At the same time, she dissects their movements and tacitly studies herself as if she were both the subject of the action and the object of her philosophical analysis.

Beauvoir magnifies her gallery of female portraits and endows them with anthropological depth. Did she encounter such models in real life? Or does she imagine them from her writing desk? She draws from her literary, mythological, and cultural knowledge, referencing the relationships of Liszt with Marie d'Agout, Hugo with Juliette Drouet, or those found in the novels of Emily Brontë and Katherine Mansfield. She also includes references to friends like Violette Leduc. Her approach remains unrestricted, and she happily moves among references of varying statuses. She collects her sources according to the demonstrations, evoking realities or inventing characters. She does not limit herself to using literature as a mere illustration of philosophical theses; she employs empathy and distance. Beauvoir embodies herself through her characters, breaking them down with clarity and mastery. In short, she pretends to lose herself in the psychology of the characters in order to maintain an overarching perspective and control the theoretical analysis of behaviors. Her writing is characterized by a constant splitting.

The analysis of "feminine" roles is aimed at emancipation. Beauvoir titles her final chapter, "Towards Liberation," and charts a course from immanence to transcendence. In political terms, she shows the path to independence and economic and social equality, which should lead to "an inner metamorphosis." What will happen then to love relationships, and how will women be able to experience love without dependence? Beauvoir explores the horizon of freedom in the realm of emotions by advocating for the ideal of "authentic" love. This term—as we have observed repeatedly in the proponents of truth, sincerity, and transparency—remains difficult to define and often gains meaning through its contrast to inauthentic behavior. Beauvoir continues to reflect on the concept of love, drawing from Hegel and the struggle of consciousness: "Authentic love must be founded on reciprocal recognition of two freedoms; each lover would then experience himself as himself and as the other; neither would abdicate his transcendence, they would not mutilate themselves.[97]"

No more identification and offering of freedom as a pledge of love... the two will love each other by remaining two freedoms in action. But liberty exists only in the project, the tearing away from the petrification imposed by the other's gaze, and Beauvoir cannot accept an ideal of love that would lead to the fusion of the lovers. Can the struggle of consciousnesses end without risking bad faith, complicity, and the fading of the loving consciousness into

____

97. *Ibid*, pp. 798-789

the "en-soi" of love? Beauvoir, like Sartre, maintains the movement of uprooting, which guarantees the exercise of freedom, so that the "we" of love supposes a perpetual tension, if not a war against the engulfment. The works composed by the couple just before the writing of *The Second Sex* testify to this infernal overcoming. *L'Invitée* and *Huis clos* show couples who lie to each other, act out roles, and are forced by third parties, lovers, to come out of their bad faith. The third party is diabolical but saves by denouncing the lie of fusional love. And we know from their accounts and correspondence that Sartre and Beauvoir never ceased to live their sentimental and liberal relationship in this way, experiencing their reciprocal freedom in the presence of third parties whom they associated with or expelled. *The Second Sex* can thus be read in the continuity and coherence of what Beauvoir officially wrote and lived. However, her writing is contemporary with another writing and another life.

The meeting with Nelson Algren radically changed Beauvoir's representation of love. She discovered the experience of fusion and absolute desire. Sexuality certainly plays a decisive role, but it is not reduced to only physical pleasure because it engages a desire to constitute a Whole with the beloved. Among the different accounts she gives of her relationship with Algren—in *La Force des choses, Les Mandarins*—her correspondence gives a new voice, which may be surprising if we compare it to the theses developed in *The Second Sex*. A few months after the beginning of their affair, she begins to describe this upheaval, mixing analysis and declaration. She explains that she arrived in

Chicago tired of the speeches and theoretical discussions she had endured on her university tour and wanted to be seen as a woman and not as an intellectual. She recalls first the physical seduction and then the quick confirmation of a great love: "first I loved the way you loved me, and then I just loved you myself. Now it seems to me I know you since a very long time, it seems to me, though our love is so new, that we have been friends all our life long. Dearest, *night and day I feel wrapped in your love, it protects me against every unpleasant thing; when the weather is hot, it is cool, when the wind is cool, it is warm; it seems to me I'll never get old, I'll never die as long as you love me.*[98]"

To be a woman under the gaze of a man, to feel oneself existing through him, to receive one's reason for living only from him—this is in contrast with the project of the independent woman. In *The Mandarins*, under the guise of the novelistic characters Anne Dubreuilh and Lewis Brogan, Beauvoir insists on her sexual intoxication: "He was already pressing me to him, a furnace of flesh was imprisoning my lips, a tongue was probing my mouth, and my body was rising from the dead. I staggered into the bar as Lazarus reborn must have staggered.[99]" This description conforms with an existentialist approach of the desired and desiring body, the body *for oneself* (the "lived body," says the phenomenologist) becoming the body *for the other* in an experience of reciprocal incarnation.

98. Beauvoir, Simone de, *A Transatlantic Love Affair. Letters to Nelson Algren*, New York, The New Press, 1998, p. 40.
99. Beauvoir, Simone de. *The Mandarins*. Translated by Leonard M. Friedman New York: W.W. Norton, 1991, p. 339.

The reference to the resurrection, however, suggests a new life through this love—a radical transformation that involves the entire consciousness, its emotions, and its imagination. The remainder of the correspondence highlights the complete surrender to a passion where individual identities vanish. The lover feels the absence of the loved one; she has joined Europe but cannot fill the emptiness she feels, so much so that she feels incomplete: *"I am glad to suffer by you, I am glad to miss you so badly since you miss me too. I feel as I were you and you were me.*[100]*"* And throughout the letters, the devotion to the beloved intensifies: *"I belong to you and I just feel you with body, heart, soul, all day long, just as I feel myself [...] I am your loving little frog,"*[101] she wrote on September 26, 1947. Of course, no lover is immune to using expressions that border on the ridiculous, and these quotations are not meant to undermine the image of a philosopher with rigorous language. The most notable aspect is the self-abdication expressed here by a theorist who advocates for the individuality of lovers. The beloved has become the entirety of desire; he fulfills all roles: the beloved, the friend, the husband, and the lover, as the lover refers to him. He is the dominant animal, the Chicago "crocodile" who can devour his small, submissive prey: the builder Beaver has transformed into a small French frog. Contrary to what she writes and recommends in *The Second Sex*, Beauvoir renounces her independence: *"It means now my happiness is in your hands, and in a way I should rather*

---

100. Simone de Beauvoir, *A Transatlantic Affair, op. cit.*, p. 50.
101. *Ibid.*, p. 67.

have kept it in mine. But, well, it is done now; I cannot help it any more. I have to admit this dependence. I do it willingly since I love you."[102]

Without a doubt, the language of correspondence primarily serves an expressive function and cannot be compared to the language of theory. One is a personal address, aimed at touching the addressee with the emotions it describes, while the other aims for conceptual generality and is directed towards a supposedly universal reader. However, Beauvoir cannot help but theorize, based on her experience in love, about what she feels and, in particular, the overcoming of the dualism between mind and body. In *Le Deuxième Sexe*, the phenomenologist explains that she sees her body as a project towards the world; she is this body as her free and active conscience, grappling with the situations that she modifies. On the other hand, the lover becomes one with her desire for another; she merges into him, no longer experiencing a sense of lack: nothingness has disappeared, and love allows the lovers to exist in the fullness of Being without any division. *"With you, from pleasure to love I never felt any difference, as I never felt any difference between my body and my spirit. I am a whole woman longing for you. I am nothing else now but that burning, proud, impatient, and happy longing for you.*[103]*"*

In a happy blur, the lovers become mimetic and synchronous; they say "I love you" to each other

---

102. *Ibid*, p. 71.
103. *Ibid*, p. 193.

simultaneously, living without their freedom and possessed by a single love. "A new woman," Beauvoir writes, "a real woman whom the man treats as a woman, a woman who feels herself to be something other than a leading woman," she makes her double say in The Mandarins. And readers of The Second Sex may wonder if it was the same person who wrote the letters to Algren, as if Beauvoir had split herself, replaying a somewhat naive dualism and suggesting that she is "herself" only in the arms of her lover. When she reports to Algren on the success of her book and its media coverage from the United States, she is amused to think that he does not make the connection between her and the author. Even more surprising are the gestures and behaviors of love life, which are undoubtedly ordinary but the opposite of everything that Beauvoir deconstructed in her philosophical book. She embodies the figure of the wife even in her most conventional roles.

The woman who had formed a pact of freedom, without marriage, with Sartre wears a ring that Nelson put on her finger and that she will keep until her last days. To demonstrate her loyalty and absolute obedience, she promised: *"I'll come to you, and you'll see, honey, next time I'll be nice and quiet and obedient as an Arabian wife (but they talk too much, you know)."*[104] A recent visit to Algeria with Sartre had led her to observe the domestic isolation and social alienation of Arab women. The reference becomes humorous here; it is no longer a question of feminist criticism but a love game where Beauvoir is

---

104. *Ibid.*, p. 226.

amused by voluntary servitude. The Thousand and One Nights have replaced Hegel and Marx. To complete the reversal, the philosopher, who has described with such finesse the psychological and phenomenological stakes of the domestic tasks in which women are trapped, begins to imagine the perfect life with Nelson by promising to be his housewife: *"Oh Nelson! I'll be so nice and good, you'll see. I'll wash the floor. I'll cook the whole meals,"*[105] The discrepancy is too glaring not to be ironic, and no doubt Beauvoir plays the maid and the cook, roles she associates with an intense sexual life since she plans to make love ten times a night and ten times a day.

How much of the comedy in these letters represents Beauvoir in contrast to the ideal she theorized in The Second Sex? And if she plays the submissive woman, what degree of truth does she discover in this role? Even if the tone is sometimes humorous, it is always exalted, and the emotional charge that carries these letters cannot limit their writing to a literary exercise. The suffering, the ecstasy, the jealousy, the passion, the tears, and the anguish are expressed there without makeup. There is no doubt that Beauvoir lived these emotions intensely. This extraordinary gap constitutes an enigma and a source of reflection on the relationship between theoretical affirmation and lived existence. To reduce such a distance by rejecting the correspondence in a private domain, inaccessible or of little value compared to the philosophical work, is laziness. And the morality that would condemn

---

105. *Ibid.*, p. 324.

hypocritical behavior deprives itself of understanding the psychic complexity at work in elaborating ideas.

The reactions to the publication of this love letter were violent, commensurate with the challenge of understanding the contradictory concomitance of writings and lives. The misogynists found in it a kind of revenge, showing that this bas-bleu of Simone de Beauvoir was a "real" woman, available to sexual pleasure, according to their criteria of female nature. Conversely, many feminist theorists felt betrayed. Their philosopher had to adopt exemplary conduct by the principles of her founding book. The revelation of amorous behavior that compromises with the norms of female alienation seemed to them an unforgivable cheat. Some less committed commentators have tried to interpret Beauvoir's attitude by pointing to her jealousy and tacit rivalry with Sartre. During those post-war years, the couple lived in similar love situations, and each would have exercised emotional one-upmanship. Sartre had a passionate relationship with Dolores Vanetti, whom he had met during his trip to the United States in 1945 and to whom he dedicated several books. This love lasted five years and threatened the bond with Beauvoir, who reports, in *La Force des Choses*, tumultuous negotiations between the couple on the distribution of the trips made with Dolores and Nelson. Another interpretation, less focused on marital conflict, has suggested a division of Beauvoir's personality between her body, devoted to Nelson, and her mind, loyal to Sartre. This rather simplistic dualism, based on the discovery of physical pleasure, cannot, however, provide the key to explaining the simultaneous writing of *The Second Sex.* It seems to us much more interesting to understand the compatibility, almost schizophrenic, between experience and theory when they oppose each other. Another psychology than that of characters is necessary to understand the contradictions, the lies, and the articulations between lives and writings, especially since Beauvoir's passion for Algren is also lived through words: the division is held in writing itself.

The split in Beauvoir's personality can be observed, at a minimum, in the multiple voices she chooses to narrate her life. Thus, her relationship with Algren is described through four series of texts with very different statuses and contemporary to this passion: in *L'Amérique au jour le jour*, in 1948, she tells the story of their encounter from a cultural and sociological perspective and integrates it into Chicago, the city's underworld, and the Polish bistros. The adventure is an episode of a travel journal written by a French intellectual. On the other hand, *Les Mandarins*, in 1954, is a work of fiction. However, this essential book tells the life of the novelist, particularly her sexual passion for Algren, to whom the book is dedicated. In 1963, Beauvoir wrote La Force des Choses in the style of a memoir, showing herself to be reasoned and analyzing with distance the history of a relationship that was coming to an end. Her letters to Algren reveal another version of their love: their moments of joy or disarray. Beauvoir recounts her life, expresses her feelings, and invents characters through these writings. Where is she? Does she pastiche herself in each of these stories? It is impossible to decide, as the codes of writing imply, from the beginning of a sentence, standards, and representations that forbid judging any of these texts as authentic. From the outset, writing life is a transformation of the reality narrated. What is most instructive, however, is the diversity of versions and their discrepancies, with no privileges for any of them about the "truth". Only the tension between the writings can give an idea of the lived truth and the multiple personalities because Beauvoir multiplies herself by multiplying her stories.

The Second Sex does not mention Algren's presence, but this text can also be included in the writings that "express" Beauvoir's love life. This proposal is paradoxical insofar as the book's theoretical arguments go against the life lived. Expression is understood here as a complex articulation, not a more or less masked and decipherable representation of lived experience. *The Second Sex* expresses something of Beauvoir's life precisely through its discord and inconsistency with the letters written simultaneously. Hypotheses of another nature must be formulated. The first is to think that Beauvoir deciphers the traps set for her lover when she meets them. The Second Sex would then be the antidote to the dangers incurred in the experience of passion. With Algren, Beauvoir risks letting go, which leads her to lose control of her freedom. However, she curbs this chaos by analyzing it and articulating her feelings in a lucid and rational examination, which makes the material of her book all the more voluminous as it covers the most intense periods of her love. Its extent would testify to the psychic tension between the passionate experience and the will of control through theoretical writing. The analysis and theory make it possible to introduce a reflexive distance and not to let oneself be immersed in the ocean of emotions and imagination. Naming the real ensures relative control, even if it means lying to counter its devastating power. Beauvoir struggles against the temptation to leave Paris, to abandon Sartre and her intellectual career to go and live with Algren.

However, we cannot fully credit Beauvoir's passionate temptation in her correspondence. Her desire to leave everything to marry Algren may be nothing more than a fantasy she toys with. She scares herself; she enjoys the idea of breaking away from the image she has created of herself as an independent woman. Undoubtedly, she understands the thrill of destruction, especially since she sees it as a possible rebirth. This introduces a second hypothesis: Beauvoir allows herself to express her desire for surrender and play the submissive woman because she has a safeguard in place—her theory of the independent woman. She can balance on a tightrope and take risks because a safety net of hundreds of pages prevents her from falling completely. She plays this game knowingly: she understands the dangers of her passionate relationship with Algren and experiences its limitations. She references her work on *The Second Sex* in her love correspondence, and in La Force des Choses, she also notes the simultaneous occurrence of her love affairs with Algren and the public success of her theoretical book. Ambivalence is present, although it is unclear if it is controlled. Indeed, the game can be played in both directions: Beauvoir plays the role of both the dependent and independent woman, and there is no doubt that she experiences these roles intensely, as evidenced by the tears and despair that permeate her texts when describing her passion.

These writings serve psychological purposes. While we readily recognize this in fictional or autobiographical works, we struggle to acknowledge it in theoretical texts. The proliferation of Simone de Beauvoir's writings, particularly when they revolve around the same events but are presented in different genres, provides insight into this psychological investment. The "contradiction" allows us to grasp its complexity and strength when it permeates speculative and abstract language. The distinction between literary writing and philosophical writing is as simplistic as the division between feminine writing, with its imagination and emotions, and masculine writing, with its concepts and rational control. The stark contradiction between *The Second Sex* and the Letters to Nelson Algren instead points us towards a double life, or perhaps even a multifaceted life, in which the author navigates without a secure position. She represents and reflects on what she is experiencing and continues to live this life through her words.

The disharmony between Beauvoir's theoretical treatise and her love correspondence reveals, above all, an availability of the self that experiences multiple lives. Commentators have not emphasized enough what makes the epistolary writing dedicated to Nelson Algren so unique: the letters were written in English. Writing in a foreign language is more than just an exercise in translation. Beauvoir lived her love in English; she pronounced the words of desire and expressed what she felt, told, and thought about her life in a new language. Not only did she integrate a different linguistic imagination, but she could live and speak experiences that she would not have lived in the same way in French. Expressing desire in a foreign language often encourages disinhibition, as the taboos of the so-called mother tongue are lightened. A kind of innocence and shamelessness thus characterizes Beauvoir's letters. When she talks about her trips to Chicago to join Algren, she admits she "changes her skin" by becoming a woman in love and being loved. Yet the transition from one personality to another is not as controlled as a change of apartment. Beauvoir experiences floats, syncopations in her transatlantic life. Sometimes, she thinks she recognizes Algren at the airport when he is elsewhere; she projects the desired image onto other faces and suffers from *dissociative disorders*. The object of her desire seems metastable as if she is not sure to recognize him after months of absence and substitute imagination. The regulated distribution between her two lives supposes a kind of "schizophrenia", as she confesses in *La Force des choses*. She revels in the possible existences she could lead with her lover in Illlnois or Mexico, ready to become an American or an Indian. She makes her double say, in *The Mandarins*, "It would be necessary to have several lives[106] ". Writing allows her to imagine them and to put some order in this vertigo of a multiplied self.

---

106. Beauvoir, Simone de, *Les Mandarins*, op. cit. in vol. II, p. 228.

The impression of schizophrenia that Beauvoir confesses suggests that she compartmentalizes her life and her writing. But these existences are not watertight; they are articulated according to complex and contradictory links regarding her theoretical production. In writing *The Second Sex,* Beauvoir compensates, controls, deludes, and lies to herself. Such waverings do not invalidate the relevance of her philosophical opus. We have already observed in many thinkers that general truths can come from lying to oneself without invalidating the relevance of the ideas. Beauvoir says true and lies at the same time. She elaborates on "true" theses and analyses through denials and contradictions. From the tension between truths and lies can thus come a general truth. And if the reader of The *Second Sex* does not need to know the psychic hazards of its elaboration because this book remains an exceptional philosophical work, it is interesting to understand, according to an analysis of the subjective motives of the theorist, how the choice and the construction of thought are linked with a lying practice. The lie remains here to be understood without moral judgment and in the articulation of discordant desires at work in the abstract language.

Writing, whether fiction or theory, is a way of experiencing reality, and we can question this choice to exist through words, this creation of an existence that is extended, transformed, and invented in language. The relationship between Beauvoir and Algren demonstrates this emotional investment in language. He does not feel the need to verbalize their love; he lives it without representation. Beauvoir highlights his reluctance to speak and analyze. "Words are dangerous," she makes him say; "one risks confusing everything"[107] The simplicity of his vocabulary does not stem from a lack of ability; he is a writer but is content with the expressive function of the language of love. He says "I love you" without attempting to explain, describe, or interpret. When she recounts their relationship, Beauvoir portrays it through the implicit and naïve evidence of desire, and the satisfaction of their bodies does not require commentary. The reader may perceive Algren as a straightforward person from the Midwest, but his relationship to language and publication differs from Beauvoir's. Resistant to the publicity of their affair, he does not believe in the truthfulness of discourse. "The worst lie: pretending to tell each other the truth," [108] he objects to those who advocate transparency. On the other hand, Beauvoir never stops resorting to words, not only to narrate but primarily to give shape to her lived experiences.

To describe and contemplate her desire, Beauvoir employs four forms of writing, each serving a specific purpose. Through her novels, she continues her literary work by recounting her love and sensual life with Algren through her characters. "I didn't know it could be so overwhelming to make love,[109]" she has her alter ego say in The Mandarins. Under the guise of autobiographical fiction, she continues to construct an image that aligns with her ideal self.

---

107. Beauvoir, Simone de, *Les Mandarins, op. cit.*, vol. II, p. 229.
108. *Ibid*, vol. II, p. 263.
109. *Ibid*, vol. II, p. 55.

Her philosophical writing corresponds to her theoretical aspirations: she reflects on the desire she feels and imagines in other women. In The Second Sex, she devotes several chapters to women's sexual initiation. She extensively comments on Stekel's book, a disciple of Freud, about frigid women, and she develops numerous generalizations about female passivity and the asymmetry of access to pleasure. She references the Kinsey report on American sexuality. She then adopts a clinical style based on physiological observations.

The third form of writing is correspondence and addressing the lover. Erotic content plays a significant role here, especially since the act of writing letters is associated with sexual longing. Beauvoir seeks to rediscover her own physicality, to reassure herself through the expression of her desire, even in the excitement that writing a sexual request provokes. She presents herself to others and to herself as a woman with desires. In contrast, she describes to Algren the failure of her first sexual experience with Sartre. She stages various aspects of her body under Nelson's gaze. She even allows herself to be photographed naked, seen from behind, in her lover's bathroom.

A fourth form of writing, presented in the autobiographical genre, can be identified as playing a prophylactic role. When her relationship with Algren ends, Beauvoir feels that her desire will disappear, and she seeks to protect herself from a depressive fall. In *La Force des Choses*, she describes a feeling of amputation: "Suddenly, at one blow, a whole piece of myself was being engulfed before my eyes;

it was like some brutal but inexplicable amputation, for nothing had happened to me.[110]" She, discover a tumor in her breast and fears that she will have to have it removed. The unity of her self is put in danger with the end of desire. Then, the story of her relationship with Algren becomes a remedy. Beauvoir draws up a retrospective and cold assessment, adopting the wisdom of reason and reconstructing her history. She describes herself as masterful, aware of the misunderstanding between her choice of an independent life and Algren's matrimonial project. The autobiographical account, devoid of pathos, contrasts with the correspondence and its unbridled style. The image of Beauvoir as an independent woman is preserved. By exposing herself in this way, she takes her anonymous readers as witnesses to a whole and complete truth that she constructs to better contain and hide her division. Exposing herself to cover herself better: transparency is the main highway to denial.

Beauvoir's contradictions teach us a lot about the psychic springs of writing, which conceals lies less intended to deceive readers than to produce lures for the writer who lies to themselves. However, the word "lie" remains too univocal, and these writings in tension reveal multiple personalities built by different language registers. Readers are tempted to denounce lies and express deception when reading Beauvoir's correspondence with Algren. How did the feminist philosopher allow herself to assert theses in

---

110. Beauvoir, Simone de. *Force of Circumstance.* Translated by Richard Howard. New York: Putnam, 1965, p. 254.

The Second Sex so contrary to what she lived, felt, and desired? However, the paradox is more complex, and it seems more accurate to observe that a writing subject composes characters, not only when resorting to fiction but also when building theoretical systems.

The lie about ourselves consists in thinking that we can control all the personalities we invent for ourselves. Beauvoir believed this, even if it meant separating her life and writing. She lived as an independent woman in Paris with Sartre, she traveled as an enamored and docile woman with Algren, she wrote The Second Sex with implacable clarity, and she got carried away in her passionate correspondence. Beauvoir had the temptation of ubiquity, the illusion of taking several points of view and immersing herself in each of them at will. She imagined herself living a gentle schizophrenia, controlled from above by an omniscient self. The practice of her different writings allowed her to believe in her control by being the object and the subject of the analysis at the same time.

Unbeknownst to her, Beauvoir experimented with multiple personalities, using words as screens. She represented herself, projected herself, hid herself, and transformed herself as much in her novels as in her philosophical constructions. The theory provided her with the masks of a universal subject to better contain an irrepressible dispersion. From there comes the impression of deception felt by readers who do not yet accept the idea that the self of the writer-philosopher is not transparent and does not adhere to their person. On the other hand, if we assume the idea of multiple personalities expressing themselves even in the theoretical language, the lie becomes the availability of the subject who divides and multiplies herself in the writing theater. Whether it is a novel, a confession, a letter, or a philosophical treatise, the author is also a character who opens doors, raises curtains, wears masks, exposes herself on the stage, or disappears behind the scenes.

Once again, we observe that the affirmation of transparency produces a decoy that transforms psychic indeterminacy into a moral choice—it is often the role of morality to mask the reasons that make us act. The harmony between life and speech, simultaneously evident and deceptive, is a fiction of the self. It proceeds from the unsaid, denial, tinkering, tricks, and lies. Through these "contradictions", writing functions can be guessed: why does a subject write, in place of what, to give form to what, not to say what? And what role does theoretical writing, in particular, play, taking on the clothes of a universal subject and expressing itself in a so-called abstract language? We detect through these more or less informed choices the function of invention and representation of writing, which can affirm one thing and its opposite, deny what is experienced, or theorize the opposite of what is experienced. A subject who writes is composed of the characters that one could have been or is in a certain way, virtually, in imagination, or theory.

Few theorists assume the imaginary and psychic dimensions of their production. Very few admit that they play characters when they write a book of theory, to confess "it is not me", or "it is me, but in a certain way, who asserts certain ideas". At most, they concede that they have changed and contradict themselves for intellectual reasons: they have advanced in their reasoning, which retains its unity despite inevitable dissensions. A little less assurance would, however, lead them to recognize: "I tried myself through some affirmations, I composed myself an affirming personality, I lived abstract existences, I countered, pursued, transformed what I felt, without really knowing what the writing brought me to say and to live. The name that allows me to sign my treatises is both mine and that of a character who expresses himself in my name." Among the rare thinkers who have assumed such multiplicity, Kierkegaard embodies a polymorphic psyche most illuminating for understanding this psychic power of philosophical writing. His practice of thinking and writing allows us to approach a "multiple personality".

Living and Thinking like a Thousand Others: Kierkegaard's Pseudonyms

What thinkers would admit that they are not the authors of their words and writings? Or at least their utterances, when arguing, do not correspond precisely with what they live, feel, and think. This inadequacy undermines the sincerity and validity of their claims. On the other hand, writers accept more willingly, sometimes thanks to pseudonyms, to play with this distance between the "I's" of writing. The history of philosophy witnesses such practices called "literary" for convenience, which allow philosophers to try out audacious theses under a pseudonym. The 18th century offers brilliant examples of essays where a thinker takes on masks without the reader knowing where the theoretical "position" of reference lies. The coexistence of several theses, in the dialogical form in particular, has undoubtedly existed since the beginnings of Socratic philosophy. However, it only takes on a genuinely theatrical and ambivalent dimension with plays where the pedagogy of the character who "knows" disappears behind the delivered thesis. Diderot proposed many versions, of which Le Rêve de d'Alembert is one of the most successful, the philosopher jumping into the jousts of a witty woman, a doctor, and an encyclopedist, risking funny and audacious materialist remarks. Where is Diderot? In each of his characters to whom he gives contradictory support. The projection of oneself in conceptual figures is both a game and a strategy, as subversive arguments need screens to be pleaded at their sharpest.

If using a pseudonym was a tactic to avoid censorship, it can also become an existential choice. For Kierkegaard, it was a way of life and thinking. The philosopher used pseudonyms to write numerous texts and explore various theoretical ideas. While he employed abstract language in the name of a universal and anonymous subject, Kierkegaard created authorial personas and fully embraced the subjectivity of each voice. This practice goes beyond stylistic preferences; it involves the existence of the writer and a particular conception of philosophy. The author, in this case, someone who takes on a name and presents reflections, asserts their subjectivity and does not hide behind the abstraction of their ideas. They do not detach themselves from their writings, but rather, "are" what they write, as one possibility of their intellectual life. Kierkegaard condemned the falsehood of certain philosophies that dissolve individuality in objective reason. Against Hegel, he emphasized the presence and uniqueness of the individual, which cannot be reduced to the grand narrative of History. According to Kierkegaard, philosophers blend imagination into rational systems to deceive themselves. Impersonality, to him, is a form of cowardice among thinkers who seek to evade their responsibility. Anonymity is only a means of avoiding the contradictions between one's lived experiences and the ideas one professes.

On the other hand, Kierkegaard defends the writer's individual and existential commitment in their works. Therefore, he insists on having his authorship recognized in each book, even if he invents new names. A pseudonym represents a proposal of personal existence, not merely a compositional role. This practice challenges the traditional distinction between the ordinary self and the authorial self, which has been extensively discussed. Two perspectives have long divided readers: some believe that an author's life is expressed in their works through different filters, while others argue for a fundamental distinction between their psychological life and their creative life. Even before Proust's famous "Contre Sainte-Beuve," which supported the latter perspective, Kierkegaard engaged in this debate with an original approach. He refused to separate the author's self from the writer's self, while simultaneously denying the unity of each self. He went beyond contemplations on the self and its masks by exposing the interior and authentic self as an unclaimed fiction, a borrowed identity, a perpetual illusion. Conversely, the selves embodied by his pseudonyms actively shape what they write; they draw from external sources to explore various possibilities and experiences. These potential selves belong to the writing subject as virtualities that are actualized through their written propositions.

A psychological interpretation of pseudonyms suggests compensatory strategies in an individual who lives vicariously. As a writer uses imagination, the philosopher would adopt abstract speculation to experience spiritual emotions. However, this psychology overlooks the power of existence that the practice of pseudonyms offers. To understand what is at stake in the complex interactions between lived existence and the affirmation of thought, it is more interesting to analyze the affirmation of a potential self in theory rather than unconscious motivations and regression to infantile determinations. In the realm of abstract production, contradictory transfers and masquerades occur, through which life projects are realized and feelings, hopes, and desires are experienced. The lived experiences of thought have their own reality; they simultaneously involve the personal ego and all egos in both virtual and actual forms. The lives that pseudonyms engage in are not pseudo-lives, nor are their emotions pseudo-emotions. They are actualized through writing and thought. When Kierkegaard defines himself as a detective who follows higher interests to discover the true and the false, he willingly experiments with illusions, making them his own, without the specter of illusory authority.

The pseudonym, as understood in this way, authorizes existences and recompositions of the self. It corresponds to "lifestyles" in the sense that Foucault formulated it, extending the notion beyond a concern for the ego, to describe how ancient philosophers crafted their lives as a work of art. Indeed, the subjective commitment, as Kierkegaard conceives it, is not a fabrication because it does not construct a singular self that strives for wisdom, balance, or perfection. It is not driven by will. The investment of a subject in theoretical elaboration remains open to the enticements and contradictions they experience, sometimes perceiving them with clarity, at other times blindly navigating through them. However, not knowing exactly what we are constructing does not prevent us from wholeheartedly committing to it. These alternative existences allow us to inhabit worlds of our own invention. They can become the subject of alternative biographies, with a subject orienting themselves towards imagined lives from which they develop other personas. Kierkegaard embraced being himself while adopting other lives, wandering and making mistakes, but fully exploring these contemplative lives. He forged existences by assuming authorial names for himself and established them as places of convergence and divergence, blending his doubts with his spiritual ambitions. The "given" name we receive at birth remains a contingent fact, albeit charged with memories, and those that we invent also become attributes of the self and adopted personas. Each pseudonym, far from being a mere mask, is a genuine proposition of existence.

If we do not ultimately know who Kierkegaard truly is, his multiple names convey profound truths. In 1846, he felt compelled to explain this practice: "For the sake of form and order, I hereby acknowledge, something that really can scarcely be of interest to anyone to know, that I am, as is said, the author of Either/Or (Victor Eremita), Copenhagen, February 1843; Fear and Trembling (Johannes de Silentio), 1843; Repetition (Constantin Constantius), 1843; The Concept of Anxiety (Vigilius Haufniensis), 1844; Prefaces (Nicolaus Notabene), 1844; Philosophical Fragments (Johannes Climacus) , 1844; Stages on Life's Way (Hilarius BookbinderWilliam Afham, the Judge, Frater Taciturnus), 1845; Concluding Postscript to Philosophical Fragments (Johannes Climacus), 1846.[111]" The list, though far from exhaustive, serves as more of a paradoxical explanation rather than a confession, as Kierkegaard states that he both is and is not his pseudonyms. The selection of these names carries a strong sense of irony, with their Latinized form that conveys erudition and the use of aliases as pseudonyms. Kierkegaard deliberately maintains a distance from any notion of paternal relationship with his names, as if each one possesses its own autonomy and he does not need to impose his personality upon them.

---

111. Kierkegaard, Søren. *Kierkegaard's Writings*, XII, Volume I : Concluding Unscientific Postscript to Philosophical Fragments. Translated by Edna H. Hong and Howard V. Hong. Course Book. Princeton, NJ: Princeton University Press, 2013, p. 625.

Recognizing pseudonyms seems complex: these fictitious authors are not his sons, nor even his doubles; they exist on their own, and we cannot treat them as secondary avatars of the thinker named Kierkegaard. The specialists of the philosopher are tempted to take a global point of view and integrate them into an intellectual path. In fact, these names were used for four years. The notion of a complete "work" in retrospect leads to isolating them in a sequence that would follow religious speeches signed with the family name. However, Kierkegaard continued to use these pseudonyms after this period, and, above all, this usage raises questions about his relationship to his family name: is "Kierkegaard" just another name imposed by civil status and filiation? Does the person who signs with this surname fully recognize themselves in it?

The desire for exegesis is to unify the pseudonyms within a system where each one would play a specific role, imposing continuity and unity on the work. Interpreters are hesitant to acknowledge the fragmentation and multiplicity of a personality and its thoughts. However, the pseudonym is not merely a temporary borrowing; it also reflects a personal disposition and a way of thinking. Kierkegaard rejects the idea of a totalizing point of view, allowing himself to be everywhere like God, overseeing all consciousness. He is neither the sum nor the reason behind all his pseudonyms. At most, he acknowledges that Providence may hold the key to his path and his multiple existences. On the other hand, humans like him are destined to live in the contradictions and lies they create for others and themselves.

No overview can capture the truth of all his names. And when he contemplates an assessment of his works, Kierkegaard turns to a pseudonym once again! In *The Point of View of My Work* as an Author, in 1849, when he believed his life was nearing its end, he envisions a coherent picture of his intellectual and spiritual evolution as if he had followed a predetermined plan. He distances himself from the moments of his existence, organizes them into stages, and explains his progression from aesthetic works towards religious writings under his own name. But he hesitates to publish this intellectual autobiography and gives up: "I cannot present myself in an entirely true light." His pseudonym, Johannes de Silentio, could portray Kierkegaard, but not himself. Only a summary will be published in 1851, and the rest posthumously. With this explanation, Kierkegaard claims to have concluded his previous work and finally become the author of his own work. In reality, authority is never acquired; it is constructed through uprooting, hesitation, and derivation, and always remains uncertain. Far from indulging in a relativistic game where all truth would be nothing but a decoy, Kierkegaard continues his search for true meaning while admitting that he cannot fully attain it. The final stage of his quest illuminates the preceding ones while remaining in the shadow of a yet to be revealed light. Despite this path and these stages, chronology alone cannot provide the truth of an edifying journey; it only reflects the different facets of a subject with multiple faces.

Despite Kierkegaard's Christian fervor, the proliferation of perspectives and positions of authority indicates a constant concern that there will be no definitive revelation to conclude. Consequently, the relationship between lies and truth is reversed. The pursuit of truth assumes the duplicity of the individual who embraces the famous either/or. Kierkegaard does not even present this alternative as a method of weighing the pros and cons. This way of thinking surpasses mere willpower and corresponds to "stages," states, and dispositions, which the author refers to as "aesthetic life," "ethical life," and "religious life." However, readers would be mistaken to see only a progression towards good in this. Kierkegaard specifies that this triple perspective has existed since the beginning and will continue until the end—he can never firmly stand in one place of truth. For sometimes, the truth lies at the heart of deceit. While he believed himself to be in the aesthetic stage, Kierkegaard was already in the religious stage, present from the start, even when experiencing despair or indulging in sensuality.

Kierkegaard admits to writing the opposite of what he lives. The most mystical texts are sometimes conceived while leading a non-religious life, and conversely, the most licentious texts can emerge from moments of asceticism. For example, "The Seducer's Diary" was written in a cloister while the author was reading religious works. No matter the style of writing—austere or libertine, philosophical or literary—none can escape the interplay of truth and lies because truth does not reside in any fixed location and is expressed through fertile falsehoods. It remains subject to partial utterance, to a subject who embodies a version and its antithesis, experiments with them, experiences them, and lives contradiction as a mode of existence. Never tranquil and perpetually concerned, the seeker of truth cannot wholly reside in any single mode of life and thought; they must navigate multiple perspectives.

Using pseudonyms thus assumes a philosophical significance. Few thinkers have dared to multiply pseudonyms like Kierkegaard and explore their logical, political, and psychological functions. His approach introduces a fundamentally new understanding of the pseudonym. It is not merely a means to evade censorship for authors who conceal themselves behind assumed names. Instead, it subverts the authoritative stance that a thinker assumes in their writings. By not taking full responsibility for a work they do not sign with their own name, Kierkegaard does not advocate for the author's irresponsibility; rather, he claims not to be entirely confined within his writing. He alters the polemical role played by such texts, often pamphlets, which invent an enunciator to adopt a critical and transgressive position. Kierkegaard proposes embracing a thesis and its opposite, engaging in a dialectic that does not seek to resolve the contradiction. The pseudonyms do not embody pseudo-theses that the author presents surreptitiously, as in a Socratic dialogue, to reveal the truth. Instead, they generate tension between contradictory hypotheses and create continual gaps within the enunciator, who can entertain conflicting thoughts.

Through his pseudonyms, Kierkegaard seeks a position of detachment: he explores various lifestyles and thoughts without passing judgment or imposing a pedagogical trajectory. He embraces their existential richness while maintaining a moral and emotional distance, allowing him to breathe life into these fictional authors.

"My pseudonymity or polyonymity," he writes, "has not had an accidental basis in my person (certainly not from a fear of penalty under the law, in regard to which I am not aware of any offense, and simultaneously with the publication of a book the printer and the censor qua public official have always been officially informed who the author was) but an essential basis in the production itself, which, for the sake of the lines and of the psychologically varied differences of the individualities, poetically required an indiscriminateness with regard to good and evil, brokenheartedness and gaiety, despair and overconfidence, suffering and elation.[112]"

Like a writer who creates characters, Kierkegaard aims to bring his thinkers to life, complete with their theses and ways of life, as if they existed independently of his own psyche. In doing so, he can take these theoretical positions to their extreme consequences without fearing the disapproval of his readers. We may find it amusing that an author would attempt to detach himself from his characters or concepts. However, this indifference actually creates less distance for the audience than fully immersing oneself into another existence, with its own hopes, anxieties, and mistakes. By adopting a pseudonymous author, Kierkegaard chooses to live in the absolute and intense realm of a foreign voice.

---

112. *Id. p.* 625.

Undoubtedly, this notion of voice aligns perfectly with the nature of the pseudonym and the truths it embodies. The author's persona has disappeared; the self has shed its layers of depth and accumulated meanings. The pseudonym has disentangled them, allowing the passage of various voices that manifest in cries, words, songs, desolation, and prayers. Kierkegaard emphasized the act of listening as the royal path to truth. He is one of the rare thinkers who challenged the dominance of sight and made philosophy a matter of the ear. A passionate lover of music, he perceived thoughts through a musical lens, transcending the notions of good and evil. He presented himself as a voice from which the personal self has withdrawn. And perhaps the truth lies precisely there, in surrendering to a voice, in the pursuit of a vocal quality that corresponds to an existence devoid of falsehood: the truth is heard when the correct tone is struck.

The diversity of voices that a thinker can adopt is written in a paradoxical score without pre-established harmony. The comparison with music would lead one to think of a polyphony of authors' names, which would enter into relation with each other to constitute the choir of truth. However, the pseudonyms often play solo, even if they communicate with each other. Kierkegaard liked to build a small inner theater in which his fictional names dialogue or speak of others, thus arranging different layers of voices, fewer fugues or counterpoints than tracks that superimpose and cross each other from time to time. He, Kierkegaard by name, measures himself by their yardstick and thinks himself inferior, superior, or even foreign to their discourses. Each voice, proper or figurative, invents its scene and sometimes provides entrances for the others.

The pseudonym, thus, is more voice than face and raises the question of authenticity. Whereas many thinkers wanted to display their sincerity and made themselves all the more suspicious of lies, those who use assumed names assume the diffraction of truth and its misunderstandings. The pseudonym does not present a mask of the author; he is this author, in a singular mode, at the same time foreign to him and in deviation, that is to say, in the tension of all the possibilities of the personalities that he is and that he is not, that he could be and by which he tells the truth of his existence. The multiple diversions of self do not lead to any natural face but rather produce the echoes of the different voices spoken through the writings, those of the dialectician or the writer, the seducer or the pastor. By using a pseudonym, the thinker does not mask himself; he moves beyond his person, goes further than himself at the risk of losing himself, and has a greater chance to approach his truth.

Does Søren Kierkegaard avoid, thanks to pseudonyms, the deceptive lie that threatens the advocates of sincere truth? No doubt, he encounters it while dodging it by this clarity, or "pensées de derrière" as Pascal formulated it, which leads him to recognize the necessary ambivalence of the enunciator and his truth. He is undoubtedly among the contradictory assertors whose turns we have analyzed. Among the striking examples of a contradiction between what a thinker lives and what he theorizes is the theory of marriage published by Kierkegaard. How can a man who has never married and loved a woman passionately and broken off his engagement praise marriage? This is a common sense question like the ones we previously asked: Why did Rousseau, the educator, abandon his children? How could Beauvoir, the feminist philosopher, desire to live as a docile servant? How could the thinker of nomadism be so sedentary? How could the thinker of commitment miss a significant political appointment? Philosophical exegetes know how to answer these naive questions by despising the authors' biography or by giving the intellectual reason for the contradictions, their overcoming, and their resolution. However, we have tried to bypass these procedures to question the psychic disposition, allowing us to hold a statement while living opposite to what it supports. And Kierkegaard offers a new version of this gap.

But who exactly is praising marriage? Is it Kierkegaard, the author himself, the editor Victor Eremita, or B, this Wilhelm to whom the text is attributed and who succeeds A, the author of the aesthetic texts, and then Johannes of The Seducer's Diary? And how can we know what Kierkegaard thinks of these theses, and who wins, A, B, or Johannes? We have to listen carefully to answer. The editor says that hearing is the most precious sense, the ear remaining the organ that allows one to grasp the interiority, as in the confessional. The key word in this set is "secrecy". The fictional editor says he found these papers in the false drawer of a secretary he bought at a flea market. He presents this piece of furniture as a metaphor for the human being, with an exterior and a hidden interior. The papers come from three supposed persons, without the editor emphasizing one more than the other. We understand that Kierkegaard is each of them, or at least could be, although they support contradictory theses. And especially, none of them will definitively win the philosophical game: " Thus, when the book is read, A and B are forgotten; only the points of view confront each other and expect no final decision in the particular personalities.[113]" We will thus examine the praise of marriage as a version that is not edifying but plausible and supported by Kierkegaard who has invested himself in this very ample and argued text.

The apology of marriage is a response to the "aesthetic" life led by A and praises the permanence of love guaranteed by this institution. Against the objection of a decline of passion in married life, B affirms marriage realizes this love. Married life supposes a life in good understanding from which lies have disappeared, the spouses declaring everything to each other, which B embodies in person, citing his harmonious couple as an example. The reader, who has some information on Kierkegaard's life, thinks of his practice of secrecy, which prevents him from admitting who he is to Regine Olsen, the woman he loves. The pseudonym B then seems to be addressing Kierkegaard, as if to a contradiction and a friend. He criticizes Don Juan, whose figure is dear to the philosopher, and denounces

---

113. Kierkegaard, Søren, *Either/Or*. Translated by Edna Hatlestad Hong, and Howard Vincent Hong. Princeton, N.J: Princeton University Press, 1987, p. 14.

his conquering conception of sentimental life. One needs more strength to preserve than to conquer, he declares.

Why does a bachelor write a eulogy of marriage? A first listen lets you hear the nostalgia for the ideal union, hoped for with a loved one. Kierkegaard thus marries by way of theoretical imagination. The language of abstraction allows him to live this love that life has disappointed. By philosophizing on marriage as a superior expression of love, Kierkegaard leads a love life with his dream wife, thanks to the pseudonym. The enunciator B, referring to his marital happiness to build the philosophical theory of marriage, would be a double of the author. In fact, Régine Olsen is present in Kierkegaard's texts, explicitly or by allusion, and sometimes her name has been crossed out. In his Diary, he devoted long passages to her, then tore out the pages or covered the lines in ink with loops that archivists have been able to decipher thanks to the microscope.

The beloved woman remains present, even in her effacement, and her figure haunts the philosopher's writing and reflection. Kierkegaard has broken off his engagement but remains in the alternative that preceded his decision. He even envisions writing a book based on this breakup, which would be entitled Guilty? / Not guilty?. While he tries, for Régine's sake, to make her believe that their relationship is a sham, he continues to imagine himself married to her. He loves and cannot forget her: "She has not become any theater princess so she should, if possible, become my wife. [...] Had I not honored her more than myself as my future wife, had I not been prouder of her honor than of my own, I would have held my tongue and fulfilled her wish and mine, let myself be married to her—so many a marriage conceals little stories. I didn't want that, she would have been my concubine, and then I would rather have murdered her.—But if I were to explain myself, I would have had to initiate her into terrible things, my relationship to Father, his melancholy, the eternal night brooding deep inside me, my going astray, my desires and excesses.[114]" The reasons that Kierkegaard gives for his rupture remain obscure and the fact that they are written in his Diary, then crossed out, does not guarantee their additional authenticity. Does he himself really know why he broke up with Régine, and are his ethical arguments or the admission of his weaknesses not an attempt at self-justification? Each statement testifies to a continual decentering, and none can be elected as that of the true Kierkegaard.

In which voice does he recognize himself then, and with which one does he feel bound body and soul? It is impossible to decide. The reader would rightly be indignant: "You, Kierkegaard, have defended the opposite thesis; it is not serious!" But the use of pseudonyms leads to thwarting this objection and frees the author from having to justify a position in his own right. Multiplicity and ambivalence push back this fiction of a unitary subject who would give reason for all the ideas he has built up during his existence. Resolving the contradiction between

---

114. Kierkegaard, Søren. *Kierkegaard's Journals and Notebooks*. Volume 2, Journals EE-KK. Translated by Niels Jørgen Cappelørn and George Pattison. Princeton: Princeton University Press, 2008, pp. 164-165.

self and self is no longer necessary, even if the articulation between contradictory positions remains a vital tension. To live by adopting several voices and singing several tunes according to the crises of existence is the way to the truth, which must pass through various partitions.

Music allows Kierkegaard to formulate the alliance of unity and multiplicity. It provides him with both the experience and the language to evaluate life through the timbres of voices. The voice of B corresponds to the praise of marriage, while the voice of A corresponds to spontaneous erotic steps. In this text, Kierkegaard comments on Mozart's operas to define different types of libido. Each opera corresponds to a pattern of desire: The Marriage of Figaro, through the character of Cherubino, shows a libido without a specific object, hesitating between two women. On the other hand, The Magic Flute, with Papageno, illustrates a scattered libido that is scattered in indistinct diversity. Finally, Don Juan embodies a libido that has defined its objects, combining joy and power, and enjoying its idea of desire. Through these conceptual characters, does Kierkegaard project his personality or ideal? Nothing is certain because these figures only exist in music. Don Juan "dissolves, as it were, in music for us; he unfurls in a world of sounds.[115]" Don Juan is more like a piece of music than a person, and Kierkegaard even explains that he walks away from the stage to forget what he sees and to immerse himself in the music. While he would have done anything in his youth to have a place at the opera, he now simply

---

115. Kierkegaard, Søren, *Either/Or, op. cit.*, p. 134.

listens to the work through a partition. The transformation of bodies into musical substratum finally gives us an understanding of the status of ideas in the philosopher's mind: they are valid as harmonic propositions, and the thinker listens to them to experience their accuracy and intensity. Theoretical positions are then measured by this ability to compose a musical piece, to be listened to or sung in accordance with the agreement of life and thought.

What meaning can be given to lies and truth in this opera of pseudonyms? Kierkegaard does not avoid the question and admits that changing names and alternating contradictory theses are deceptive. He acknowledges a double fraud: not showing what one thinks and saying the opposite of what one lives. This surprising and courageous admission allows us to reconsider the philosophical and psychological functions of lying. First, a pedagogical alibi can justify the use of deception. A thinker can knowingly lie while having an idea of the truth that they do not wish to forcefully impose. Using "thinking from backward," the author believes that his listeners or readers cannot directly access the truth. Because they live in illusion, it is necessary to speak to them in their language and proceed through deception. "What, then, does it mean "to deceive"? It means that one does not begin directly with what one wishes to communicate but begins by taking the other's delusion at face value.[116]" Kierkegaard employs a Socratic

---

116. Kierkegaard, Søren. "Collation of The Point of View for My Work as an Author», Danish Editions of Kierkegaard's Collected Works." In Kierkegaard's Writings, XXII, 22:309–310. Princeton: Princeton University Press, 2016, p. 54.

maieutic here and bypasses the negative, which he refers to as the "recourse to the corrosive," in order to engage in dialogue with unbelievers or with Christians who believe themselves to be Christians. Through his words, he uses the language of "aesthetics" to better reach the "ethical" and the "religious". However, this strategy remains too simplistic, and the recognition of lying goes much further than a pedagogical method.

To think that humans live in error is also to recognize one's own illusion. To accept that one is mistaken, in the double sense of an error and of a self-illusion, leads to a paradoxical lucidity: not to be fooled by the fact that one is fooled. The thinker, conscious of this possible deception, distrusts oneself while assuming it. Such is the second level of the lie, which implies working against oneself. By annihilating oneself in the person of a pseudonym, Kierkegaard experiences deception as a test of life. He knows he has to go through the lie because the one who thinks he can escape it is the greatest of liars. The practice of lying, as a necessary illusion to hope for some truth, takes the form of imitation, projection, and introjection, all modes of life or non-life. Kierkegaard says he spies on himself through his pseudonyms. By becoming another, by abolishing his personality, he looks at the world with different eyes, he looks at himself with foreign eyes, he also experiences himself in a life and a thought that give him other forms of existence to know affects and ideas that are potentially his. He erases himself, while knowing that even silence can be a lie. To speak from silence, like his pseudonym Johannes de Silentio, consists in denouncing the frank saying of the truth while guarding against the lures of a truth that would be held outside language. It is necessary to speak, think, write, and live a lie to escape the arrogance of a subject who believes himself to be in the truth, untouched by any illusion.

The possibility of reaching one or more truths requires a double movement of immersion and withdrawal. The practice of lying comes less from a concession to a world that wants to be deceived and lives on illusions than from a will to annihilate oneself and not to be impressed by one's own person. Kierkegaard decided to live as much away from the world as in its heart. He does not seek to be recognized as a great philosopher by inscribing his name in the great book of thought. He despises those who make themselves exist through their ideas, who conceive their concepts as trademarks. Against this authority, he lives styles of existence, thoughts, and lives, by "supporting" his pseudonyms. He exists in them, truths and lies; he immerses himself in the world through his potential lives, becoming a flâneur, melancholic, seducer, pious, cynical, or exalted. By empathy, he experiences these deceptions as great existential trials. The pseudonyms offer him incognito truths.

Kierkegaard's movements, among his invented names, finally show us that the game between author and enunciator is not reserved for literature and that philosophy can also resort to this technique. The writer Pessoa created dozens of pseudonyms to which he gave biographies, which we call "heteronyms". This multiplication generated a protean work, composed of a multitude of thoughts of which the poet wanted to be the "guardian". In philosophy, it produces an effect that is even more corrosive as it touches on the nature of reason and truth. More than a tactic intended to hide the presence of an authorial self in the formulation of ideas, the use of pseudonyms calls into question the unity of the thinker. It challenges the illusion of sovereignty in their reflection. Who speaks when I speak? This question could be asked by anyone who risks speaking the truth. But the act of making an assertion, whether in the form of sentences or arguments, gives the subject the impression that they are one with what they say. And very few philosophers would be willing to accept such suspicion regarding the authority of their thoughts, as the exercise of reason relies heavily on the belief in its mastery, even if acquired through methodical doubts and logical questioning. Adopting multiple personalities does not imply for everyone a renunciation of authorial responsibility or the construction of truth. Instead, this multiplication of the self leads to the experience of a thesis and experiencing it as a mode of existence. Thanks to the pseudonym, the subject who writes not only adopts arguments but also a disposition towards others and the world. They embody them in their body and soul.

What appeared to us as a contradiction, or even a lie, can thus be classified as multiple personality. This term, borrowed from the classification of mental disorders, has been the subject of controversy[117]. However, exploring

---

117. See Hacking, Ian. *Rewriting the Soul : Multiple Personality and the Sciences of Memory*. Princeton, N.J: Princeton University Press, 1995.

the potential lives that a subject creates brings about a tremendous conceptual richness. Beyond its psychiatric use to describe the uncontrolled transition from one personality to another, we use it here to describe this multiplication of a self that is both dissociated and associated with fictional characters, and intensely lived. Literary invention is one of the ways in which multiple personality is expressed, and literary analysts have long observed these lived experiences through proxies; these projections can lead an author to identify with one of their characters and alter their relationship to the world by imagining possible existences. The famous "Madame Bovary is me" has thus given rise to several interpretations of Flaubert's personality. When it comes to assertors, especially those who use the language of abstraction, the stakes seem even more complex because the use of multiple personalities calls into question the very nature of language and the trust placed in it.

Literature allows writers to assume different personas, as the contract between reader and writer is based on the realm of imagination. In contrast, theory is bound to truth. The notion of authority becomes more troublesome when a thinker claims that all of their statements could be attributed to others, while also asserting that nothing is truly their own. Those who dare to adopt multiple persona-lities, like Kierkegaard, not only confuse their readers but also challenge the coherence of their own reflection and all of thought itself. By embodying different identities, sometimes in opposition to each other, they navigate the various facets of truth. Pseudonyms, used as modes of existence, signify a multiplicity of selves and allow for an extraordinary richness of speculation. However, even a singular name can encompass such multiplicities. Simone de Beauvoir provides a striking example, formulating ideas that contradict her own experiences, employing theory, analysis, novels, diaries, and correspondence to live and write contradictory lives, exploring a position and its opposite, all while attempting to reconcile these contradictions in retrospect.

Language predisposes us to unifying ourselves, particularly when wielded with the force of affirmation, the most powerful tool of denial. Singular philosophers have fought against this temptation and displayed multiple facets of their selves, like Nietzsche, whose Ecce Homo presents a series of metamorphoses. Reflecting on his life and works, Nietzsche presents his authorial self with grandeur, while acknowledging that his thoughts emerge from moments, travels, and music. He lived through intense experiences without always fully comprehending them, likening his works to elephant pregnancies. Who is he at the end of these processes? He exposes himself in the very act of veiling and transforming himself. He never ceases to assimilate his contradictions and embrace new ones; he embodies both strength and perpetual melancholy; the descent looms, and he endlessly walks and flees, like a multiple personality named Nietzsche. If we were to reinterpret the history of philosophy through this lens, we would discover numerous instances of multiple personalities, even among the most self-assured thinkers.

Through such experiences, both in life and thought, we gain a better understanding of the contradictions between experience and theory. These apparent falsehoods arise from the interplay between potential selves that reside within the same individual and manifest themselves in abstract constructs. Each assertor finds psychological solutions, some of which lead to general truths. The theater of their multiple personalities engenders discordance as these selves avoid, engage in dialogue, or clash with one another. Moods, circumstances, and interests determine their relationships and the dominance of a particular self at a given moment, ultimately shaping the boundary between truth and falsehood.

Lies and Posthumous Truths

Are there situations that are conducive to telling the truth or telling a lie? Sometimes, thinkers who are aware of the discrepancies between their lives and their assertions take steps to reveal certain truths. They anticipate and reveal an alternative, more "true" personality. Often, they delay this moment. Many reserve certain revelations for after their death, what are known as posthumous truths. What concept of truth does a person have that they feel must be declared once they are no longer alive, so they do not have to face the consequences in vivo? They project an image of themselves that they will leave behind after their death, either by controlling the information they leave behind or accepting the uncontrolled consequences of their legacy. The first intention is most likely a desire for posterity. Many writers, artists, and philosophers have contemplated the future of their work, even their destiny, after their own existence. They have sometimes crafted a narrative of their lives that blends the significant and the mundane, based on an artificial distinction between momentous events and those of everyday life, preemptively safeguarding themselves from malicious interpretations. Chateaubriand's Memoirs from Beyond the Grave provides the best example. Simultaneously, his masterpiece serves as a stylistic monument, a reflection on the times he lived in, and an autobiography that does him justice. In general, dreams of glory have fueled the imaginations of authors, nurturing their hopes of securing a place in the pantheon of humanity or finding the well-deserved readers they had longed for. The practice of writers and thinkers preserving archives during their lifetimes often bears witness to the construction of a self-portrait through selections, omissions, falsifications, and many compromises with the half-truths of existence. These self-portraits by anticipation, more or less orchestrated, avatars of multiple personalities, become enigmatic when authors intend to expose unfavorable truths they deemed unspeakable during their lifetimes.

The fear of a post-mortem revelation may lead an individual to clean up their affairs to eliminate compromising traces. However, authors contemplating damaging posthumous revelations have a complex representation of themselves and their unity. Kierkegaard left the manuscript supposed to explain his work with the note "not to be opened until after my death". Publication during his lifetime would force him to answer for a homogeneous personality, for a unique truth about his existence, whereas he knows his division and multiplicity. Unity and authority seem to be accessible only after death, once it is no longer possible to experience other existences. The Point of View of My Work as an Author will appear in its entirety four years after the philosopher's death. However, it would be illusory to unquestioningly believe in such an "explanation" which, under the pretext of having been revealed post-mortem, would expose "the" truth of the author. This "definitive" version remains a reconstruction, at a given moment of existence, indeed proposed as the ultimate, but dependent on this desire of a retrospective unity and thus relative to the time of the writing at the end of life. A unitary image is well revealed, adding to the others and building a totality as one of the author's possibilities. This will of posthumous unity by anticipation conjures up the anguish of the final dispersion.

Sometimes, thinkers leave it to future readers to put together the pieces of a fragmented personality. Beauvoir's love correspondence, whose extreme distance from her philosophical work we have analyzed, was not found like a secret unearthed in the closets of a dead author. She accepted, even wished for, its publication, but she postponed it beyond her existence, probably considering, like Jean-Paul Sartre, that her death belonged to others. During their lifetime, individuals may modify the meaning of their past from what they recover and project into the future. Once dead, they can no longer change or control this life that has become an en-soi, a block of meanings interpretable by others. Beauvoir finally assumes the contradictions of her multiple personalities, composed of incompatible desires, by delivering them to her posthumous readers. The truth is thus said with delay, published "in full and final settlement", at least "a truth" that brings to light the sidesteps, the half-lies, the arrangements with the potential selves, and that will be transformed again by the new truths given by the following generations.

The revelation of truth condemns one to be accountable to those who seek it. This accountability leads to postponing the publication of unmentionable facts or thoughts. One solution is to erase the embarrassing traces or to affirm the silliness of any "personal truth" theoretically. These remnants of existence, unfinished manuscripts, and intimate correspondences become the prey of truth-seekers. Slag of work or waste of life, these relics of existence testify to the accommodations with oneself, what Deleuze called "dirty little secrets" which he believed psychoanalysts feast on. Yet the thinker of the "impersonal" life had accepted a series of filmed conversations in which he exposed himself "in person," sparingly delivering biographical elements amidst philosophical statements made in his name. Of course, the form of *L'Abécédaire*[118] radically thwarted any confession or life story, but Deleuze was adamant that these interviews would not be broadcast until after his death. Their publicity would not commit him to answering, to holding a personal

---

118. Gilles Deleuze, Claire Parnet, Pierre-André Boutang, *L'Abécédaire de Gilles Deleuze*, boxed set of 3 DVD, Montparnasse Edition, 2004.

position. Although he showed his body and his subjectivity, he humorously imagined himself as a pure spirit addressing those who would turn the tables to summon the voice of a dead man. Unlike Montaigne, who, in the Essays, affirmed that he was the subject of his book while assuming, in the present, the trembling variations of his self, Deleuze rejected in the beyond of his existence any discourse involving his particular person. And he was still reluctant, in his interviews, to reveal names or personal stories despite the posthumous diffusion. He postponed as much as possible—except for a concession at the end of his life, when excerpts were broadcast during his lifetime—his exposure to biographical curiosity. The postponement of these filmed "truths" reveals, above all, an imaginary cross between, on the one hand, the acceptance of showing oneself in person, flesh and bone, in the process of disserting and, on the other hand, the illusion of having become invisible and disembodied, without the need to respond, without the burden of judgment. Being heard after death contributes to the utopia of an impersonal self, to the becoming ghost of all thought.

Whatever the reasons for these small adjustments or great anxieties, the status of post-mortem truths, personal or general, posted or whispered, remains ambiguous. And readers would be mistaken to consider them as superior truths on the pretext that the author did not want or could not assume them during his life. They are also the object of a more or less conscious displacement of the representations an individual forges of himself, lying voluntarily or not, imagining himself surviving in them according to their unpredictable effects. The posthumous truths exist only in the eyes of the interpreter, freed from the author's control. An anecdote provides a testamentary allegory: a son discovers that his father, a printer during his lifetime, has left a few sealed letters in his workshop. On one of them is written the words "Do not open." This injunction, paradoxical for a legacy, disturbs his heir, who wants to respect the will of his deceased father and, at the same time, know what secret he is keeping. He suspects terrible truths and fears devastating revelations. After long weeks of doubts and moral scruples, of the craziest interpretations of his father's existence, radically modifying his image, he opens the envelope. He then discovers a series of cards written "Do not open" for the printer's clients.

Posthumous publications are given a higher coefficient of truth, but they remain dependent on a projective imagination, either that of an "author" who has constructed a personality for the survivors or that of readers who satisfy their desire for a unifying truth. These post-mortem data remain fiction and are built from a legacy, voluntary or not, which takes on the appearance of objective reality. The illusion of finally knowing an author's personality comes from the belief in the testamentary value of some writings or biographical elements. These documents generally offer only one more perspective, another shaping of the nature of the deceased, and not a retrospective truth that would provide the key to their existence. Thus, the Journal de deuil, published some thirty years after Barthes' death, reveals his deep depression at the time of his mother's death. However, it does not reveal a more relevant truth than La Chambre Claire, his theoretical book on photography, in which he incorporates the maternal figure in his analysis of the imprint of reality on an image. Barthes is neither more present nor more "real" in these scattered notes, not intended for publication. He is just as present in the concepts he invents to analyze the photographic gaze.

The impression of breaking into the dead man's room and finding manuscripts creates a lure of truth: the investigator transforms the remnants into a secret and believes he has access to a hidden meaning. He invents a depth and establishes it as knowledge. However, these truths, acquired behind the author's back, exist only through the relative contingency of any inheritance, depending on whether it has been anticipated. They are formed through the pseudo-discoverers' representation of a "life". The biographical canons that determine our idea of existence lead us to assign a false authenticity and positivity to the post-mortem documents. This belief operates on the illusion of an established division between truth and falsehood, as if the boundary could be drawn from outside of an existence, in the eyes of the archivist who decides what is authentic. However, the data constituted by these archives or by these post-mortem facts has no more truth than the author's own discourse on their own life. Or at least, this truth is only another version of existence, certainly of a different nature since it is formulated from the outside. It remains suspended on a particular conception of truth, and it does not allow us to say, "Here is the truth restored" or "The author told stories, and here is what it really is". Instead, our analysis of the dispersal of the writing and thinking self suggests that existence is constructed amidst the tensions between discourses and practices of life, and that truth is told through lies. The apparent contradictions between declared theory and lived life are part of the multiple existence of a consciousness that projects itself in fiction, thoughts, images, and concepts. While it may be tempting to denounce a lie by opposing it to the truth of the facts discovered after death, we know that the lie is a way of speaking about oneself and of existing as a being of language. The "theoretical life", even when it seems to contradict the so-called ordinary life, also belongs to lived existence. Its virtual nature does not invalidate it and does not take away an inevitable reality from it, especially when it produces works of thought. The books, which are both fictional and theoretical, are extensions of existence, lived propositions, acquiring a status of truth.

The posthumous truths, derived from revelations after death, cannot be considered more reliable than the "lies" told during the author's lifetime. They serve as metaphors of the self, expanded and divergent versions that contribute to the contradictions experienced before death. The word metaphor indicates the transfer of these renewed constructions of the self without assuming a primary meaning: the metaphors entangle the figures; they metaphorize other metaphors by multiplying the projective movement of the self. These displacements do not have a core or pre-existing real personality. The invention of selves through theory and abstract assertions participates in the multiple characters, and the self "authenticated" by posthumous truths continues the complexity of these ongoing self-representations.

Whether open or sealed, posthumous truths are neither transparent nor profound, and to understand their nature, it is essential to grasp what sustains them: the circumstances in which they are spoken, the psychic intentions, the meanderings that led to their declaration. The fact that they are verifiable and have conceptual, logical, and universal relevance... is a different level of analysis. Their success and adoption by other speakers do not prevent us from observing how they are made and their psychic functions. Their contexts, formulations, addressees, reverse sides, and the lies they uncover are interwoven with them. There is no need to refer to great thought experiments to observe this. Our relationship with the truth is closely tied to the situations in which we speak it. Why are we willing to answer the most intimate questions in a doctor's office, even if they are unrelated to the consultation? Dialogue protocols establish specific discourse modalities, protected by professional confidentiality, and more or less conducive to confessions. We could broaden the inquiry to the various circumstances of everyday life to analyze the interplay between truth and lies. For example, the "pillow truths" that an individual might be more inclined to share under the pretext of sexual intimacy. Or the truths that a traveler confides in an unknown interlocutor whom they will never see again. The truths that arise from personal confessions have nothing in common with logical or philosophical truths, but their modes of expression can teach us much about abstract assertions. The ordinary situations in which truths and lies are formulated offer a vast and underexplored field of study. They prompt us to consider, in abstract statements, the conditions of enunciation, whose role extends beyond the context and whose complexity provides valuable insights into the forms of lying and truth-telling. An archaeology or psychology of thought allows us to perceive the circumstantial nature of any truth.

The dialogical form in which a thinker exercises truthfulness particularly emphasizes the importance of these enunciative devices, especially when they appear posthumously, as a conversation from beyond the grave. The address to an interlocutor oscillates between explanation and confession. Either it imposes a norm, with the risk of a standard that leads the enunciator to format their words and tell a conventional truth intended for posterity, or the listening of their truth by another obliges them to accept a meaning that they do not control and to compose with an indeterminate reception. The lie to oneself, this bad faith of a subject alone "facing" oneself, must be confronted with more or less docile listening. Indeed, the dialogues of a thinker with an appointed interlocutor often give the impression of a pedagogical exercise intended to explain the coherence of their ideas. Sometimes, the author feigns to split themselves, such as Rousseau with Jean-Jacques. However, personal confidences are often mixed with general truths. The exchange remains closed if the interlocutor is only a stooge; it opens when confidence provokes unexpected truths. Sartre's dialogues with Beauvoir, published in Adieux, a Farewell to Sartre, after Jean-Paul's death, offer a fine example of the philosopher combining reflections and confessions, accepting the gaze of a privileged witness of his life and abandoning part of his will to master it. Deleuze also, answering Claire Parnet in *L'Abécédaire*, lets us hear more than an explanation of his concepts. He unwillingly delivers truths charged with affect, detectable in his physical reactions and particularly in his voice. In a dialogue, the tricks of truth and falsehood are heard, even if we lack the codes to decipher them. A thundering assertion or a trembling utterance, a silence or a stammer, reveal movements underneath the language, underlying fractures, and struggles, audible even in writing. Thinkers like Kierkegaard and Nietzsche knew how much truth was a matter of tone and timbre, perceptible by the ear. Kierkegaard considered that truth comes through the voice more than through meaning. The latter, also a great music lover, boasted that he had the sharpest ears of all philosophers to hear the psyche at work in concepts. These posthumous words, confided during interviews and abandoned to an indefinite posterity, provide less enlightenment than whispers. They diffuse the echoes of the lies and truths that a still-living author bequeaths in the form of murmurs.

Listening Psychically to Lies

The lie encompasses a wide range of attitudes, figures, and processes that extend well beyond the deliberate denial of truth. The intricate maneuvers observed in the philosophers we have analyzed demonstrate their speculative power. It would be unproductive to label them with contradictions that actually indicate an inherent divide in any author whose life cannot be reduced to objective facts. While these discourses may possess rational coherence, they are also shaped by complex and opaque forces. They create and develop existences. Additionally, the desire for a comprehensive work should not overshadow the richness of its creation, which goes beyond conceptual arguments and harnesses psychic energies. In this regard, the philosophers, who excel at abstraction, provide valuable material for highlighting the tensions involved in the production of rational discourses. Certainly, not all philosophical works stem from a lie, but the previously examined cases reveal a significant distortion between multiple selves that coexist within the same thinker.

At the end of our analysis, the concept of a lie is no longer defined solely by intention (intentional lie vs. unintentional lie): as a linguistic construct, this notion of a lie, burdened with moral implications, connects various paths taken in the construction of multiple identities, whose coherence is more or less controlled. The expression "lying to oneself" that we introduced at the beginning of the book remains problematic, as it relies on the fiction of a unified and objectifiable self. The self is a precarious figure that emerges from processes of subjectivization. It is divided, composite, and multiple, as evidenced by its contradictions, which are symptomatic of the divisions arbitrarily grouped under the author's name. Instead of conceptualizing "the" lie at play, we prefer to analyze the inventive multiplicities that nourish the production of abstract discourses and provide abstractors with "theoretical existences" that are lived with as much emotional and sensory consistency as so-called real lives. This truthful-lying of theory is a self-constitution, a way of being born and representing oneself within a linguistic complex.

Lying is connected to delivery. The history of philosophy states the opposite: that truth gives birth, not lies. Socratic maieutics organizes this struggle against false pretenses, doxa, and simulacra in order to bring forth Truth. It represents a movement of liberation, a model for any assertion that stages a brilliant apotheosis, the more radiant because of the great energy required to attain it. Metaphysical truth, moral truth, and factual truth all unfold according to this exact scenario. However, lies can also lead to delivery, combining childbirth and freedom.

In its simplest form, delivering a lie means giving someone a false commodity. But the deliverer might also relieve themselves by escaping the pressure exerted by the truth. Indeed, the lie, which has become intransitive, suspends the opposition between truth and falsehood, favoring the birth of an unassignable self. If one frees themselves from error by accessing the truth, conversely, one frees themselves from the dominion of truth through a lie, much like the child whom Nietzsche says lies innocently. Unrepentant liars free themselves from the obligation of truth by becoming chameleons, ready to assume any role that allows them to multiply. Lying gives them a new identity. By adopting multiple roles, liars do not truly know who they are, but they escape the demand to be singular and transparent to others. The child liar does not deny the truth; they run away from it. In this escape, pleasure, freedom, and obliviousness intertwine. Morals dictate their repression, but a discerning ear discovers the polymorphic power of the lie.

The Three Ways of Lying

The psychic economy employed by the lie testifies to its affirmative power. It manifests itself in three ways: first, through a binary opposition between truth and falsehood. The more the lie entangles the truth, the greater the satisfaction from the revelation. Second, the lie maintains denial and reveals the truth through the resistance it faces. And third, the lie escapes the dichotomy of true and false and creates new truths. This involves an economy of expenditure rather than compensation. Affirmation is no longer the opposite of negation; it eludes verification.

The first scenario creates a stage for the triumph of truth. It resembles a police or judicial pursuit that compels the liar to tell the truth, eventually leading to their release. The contradiction generates a repetitive force that excites desire and seeks its explosion, when the secret is revealed and there is a sudden outburst. The energy of denial, haunting and persistent, is experienced over time, while the energy of confession is instantaneous and explosive. The redemption of Raskolnikov confessing his double murder offers a vivid scene. The lie finally crumbles; the culprit admits, acknowledges, and affirms that yes, they committed the crime they were accused of. He was fleeing, but now he is saved.

The moment of confession often evokes both fear and pleasure, for both the author who confesses and the recipients of the declaration. The staging of the revelation goes beyond a mere police story, as it taps into the mystical desire for truth and satisfies it with a kind of epiphany. Truth emerges from the body and miraculously restores order; everything falls into place after the illumination. Integrity is restored, guilt and innocence are distributed, and the distinction between truth and falsehood is reestablished, making the obscure motivations that distorted reality secondary. From this point on, the light is set; truth has been delivered. Watching the performances of televangelists who publicly confess their faults, we can surmise that they provide their audience with a twofold pleasure.

They allow us to simultaneously indulge in the pleasure of judging, condemning, and belittling, while also contemplating the naked truth revered in communion. Theorists of spectacle call it the purgation of passions, or rather, compulsive enjoyment for the despiser of vices, in the face of their own abjection that criminals expose in their place.

In the binary scenario of truth and lies, the nature and severity of the fault are irrelevant, as long as it allows the triumph of "yes" over "no." "Yes, I had a guilty relationship with another woman," confesses the senator or the transient hero of a television show before the cameras. "Yes, I resign, divorce, and vanish for you. I reveal all the evil to offer you the apotheosis of good." The ritual of confession exposes a perverse mechanism that confessors understand. Some priests report having to moderate the confessions of their faithful at times, suspecting their satisfaction in recounting sins. But for confession to have a powerful effect, it must follow a struggle between lies and truth, to the point of a denial that resists pressure and eventually gives way to a breath of confidence or the clamor of a public declaration. The economy of enjoyment is contingent upon this internal torment, which is followed by a liberating expulsion.

The collective exhibition of lies functions on the spectacle of their suppression. It is captured by this sacrificial ritual that nullifies them, erasing the effort and tension that sustained them. Truth shines with its brilliant light, unquestioned because it is closely tied to the pleasure it has incited. However, this dramatization of a singular, shadowless truth may have hindered access to other truths embedded within the very tension of the lie. Liars say "yes" once, but they have said "no" multiple times, and their denials are not equal, formulated at different stages of denial. How can we access the truths entwined within the utterance of falsehood? To comprehend the tricks and power of lies, we must set aside moral judgment and restrain the impulse that fuels it.

The second path followed by the psychic economy of the lie is understandable if we set aside the binary opposition of truth and falsehood. Rather than hoping for the explosive revelation of deceptive discourse, maintaining it, observing it, and listening to it can provide significant benefits. Adopting this attitude, Freud wrote a small text entitled "Die Verneinung" in 1925, translated into English as "Negation," to explore the concept of denial. In it, he highlights a paradoxical phenomenon in certain patients who propose a hypothesis only to immediately renounce it. "You ask who this person in the dream could be. My mother... it's not her." And Freud concludes, "So it is his mother." The desire to deny a possible truth is evidence of the relevance of that truth. Otherwise, there would be no need to state it. A conscious liar often exposes themselves through their suspicious and preemptive will to dismiss an accusation even before it is made. On the other hand, the unconscious liar speaks and deceives themselves. Freud subtly analyzes the moment when a repressed thought breaches the barrier of speech and enters consciousness in the form of denial. The process he elucidates gains strength through the speaker's lack of awareness, as they discover the truth through its repression. The mother has revealed herself in the substitute image that appeared in the dream. The patient suddenly "sees" her and then banishes her back to the depths of their unconscious.

Analytical listening offers a constructive approach to understanding lies. It resists the impulse to declare the truth and denounce the speaker's self-deception; it overrides our desire to judge. When the truth content of a lie is suspended from analysis, its status and function radically change. It is no longer a conscious intention to deny the truth; it becomes one of the manifestations of truth. Freud had already employed this type of reversal when faced with hysterics whose gestures and speeches were, in his opinion, neither comedic nor dishonest. By listening to the words of denial, the psychoanalyst hears the voice of the unconscious. They can decipher the meaning behind the negative statements: "No, it cannot be true, and if it were true, I would not have said it!" At this point, the goal is not to contradict the speaker and force them to acknowledge the truth, but to allow them to deny it so that the work of acceptance can commence. Gradually, the repressed content becomes integrated into a broader awareness. Freud uses the spatial metaphor of inside and outside to illustrate that the patient must bring forth something that is their own, like a part of their body, and then successfully expel it to detach themselves from it. To achieve this separation between the liar and their lie, one must allow the words of denial to flow back and forth, grow accustomed to listening to them, and better understand their depth and connections. Lies resonate with multiple motives and intertwined narratives. While

Freud relies on a conception of expression that implies depths and surfaces, we can nonetheless analyze these fictional lies as processes of subjectivization that interact with each other without necessarily originating from the same depths of the unconscious.

In this second way, the lie and the truth are closely intertwined, revealing themselves through each other. Denial is a clue, but sometimes the liar does not even feel the need to deny the truth. The supreme authority of the lie is then the derivative affirmation. Instead of hiding or denying, the liar utters parasitic truths. They aim to distract, to divert attention, like people with anorexia pointing at the plate of others while they make their own food disappear. The designation of a reality that aims to hide another one does not always concern an intentional lie. It can mobilize screens that allow the speaker, consciously or not, to avoid confrontation with a disturbing truth by substituting another fact for it. Psychoanalysis identifies assertions under the name of the screen or the cover when a memory or an interpretation given by the patient has the function of masking unmentionable content. This type of assertion needs frequent re-actualization and substitution as it loses its hiding power.

On the other hand, the third way presents the robust version of the deceptive assertion: the obstinate and self-sufficient construction of a "counter-truth"—or alternative fact—that has the beauty of intellectual coherence. Instead of the anarchic disorder of the screen assertions, this one presents an ordered logic and sometimes reaches the strength of a system. The philosophical theories that we have studied belong to this endogenous truth. The systematic assertor does not feel a duty to authenticate their statements since their speech is not based on factual veracity. If they declare themselves authentic, sincere, and transparent... it is by adhering to their sole position of enunciation and not by referencing their "life". They can lie to themselves in developing their assertions and take others hostage to their performance. As a child of their speech, they exhibit their affirmative enjoyment.

Libido Affirmandi

The excessive use of affirmative speech can manifest itself in various degrees of intensity. It may be limited to a repeated but low-intensity usage, which we can refer to as the speaker's interventionism. The assertion is not necessarily transitive, and it can change its focus when the asserter does not identify with a particular idea. Most importantly, individuals desire to speak as much as possible because the act of speaking becomes the affirmation itself, with the content becoming secondary. This attitude is often evident in people who monopolize conversations in social settings, as they want to be recognized by being listened to. However, it would be a mistake to reduce affirmative speech to a mere desire for power, as we would then fail to acknowledge the discordances of individuals who are too closely aligned with their speech. An excessive presence in the delivery of speech is a sign of inauthenticity. The more emphatic the self-affirmation, the more we can suspect that the individual is vulnerable and in need of noisy reassurance. Writers understand the significance of such vulnerabilities and account for them in their use of language, particularly when multiple voices are involved. In her work, Sarraute skillfully depicts characters who continuously assert themselves and delight in employing concepts and significant terms ending in -ism. Yet beneath their words, she subtly introduces barely audible micro-events that lead to a collapse of meaning and bring about catastrophic consequences. In contrast to the general chatter, the introduction of a silent character is enough to disrupt the harmonious affirmations of the speakers and make them aware of their fragility.

Affirmative interventionism naturally finds expression in public speech. Through declarations, podiums, debates, and petitions, those who affirm themselves, whether in the role of experts or prophets, create fertile ground for the media. Apart from their legitimate assertions, they are always ready to intervene when called upon. This meets the need for evaluations that the media must fulfill. The media, in turn, incites and maintains the desire of listeners, who then adopt the speeches in order to mimic the evident affirmers, seeking this enjoyment of affirmation in their everyday lives. If sociology examines the strategies of position in the intellectual field, this logic of interest also gives rise to a psychic economy in which affirmative enjoyment is exercised. The incessant need to speak in public spaces, to express an "opinion," or the frenzy of writing that compels certain authors to publish as much as possible, continually churning out books to avoid the anxiety of a pause in their affirmative presence... all these behaviors demonstrate how much affirmation is also a mode of existence, subjected to the imagination of the self.Intensive assertion can be seen not only in speech but also in text, if we know how to interpret it. The ways of asserting, their rhythms and patterns, can be read like voices, offering more than just stylistic forms. It is important to note that there is a wide variety of assertions—true or false, oral or written—and using a positive sentence does not necessarily imply deceit (otherwise, every speaker would be a liar!). Discussing statements like "the universe is infinite" or "the law applies to all" can be done within different frameworks of scientific or moral truth, without involving personal motives. However, the way an assertion is made—its context, emphasis, the involvement of the speaker, and the target recipient—requires careful reading and attentive listening to understand its impact.

The act of asserting requires an interlocutor, real or imagined, who must validate the speaker's self. Beyond the content of the argument itself, assertors establish their existence through the act of addressing their ideas or theses. These ideas become the basis for their identity. While arguments are often presented as containing a truth that leads to agreement or disagreement, it is important to consider the emotional investment of individuals who believe in an idea. They may have faith in it, even feel passionate about it, devoting a significant amount of their energy and time to it. These individuals may associate their sense of self with their assertions, constructing a self-portrait that can exist in their imaginations.

The psychic investment in an idea reaches its peak when the assertor is, or imagines himself to be, its creator. Being the author of an idea is not obvious, and this formula has been debated since the origins of philosophy. Freud slyly targeted this ambiguity of philosophers who affirm the universality of concepts while identifying them with their authors: Socrates and the truth, Spinoza and the conatus, Leibniz and the monads, Descartes and the cogito, Hegel and the Spirit... Freud had a ambivalent relationship with philosophy, both admiring and critical, as he was wary of the excessive use of abstraction. In "The Question of a Weltanschauung," he mocks the idolization of concepts by their creators. However, his rivalry with philosophy prevents him from singularly analyzing the psyche of philosophers who dedicate their lives to abstract notions. His irony instead applies to the "history of philosophy," which is unhistorical and idealistic because it presents philosophical ideas as independent entities produced by a philosopher, regardless of their contexts. The hagiographic dictionaries of philosophy create the illusion of an organic unity between thinkers and their ideas, while in reality, thought is constantly shaped by various diverse discourses and tensions inherent to the individual who thinks.

Although reductive, Freud's observation about the idolatrous relationship between an author and the concept that identifies him encourages us to question the motivations behind theoretical affirmations. Those familiar with philosophy would rightly argue that assertions are not highly valued in philosophical discourse, as the primary approach is often centered around dismantling preconceived assertions, introducing astonishment, worry, doubt... However, assertion is not merely the expression of a truth. Once again, it is essential to differentiate the content of meaning from its psychic investment: asserting oneself in speech, debate, or thought does not necessarily mean making grammatical assertions. The affirmation of oneself takes various forms, involving different processes of identification, fixation, and repetition focused on a thesis. Therefore, the act of devoting one's life to developing an idea, investing all one's energy in writing a treatise, or being an advocate for a particular thought must be examined from both a psychological and existential perspective. Among the cases of affirmative over-investment, philosophy is enlightening due to two features: the indeterminacy of its status and the recourse to an abstract language that identifies it. The necessity for each philosopher to say or remind what philosophy is testifies to the first characteristic. This word designates diverse uses that sometimes have nothing in common. The retrospective unification of the various discourses in a "history of philosophy" cannot hide the disparities between the approach of a Cynic in ancient Greece, the construction of a metaphysical system in the classical age, and the analysis of language by Anglo-American thinkers of the 20th century. And if the word philosophy is commonly used, according to an illusory genealogy, it undergoes redefinition each time. Philosophical practice pledges its status because it is never definitively seated: whether it seeks truth or proposes a way of life, whether it promotes action or contemplation, whether it offers a vision of the world or criticizes common values, whether it clarifies or invents concepts... an affirmative intention is always required to establish the legitimacy of its discourse.

The ideas that this or that "philosopher" defends require an additional affirmation, a linguistic act, and not only an argumentative content. Indeed, the permanent redefinition of philosophy engages the philosophers all the more since it implies the choice of a language with which they identify their practice. This investment of language constitutes another salient feature of philosophical affirmation. Attention to the linguistic and stylistic features of the discourse, often ignored or even underestimated by practitioners of philosophy who only see it as formal analysis, allows one to grasp singular psychic energy under the argumentative conviction.

To affirm, declare, define, state, propose, assert... the analysis of these discursive modalities opens an immense field that allows us to read philosophers differently. Among so many stylistic standards, which attract the attention of too few analysts, the use of the verb to be testifies to this libido affirmandi, this desire to assert. Declarative omnipotence is manifested in ontological definitions such as "man is a social/thinking/speaking animal...", "the beautiful is...", or "love is..." The reference to the Socratic method, which in principle poses the question "what is," stirs up the enjoyment of definitions, whether one subscribes to its metaphysics or not. The concern for definition is self-evident for many philosophers, so much so that it is linked to rigorous reasoning. Is it not necessary to define what we are talking about to reach clear and delimited concepts? Other philosophical practices could contest this obviousness, but it retains its force of attraction by confirming the power of a language that establishes truths through its declarative virtues. Affirmative performance is rarely heard because theoretical argumentation often overshadows it. It involves a psychological disposition in language: an imposition in which a speaker claims to speak, declare, or impose a truth. This demand becomes even more powerful when it relies on an abstract and formalized language, requiring others—whether readers or listeners—to respond with the exact words and adopt the same linguistic register. Without this, they are deemed inferior and dismissed. It's like imagining a peasant fighting against an aristocrat using completely different weapons. The deliberate choice of abstract language also raises numerous questions beyond its intellectual value. The use of conceptual generalities and theoretical hyperbole extends beyond mere linguistic technicality, drawing on a psychological energy that involves the representation of an ideal self.

The desire to affirm enters into a strategy of enjoyment that deploys ruses and weapons, composes with resistances, and establishes territories. It is part of a psychic economy that opposes pleasure and displeasure, love and death, affirmation and negation. Paying attention to these conflicts allows us to understand the shocking contradictions of great assertors who led lives opposite to what they profess or theorize. Negativity sometimes acts at the heart of the theses in which we sincerely believe. The apparent contradictions, particularly evident in some philosophers, highlight the divisions within any heavily invested statement. The strength with which we affirm a truth is the measure of the repression of its opposite: the affirmation contains a hidden negation. This secret affects it and works on it to the point that it becomes excessive and takes on marvelous appearances. Psychoanalysis has provided the term "sublimation" to understand the sexual investment of intellectual ideals that have replaced other objects desired. We do not adhere to these overly general interpretive frameworks and prefer to respect the complex and multifaceted nature of the affirmations that the notion of sublimation encompasses in a logic of symptoms. Indeed, affirmation does not necessarily encounter resistance from the superego or, at the very least, does not concentrate its energy there. When it constructs a lie and gets carried away, it creates an untruth that constitutes its infinite resource. Nothing stops it, in a way, and it can continue to repeat, develop, and transform by drawing from this source. It does not encounter a prohibition that would force it to move; rather, it is pushed by drift without limits and can multiply its forms by moving forward. It takes pleasure in its own lie and its prolonged strengthening.

Therefore, affirmation is not the symmetrical opposite of negation. Instead, it seems compatible and even complicit with negation, to the point of sometimes providing its expression: the affirmation carries within it an unacknowledged negation; it is intended to hide and, even more, to produce a denied truth that it transforms, shapes, and inflates. Precisely, the forms of verbal inflation indicate this tension between truth and falsehood that characterizes an over-invested affirmation. The word "assert" carries the meaning of firmness, suggested by a common etymology (adfirmare). To become firm, to hold firm through affirmation, that is the fantasy of self-generation, which allows one to imagine an ideal self, symbolized by an intellectual construction, a splendid idea, a thesis as unyielding as steel. The desire to affirm produces firmness of speech, tumors, and multiple appendages from an internal lie at the heart of the words. Pinocchio's nose presents the most naive, hysterical version of this. The oratorical or written energy of the assertor generates excessive verbal appendages driven by the conflict between truth and lie.

For a Second Listening

Affirmation can be heard and listened to in tone, pace, and gestures of speakers who strengthen themselves by affirming and multiplying their prostheses. They utter their ideas with assurance, a fullness of voice that is one with the meaning they are expounding. Voice, spoken or written, fills the sonar or textual space. It imposes itself entirely on the page or in the classroom. Recently, the voice of thinkers whose recordings were preserved have become the object of study. We have already suggested that Deleuze's interviews give voice to a body of affects at the heart of his affirmations. The voices of Lacan and Barthes in their seminars have also been analyzed as such and in relation to the contents of their discourse. Comparing their vocal registers leads one to appreciate the extraordinary singularity of each and their distinct relationships to knowledge, self-control, and the audience. Barthes, who did not assume the speech of a master thinker, wrote suggestive words about the voice he would like to use in a teaching situation. Instead of an organ carrying power and imposing knowledge, he hoped for a floating voice to hold knowledge in suspense and make it available. Against the impostures of the magisterial voice, the author of *The Grain of the Voice* regularly claimed awkwardness, hesitation, and silence when he was on the radio, a slag now erased by recording techniques. The qualities of a voice allow us to hear the content of thought in a new way and to read texts differently. Indeed, we do not write as we speak, but the articulation between the spoken voice and a specific tone of writing is rich in lessons. To understand a thought requires informed ears.

The detection of lies, at the heart of the statement, supposes a deaf listening to the meaning of the words. At least this methodical deafening favors the investigation. Difficult to achieve, the exercise aims to dismiss verbal meaning. Sometimes, this withdrawal position settles without intention when tiredness or boredom seize the listener attending a conference or social chatter. In the hubbub, the surrounding speeches are transformed into an unknown language. The listener then becomes sensitive to the qualities of voices no longer covered by meaning. It certainly seems complicated to intentionally stop hearing words that we know, but with effort and withdrawal, we can perceive sound phenomena that carry affects alone. This behavior is not so crazy because meaning also passes through tones, gestures, and voice ranges. In *A Word for Another*, the playwright Jean Tardieu thus enjoyed inverting and twisting the speakers' sentences without upsetting the meaning the spectators understood perfectly. The situations, exclamations, and agreed figures allowed for the preservation of a kind of syntax freed from adequate words. Adopting this approach allows one to perceive an "affirmation" over-invested by the volume of the voice, by differences in range, durations... all qualities important to the music and revealing a reality rich in secondary meanings. Theoretical vocabulary often lacks precision to describe the singularities of a voice, the subtlety of its variations, the relation between its grain, and the psychic intention that animates it. Certainly, the indistinction between the "naturalness" of a voice, the culture that formed it, and the expression that motivates it makes a universal methodology almost impossible. Numerical analyses have nourished some knowledge by transcribing voices into graphs, allowing descriptions that remain sketchy. Despite this defect of identification, being attentive to the profusion of meaning that passes in a voice, spoken or written, and its associated gestures opens with new listening and comprehension.

The *second listening* then proceeds from the scrambling and the temporary will to no longer understand the statements. It seems anti-philosophical: Plato already had the fear of a human language that would become bird sounds. This fear continues among the supporters of a purely instrumental language, a transparent vehicle of thought. The confusion of many philosophers in front

Listening Psychically to Lies

of music comes from such a fear: the seduction of sounds risks forgetting the meaning of words. In the *Symposium*, the impertinent Alcibiades flattered Socrates by claiming that his speeches were worth the most beautiful tunes of the flute player Marsyas. Even worse, he declared that Socrates was a flute and didn't need words. According to this drunken fool, the music of the philosophers would be a breath, an "air" in which words are less important than tone and rhythm. Alcibiades suggested, without saying it, a musicality of thought. But this proposal has been relegated to the side of sophists and seduction. Philosophers hardly accept to give up on mastery of meaning. Because of a passion for music, Nietzsche was one of the few to change the paradigm and propose to think with the ears. Listening, thanks to this philosopher whose hammer was a tuning fork, became a criterion of evaluation.

This attention to the musicality of thought leads to listening to philosophy differently: hearing it not only to understand it, or rather understanding it by listening to it. Rereading it with a tuning fork is necessary to grasp its vocalities without looking for a meaning that must be put in brackets. Philosopher and musician Wittgenstein considered that music does not express anything in itself and that it enters rather into games of relations and communities of style. To locate family resemblances among philosophies could be done thanks to their musical style. One would distinguish doctrines of harmony or disharmony, of duration or syncope. One would observe orchestral philosophies or philosophies of soloists, thoughts for string instruments, and others for winds.

Resonances and sound spectra can gather in refrains and feed philosophical currents over time. The aggregates of concepts impose dominant tonalities, apocalyptic, prophetic, pastoral... It would also be necessary to integrate the accents, their repression, or their persistence in voice and writing. Foreign sonorities can be heard in certain thinkers and draw new partitions. More than metaphors, these styles are constituents of thought.

The suspension of meaning is a stage, a moment of listening, which does not remain with the a-signifying music of speeches. Second truths emerge in tones and, ways of asserting reveal a subtext that can contradict the stated thesis. Proceeding to a second listening thus makes it possible to resist the force of intimidation and conviction of a dominant voice. The excess of assertion conceals sub-layers of meaning, that is, other voices in the magisterial voice, other authors in the auctorial word. Every asserter is not a liar, but the affirmative tones constitute traces. The will to assert heard behind an assertion arouses suspicion. It invites to hypothesize the content of sentences and to detect a psychic stake, a nonconscious intention that mobilizes and overflows the speaker. The madness of truth that takes hold of Rousseau is an almost caricatural example: his obsession with affirming that he is innocent and a martyr unjustly accused by all the liars of the earth can only attract the reader's suspicion. The strategies of defense or attack justify the intensity of a polemical tone, but sometimes, the affect carries away the feverish speaker and points out the lie that tortures him. Readable and audible, the assertion thus uncovers its violence and the anguish which it curbs.

Lies are only interesting if they reveal a truth that cannot be told openly or straightforwardly. After listening to the multiple turns that the lying-true takes in abstract constructions, we can ask ourselves if no truth ever escapes the ruse despite the declarations of their authors. The claim to sincerity or authenticity paradoxically awakens our doubt, and it seems impossible to trust any statement that claims to be true. The most challenging lie to detect is that subjects foment towards themselves without clearly knowing their reasons. This doubt about the truth does not proceed from skepticism here because we seek instead to understand the psychic energies that prevail in abstract affirmations without judging their relevance. Other truths emerge under "the" declared truth in the heart of linguistic artifices.

To end the lie seems impossible, but this observation does not invalidate the desire for truth. It is even the pledge of solid thought to take up this tragic challenge. Sartre hoped for a future world where lies would disappear. Everything would be sayable; individuals would no longer hide anything from each other, and secret motivations would no longer be the norm. Everyone would tell their truth, assert their position of existence, and expose the reasons that push them to defend such moral ideas and visions of the world. Sartre did not have the happiness to live this human ideal. Kierkegaard, more modestly, reserved this genuine truth for married life... but remained single. To be able to say everything to each other would suppose that we know what is true in our words, and frankness does not guarantee knowledge.

The end of the lie remains a regulating horizon whose realization can lead to perverse effects. This world where everyone would be transparent to all would impose a tyranny of truth that would leave no shadowy area, no intimacy away from the inquisitive eyes. Moreover, this ideal redoubles the illusion of transparency to oneself. The naked, total, translucent truth is a philosopher's or moralist's dream. Indeed, we can restrain ourselves from lying voluntarily, but as for lying to ourselves—such evil remains challenging to ward off. To be aware of it assures, at *least,* the pledge of an existence as close to the truth as possible because if there is no worse liar than the one who believes in holding the truth, there is no worse individual than the one who dispenses with wanting it. The multiple personalities embodied by the philosophers we studied show fewer liars than polymorphous subjects, crossed by divergent desires, who passionately want the truth and reveal it by dividing themselves.

Conclusion

Loving works said to be "from the spirit" involves diverse dispositions. Their fascinating beauty leads us to believe in their autonomy: they stand in majesty by the power of their composition, and we admire their figures and pace. Among them we find abstract speeches—of which philosophy has given sublime examples—engaging readers and listeners to embrace both their arguments and grammar. Admiration can also lead one to guess the secrets of their production, suspending the contract of reading imposed by abstract statements and universal ideas. Theoretical constructions thus reveal their complexity and, notably, the psychic investment of their author. Such an approach centers the writing, the voice, the implicit motives, the postures, and the discrepancies. It suggests an attunement to the concepts, their resonance, their volume, and sometimes their cracked timbre, drawing a singular spectrum. The abstract statements give the illusion of an existence independent of the subjects that elaborated them. They nevertheless carry a number of sediments, gestures, and addresses informing their landscape. Such is the paradox of abstract language: it uproots itself from the impurities of personal interests to cloak itself in the anonymous truth of the universal. In denying the subjective motivations that support it, it favors the lie.

Attention to the psychic matter of abstract affirmations leads one to refer them to ordinary acts of thought and the historical and personal contexts of their enunciation, or the "life" of their authors. "Life", "person", and "author" remain very ambiguous notions and require many precisions. They do not designate an identified reality— they are constructions. Life does not hold an a priori unity and is distinct from biography, where narration invents continuities. It comprises fragments and contradictory versions and presents less an individual truth than articulations between lived experience and discourses.

To access this psychic content, it is sometimes necessary to adopt a candid listening and reading style that asks simple questions: Why is an author so keen to demonstrate this or that idea? Why do they display this desire, even this rage, to assert? Why do they choose such abstract language, and why do they engage in endless circumlocutions? The naïve or discerning observer is not absorbed by the desire to decipher an obscure text or the intimidating exposition of a thesis, even if they are of intellectual relevance. Authors are sometimes surprised at the turns their works take. In his *Dialogues*, Rousseau tries to justify the length and heaviness of his jumble of arguments "drowned in a chaos of disorder and repetitions", and admits to being overcome by uncontrolled energy. He suffers, groans, sighs as he rereads, and then, discouraged, gives up trying to bring order to chaos. Many philosophers are overwhelmed by their demonstrative will, whose unknown motive exceeds theoretical intention. Sartre could not finish his books, and as soon as he took them back to reframe them, he added new chapters to them, producing magnificent and unfinished monsters, relegating their pursuit indefinitely. This compulsive trait, encountered in many authors, indicates the intensity of psychic work in conceptualization. The profusion of writing or its contractions, its breakdowns, its limpidity or its weight, are often gauged with the measure of what they seek to express, according to the adage of Boileau, who pledges the clarity of the enunciation on that of the conception. However, they manifest mainly the psychic forces struggling in the heart of intellectual production.

The forms of argumentative works need further inquiry. On the one hand they depend on historical and cultural models that favor one genre over another—treatise, meditation, fragment... On the other, their writing is nourished at once by a desire to expose, affirm, demonstrate, and by the linguistic figures informing, soliciting, and carrying them. While labeling them "symptoms" is perilous, they at least reveal the complexity of their elaboration. They articulate intentions with varying degrees of consciousness, motives to expose an unfamiliar argument in a discourse that is not solely the instrument of thought but also its screen, its decoy.

The psychic tension at the heart of abstract constructions is all the more spectacular when it produces a gap between the "life" of an author and his theoretical affirmations, appearing to us as contradiction, paradox, or lie. If we suspend our logical mind and our moral judgment we witness, above all, the psychic shortcuts of their author. Rather than pointing out an error of reasoning or condemning the hypocrisy of a thinker who leads a life contrary to what he professes, we discover *the genius of the lie*, a discourse full of anxiety and desire, of crazy representations of the self, a language of escape and metamorphosis.

The "lies" we have analyzed show the extraordinary profusion of figures of joint affirmation and denial, composing theses in which contradictory voices are heard. Some thinkers hide a personal truth while praising the Truth. In his last seminar, delivered when he thought he was doomed to die, Foucault unfolded a philosophical theater in which he played his own role by proxy. While exalting the courage of truth, he carefully kept the secret of his AIDS. This denial produced a paradoxical confession masked under the august features of the ancient philosophers.

In other cases, the lie appears as a moral plea when a fault he cannot atone for undermines a thinker. Rousseau's paranoid delusions, which convinced him that the whole world blamed him for abandoning his children, led to the construction of a treatise on education in which he portrayed himself as caring pedagogue. After having lived through the war without heroism, Sartre became the paragon of commitment, denouncing the complicity of silent intellectuals in front of injustice and crime. The reversal of defective virtue requires intense theoretical efforts. The image of the court haunts those who must contain their anxious conscience that casts them in the roles of the accused and the plaintiff ad infinity. Were we to blame them for these tricks, we would be on the side of Truth and the Good, that is to say, of imposture. It is more fruitful to analyze the psychic motivations generating sublime works and thoughts.

No one escapes the opacity of an assertion whose motives are never as clear as their authors believe. The more ostentatious the display of sincerity, the more it reveals his lie. The *pathos* of truth and its declensions in authenticity, purity, and transparency denote a paradoxical intention. The insistence, repetition, and constant redeployment of an idea come from an unresolved tension: something does not manage to be formulated once and for all and torments the speaker to the point of obsession... As soon as we feel the need to expose a principle, a quality, or a virtue, we project ourselves in an abstract entity that simultaneously catches a psychic motive and masks it under the guise of an anonymous statement.

The famous abstract pretenders use concepts as fetishes that they refine and endlessly perfect. Radicalization and hyperbole make it possible to bring notions to the limit of understanding and to extirpate them from reality to the point that they become impossible to verify. Little does it matter that they are outside the field of experience as the beauty of reasoning outweighs its human efficiency. We thus admire the refinement and the complexity of specific arguments without feeling committed to realize them. This radicalization clears us of any application, and we can enjoy imagining ourselves as moral and altruistic, impersonal and nomadic, masterfully acted out by philosophers such as Levinas or Deleuze The success of certain arguments at times derives from the pairing of such a denial with an intellectual authority that no behavior will contradict. Abstraction authorizes us to live theoretical imaginations and to compose virtual personalities.

Lying is not always a matter of the moral sphere but rather a matter of the division and multiplicity of the self. To call these divergences between intellectual adherence to a principle and a life actually led a lie in the sense of a condemnation prevents us from understanding the psychic reasons which motivate such deviations. This is why it is necessary to distinguish between lying knowingly and lying to oneself. Analyzed as such, this self-deception allows us to approach the psychic tricks linked to abstract affirmations. Affirming an ideal while living its contrary goes beyond a simple opposition. Through ideas, we experience lives that have a proper consistency, with their effects and intensities, which can at times be on par with so-called real life. Far from a binary relation between life and thought, the connections between ideas and existence are exercised in a myriad of ways, as opposition or barter, as adhesion or intoxication. Some thinkers offer astonishing examples, such as Beauvoir building a feminist philosophy of first importance and living her love with Algren on opposite models. Instead of crying foul, we understand her as living several modes of existence, with her true personality on neither side of her affirmations. She lived through conflicting desires, situations, and choices. She lived them intensely without us being able to decide on a higher degree of authenticity for one of her existential positions.

Theoretical assertions are not necessarily adequate to the subject who states them. Ideas come from a self distinct from the self of ordinary life, as Proust asserted for literature. It is certainly more common to accept such multiplicity among writers familiar with the doubles that fiction allows. The presupposition of transparency in philosophy, which supposes an identity between the "I" of a thinker and their personal "I", or even the erasure of any "I", closes our eyes to this fertile discrepancy. Kierkegaard is the philosopher who has most consciously assumed this multiplicity of *selves* in constructing abstract thoughts. His practice of pseudonyms confuses our reading habits because he does not use them as simple masks behind which he would carry out a strategy in his name. Each alias corresponds to a position of existence that he fully lives without judging or overhanging it. He becomes each of his invented authors, adopting their ideas, feelings, and behaviors towards others and the world. Contradictions disappear in favor of alternatives. This multiplicity does not lead to renouncing the truth; rather, it suggests that its research passes through various positions of existence. Thinkers can thus compose multiple personalities without holding the key to all their inventions. They live their thought according to different temporalities and different rhythms. They project themselves into potential lives, which constitute a part of themselves; many avatars that lead them to hold distinct and sometimes contradictory theses. Even for philosophers, , whether they like it or not, "I is another."

However, the lie to oneself does not disappear with multiple personalities. They do not constitute a gallery of characters, available at will, that we would decide to embody, like an actor, becoming a cynic for a day, an altruist, an enlightened person, or a sage for another. We can undoubtedly experience heterogeneous positions of existence and, by method, preserve their singularity, but we do not know what lies between them, for lack of a director that would distribute the roles. If each of us is many, the question remains how these virtual existences are articulated with their contradictory desires, dreams, and anxieties. One who holds himself to be sovereign remains the least able to understand these enmeshments.

The impossible clairvoyance towards oneself highlights the *tragic* dimension of truth. Lucid about the lies of others, we are never sure of being so for ourselves. Specific situations encourage us, in spite of everything, to discover the subterfuges that feed the representation of our self. Psychoanalytic work thus attempts to disentangle the knots of lies and to cross the screens that a subject sets up as protection. This image lets us believe in an original core hidden behind the veil of ignorance. However, while tracking down comforting lies, psychoanalysis does not unveil a range of absolving truths. Instead, it organizes new narratives through which subjects reconstruct themselves and displace points of fixation. Its perspective is more one of healing than of revelation. Whatever the practices—self-examination, systematic doubt, psychoanalytical practice—the will to deal with one's lies finds neither rest nor end. This infinite, and disappointing quest has tragic overtones. We encounter truth by fleeing it, and it escapes us when we think we get it.

The consciousness of the lie doubly condemns to solitude. By observing others' lies, we discover the inexhaustible propensity of beings to tell stories, to lie about the reasons that make them act and display high principles. But, above all, we know how much an identical evil threatens our own position. We would like to impose the truth, force others to face it, and acknowledge their denials and impostures. However, how can we do so since these pretenses return us to our illusion and the suspicion of our own lies? Even wanting the truth can have dark motives. We can, at most, hope not to be fooled by our deception. Such an observation does not condemn all forms of discourse with universal pretension, mainly as these lures produce sublime works like those we have analyzed. The presence of the lie does not disqualify an author's theoretical engagement or the intellectual relevance of his speeches. It denotes a, sometimes evil genius, in thought.

A minimal lucidity would suppose that authors recognize discrepancies between themselves and their assertions, concepts, and principles: not the simple discord between their words and their life, but a complex relation between the personalities they create for themselves as soon as positions of authority—in the form of an "I" or an impersonal—are exposed in general formulations. On this condition, they will perhaps suspect that they are deceiving themselves, that they are writing to a singular addressee while claiming to speak to the greatest number, that they are hiding under the prose of a universal subject, that they are writing in the place of another, that they took a voice to grant themselves a unity and a continuity, to forge an invented self, an author's name they say to be their own. But that is only the predicate of a self without consistency, divided and multiple, lost in its reflections. This lucidity will grant them neither clarity nor transparency; it will rather keep them from the big deception of the master's voice.

Lies can be heard, even in writing, if we listen carefully. A thundering assertion, a stutter, a looping formula, a counterfeit tone deliver the clues of a crack in the argument or even of imposture. When it comes back to us through a recording, our voice seems foreign to us and worries us: who is speaking in this way? Which person has borrowed our tone to speak in our name? The perception of this disagreement incites us to whisper, to moderate the desire to affirm. Or to cry out the tragic lie of existence lived without knowing it. By frequenting the great speeches too much, we sometimes become detached from their score and no longer hear the reassuring music of meaning. They disintegrate and sound false… then they recompose… and, little by little, they rustle with unheard-of truths.

Table of contents